Sex, Love, and Marriage

in the 21st Century

Sex, Love, and Marriage in the 21st Century

The Next Sexual Revolution

Edited

by

Robert T. Francoeur
Martha Cornog
Timothy Perper

toExcel

San Jose   New York   Lincoln   Shanghai

Sex, Love, and Marriage in the 21st Century

Editorial Services by Ray Noonan, Ph.D.,
ParaGraphic Artists, NYC, http://www.paragraphics.com/

Published by toExcel,
an imprint of iUniverse.com, Inc.

For information address:
iUniverse.com, Inc.
620 North 48th Street
Suite 201
Lincoln, NE 68504-3467
www.iUniverse.com

ISBN: 1-58348-366-7

LCCN: 99-64067

Printed in the United States of America

About the Editors

Robert T. Francoeur, Ph.D.
is author of
Eve's New Rib and *Hot and Cool Sex: Cultures in Conflict*

Martha Cornog, M.A., M.S.
is author of
For Sex Education: See Librarian and *Libraries, Erotica and Pornography*

and

Timothy Perper, Ph.D.
is author of
Sex Signals: The Biology of Love

With a Forward on
"The Spiritual Challenge of Sexuality"
by
William R. Stayton, Th.D., an American Baptist minister, relationship counselor, professor of psychiatry and human behavior at Jefferson Medical College, and professor of human sexuality at the University of Pennsylvania

Contents

The Spiritual Challenge of Sexuality Today   xi

An Important Comment   xvii

Part One   Redefining It All   1

The Full Picture
     Annette Covatta   3

1. A Southern Rural Pastor
     Maude's Friend   7

2. Sunglasses and Baseball Caps
     Colin Flaherty   11

3. The Story of a Single Pastor
     Alicia Smith   15

4. This Is My Song, This Is My Sacred Journey
     Henry Bullmann   21

5. The Body Sacred
     A Modern Teresa   37

6. A Nun's Transformation
     Teresa's Daughter, Not Maria's   41

Who Says There Is Only One Way to Experience the Divine?
     Marilyn Fithian   45

7. The Creative Fire of Knowing and Loving
     Peter Declan   49

8. Tantric Unions—A Quest for Ecstasy, and Agony
     Ed Palmers   61

The Tantric Sex Path to Spirit
     David Schnarch   69

Part Two   Reinventing Marriage and Intimacy   73

The Reality of Eros
     James B. Nelson   75

9. New Marital Patterns Work—If Lived with Principles and Patience
     Eleanor and John Sharp   79

10. Forty-Two Years of Sexually Open Relating
     Atwood Henderson   87

11. Growing in Synergy
     Valerie Triumph   95

12. Faithfulness in Marriage
     Art Rosenblum   99

Intimacy and the New Humans
     Ron Mazur   109

13. Searching for Three-in-One Body/Spirit
     Susan Robbins   111

14. My Personal Story of Connecting Spirituality and Sexuality
     Peter B. Anderson   125

15. Slippery Rocks and Sparkling Waters
     Kathryn Burnett   133

16. Playing Pygmalion
     Robert H. Rimmer   137

Families, Small and Big
     Jerry Jud   151

Part Three The Healing Power of Sacred Sex   155

Painting Outside the Lines
     Jerry Jud   157

17. Growing Beyond an Open Marriage
     Ryam Nearing   159

18. Dancing to the Goddess' Drum
     Carol Jud   167

19. Enriching Deep Friendships with Sexual Intimacies
    Jeremy Masefield   175

One God, One Spouse?
    Robert T. Francoeur   181

20. A Single Woman's Journey
    Cynthia   183

21. The Runaway's Story
    Judy Harrow   187

22. Reclaiming Lost Sexuality—A Man's Journey
    Lawrence Davies   195

Sex Before and After the Resurrection
    James B. Nelson   199

A Reflection   **201**

Suggested Readings   **215**

The Editors   **219**

The Spiritual Challenge of Sexuality Today

William R. Stayton, M.Div., Th.D.

Sometime in the late 1970s I was asked to give a lecture at a North American Conference on Marriage and the Family in Canada on the topic "Monogamy and Its Alternatives." It was a challenging undertaking, as I had never done much thinking or research on the topic. I had, however, done a lot of counseling, both in churches I served as well as in my counseling practice, of individuals and couples who were involved in some sort of alternative lifestyle. To my amazement I discovered that monogamy is not natural to any species, especially humans, and that there have been alternatives to monogamy in every major culture in history. I ended up writing several articles on the topic and outlining the variety of lifestyles that people were choosing for their life journey.

More recently, during the summer of 1996, my life partner and I went on a vacation to Nova Scotia with another couple we had known for almost forty years. Josh, the other male, echoes my ministerial interest, having been a theological professor his entire career. As I packed for the trip I decided to include the manuscripts for the stories that now appear in this book—my friend, Bob Francoeur, had sent them to me some months earlier and our vacation seemed a good opportunity to read them.

❖   ❖   ❖

William R. Stayton, an American Baptist minister, has been a marriage and gender counselor for many years, in addition to teaching in the human sexuality graduate program at the University of Pennsylvania. An assistant professor of psychiatry and human behavior at Jefferson Medical College, he has also held several offices in the Society for the Scientific Study of Sexuality and the American Association of Sex Educators, Counselors, and Therapists.

I quickly became so fascinated that I started reading them aloud to our friends at our breaks. Soon we were taking turns reading them. We became so fascinated that we ended up reading every time we had a break, in the evening, and during our car travels around the beautiful Nova Scotia shoreline. We had more in-depth conversations with this couple during this vacation than in our entire forty-year friendship. Until this experience I am sure that our traveling companions believed I was some "liberal thinker" who just reflected theoretical concepts.

As we read through these very powerful and moving stories and talked, some common themes stood out.

First, all the storytellers try to explore both their spirituality and their sexuality as they search for the meaning of their lives — they believe that there is some connection between spirit and sex.

Several years ago I wrote an article on "A Theology of Sexual Pleasures" for a theological journal. I started the article with this statement: "My story undergirds my belief that we are born both spiritual and sexual. One of the tasks of life is integrating into wholeness these two aspects of our being." One of the tragedies of modern day institutional religion is that too often we are schizophrenic. We split ourselves in two; we lose our wholeness when we split these two important aspects of our humanity. In splitting sex and spirit, we cut ourselves off from both our animal and our spiritual natures. We deny ourselves the experience of finding our wholeness, our true identity, our core self, our identity as persons who want desperately to live fully at home in our sexual/gendered bodies and brains. Our bliss is rooted in our wholeness, not in schizophrenia.

Sexuality can be defined as that part of ourselves that we experience as being male-female, masculine-feminine, heterosexual-bisexual-homosexual, erotically experiencing anything or potentially everything in our universe. Sexuality is how we experience ourselves in this world as human beings. It also determines how we relate to others, and find our wholeness in belonging.

Self is our experience of our true identity as persons. "I'm a doctor, a lawyer, a househusband, a whatever," identifies me, but it's not my true identity as a person. *Self* is our experience of being one with our deepest self, being whole, knowing ourselves intimately and being comfortable with the person we know we are deep inside.

I see *spirituality* as our search for the meaning of our human experience. It is that part of us that wants to feel connected with something outside of our self. We want to belong and not feel cut off from others, the world, and God, the Ultimate source and horizon of all that is.

Like the writers of these stories, I believe sex, self, and spirit are essential parts of the whole we are meant to be by the Creator. Like three legs of a stool, we need to experience our sexuality, our self, and our spirituality as fully as we can in order to be fully the persons we can become. It's a lifelong challenge we never quite complete, but our struggle for wholeness, our battle against schizophrenia is what life is about. It makes life very interesting and can make each of us more human. In these stories one senses a struggle with schizophrenia and loneliness in a too-fragmented world. Much of this fragmentation is the creation of institutional religion, which is why these storytellers found it necessary to explore intimacy beyond the conventional boundaries of institutional religions and society. Too often the parental, societal, and religious messages of the past were restrictive, scary, and dehumanizing when it came to dealing with our sexuality. These stories are replete with negative examples of those messages. Yet these storytellers have a consistent feeling that their sexuality and spirituality were being unified through their human experience. This they EXPERIENCED as a natural unity.

Second, the more these men and women explored their spirituality and their sexuality, the more they realized universal principles of love, justice, honesty, truthfulness, and equality. I found it so interesting that, as these spiritually oriented people explored their sexuality with different people, they also got in touch with these important universal values. Many who tell their self-histories in these pages found new meaning in the positive spiritual concepts of connectedness, intimacy, affirmation, valuing others, reconciliation, forgiveness, self-understanding, and unconditional love through the humanness of their sexuality and positive sexual exploration.

Third, as these women and men explored various lifestyles, they also developed insights into their "shadow side." They learned, first hand, about jealousy, possessiveness, sexism, negative role socialization, and exclusivity. From these learnings, they could appreciate how hurtful these characteristics were to their own personal growth and development and how destructive they could be to their important interpersonal relationships. Experiencing both sides of their human nature, they were able to grow in more positive and meaningful ways.

Reading these stories, I was reminded of an important thought I believe comes from Pierre Teilhard de Chardin, the French Jesuit scientist-mystic who tried to combine evolution and theology. Somewhere, Teilhard wrote that we are all spiritual beings in the process of learning to be human. All of these stories reflect this concept. The majority started out their explorations of life with religious and spiritual concepts. As they explored their sexual side they found some keys to the meaning of being fully human.

Finally, as I reflected on these stories, I began to see an interesting irony. Many "religious" people, especially fundamentalists and the "religious right," politicians, and media people would describe the men and women in these stories not as people in unconventional or "alternative" lifestyles, but as evil as the people of Sodom and Gomorrah. The irony is that to liken people in alternative lifestyles or different sexual orientations to "Sodomites" or the evil people of Gomorrah is to misunderstand completely the biblical story and its message. In fact, I believe, the message is just the opposite. If one explores the Bible to see what the sins of the people in Sodom and Gomorrah actually were, it becomes apparent that the issue was not about sexual orientation or alternative sexual lifestyles at all, but rather about the quality of life and of the relationships these people had with their neighbors and visitors.

Jeremiah, the first biblical writer to discuss the sins of Sodom and Gomorrah, makes this very point. "But in the prophets of Jerusalem I have seen a more shocking thing; they commit adultery and walk in lies; they strengthen the hands of evildoers, so that no one turns from wickedness; all of them have become like Sodom to me, and its inhabitants like Gomorrah" (Jeremiah 23:14). Note how Jeremiah uses the word "adultery." Biblical scholars agree that the word "adultery" in the Bible does not mean what the English word "adultery" means to most people today. It was **not** a sexual word, but an economic term that had to do with violating another man's property rights, his wife, without his permission.

The prophet Ezekiel also saw the sin of Sodom and Gomorrah in similar terms. "This was the guilt of your sister Sodom: she and her daughters had pride, excess of food, and prosperous ease, but did not aid the poor and needy. They were haughty, and did abominable things before me; therefore I removed them when I saw it" (Ezekiel 16:49-50). Again, biblical scholars tell us that "abominations" are the breaking of the laws of the Torah, the first five books of the Bible. These were not just sexual sins; they were about daily living, about food and eating, clothing, building, and the abuse of others and their possessions.

Take Jesus, as a final example, "If anyone will not welcome you or listen to your words, shake off the dust from your feet as you leave that house or town. Truly I tell you, it will be more tolerable for the land of Sodom and Gomorrah on the day of judgment than for that town" (Matthew 10:14-15; also in Luke 10:10-12).

It is the religious and political right today who violate these biblical admonitions. It is the Rush Limbaughs, Mother Angelicas, Pat Robertsons, and other fundamentalists who are like the people of Sodom and Gomorrah. They are the type of people who threaten the integrity and humanness of the people in the stories told here. They are the close-minded and inhospitable people of our day, who are restrictive and dehumanizing of individual exploration and integration of sexuality and spirituality. The religious conservative, the "religious right" who, like Limbaugh, claim "I speak the only truth … with talent on loan from God." In claiming to speak on behalf of God, they miss both the meaning and intent of the Bible.

The political right and people like Howard Stern and relationship maven Laura Schlessinger exploit, belittle, and undermine sexual and spiritual exploration and wholeness. "No more whining," Schlessinger warns. "The 'me-first' era is over. The 60s 'sexual revolution' was an aberration. We have to grow up and return to the straight and narrow of our traditional, conventional marital/sexual values. We CAN go back to 'the good old days.' We can be ecstatically happy and re-ignite the volcano in our marriage, even after 30, 40, or more years. Sex and marriage go together; when they don't, it's disaster."

The damage these people do is not only inhospitable to diversity and differences, but also destructive to all the universal principles, such as love, justice, honesty, truthfulness, and equality. In addition, they exploit the shadow side of humanity to fear and mistrust people who express these differences.

Unfortunately, when it comes to any suggestion that other lifestyles besides the celibate single and sexually exclusive married lifestyles may be worth exploring, too many people in all areas of American life, including the mainstream religious traditions, echo the ultra-conservative rightwing condemnations of the Rush Limbaughs, Pat Robertsons, and Mother Angelicas. They are not aware that many serious, respected biblical scholars see no connection between God's condemnation of the inhospitable people of Sodom and Gomorrah and people like those telling their stories here who are exploring in a responsible way the connection between sex and spirit in some alternative lifestyle. They don't realize that the ancient Hebrews had a very different meaning for the word "adultery" than we have today. As a result, men and women exploring alternatives to the presumed dominant lifestyle often have to bear an unnecessary burden of shame and guilt. Small wonder they seldom let their unconventional lifestyles be known.

The stories recorded in this book are precious because they come out of the struggle of spiritually driven people learning to be human. The people who share their stories here have provided us a rare and profound opportunity to walk with them through their life experiences and their struggle to find meaning. The insights offered and the lessons learned are invaluable to the rest of us who are struggling to find meaning to our life experiences and turn our own stories into a journey well worth traveling.

An Important Comment

The stories contained in this book tell of unconventional paths taken in the quest to join sex and spirit. Some might see in these unorthodox explorations only tales of promiscuous couplings or lewdness run amok. But these are not stories of wild thrill seekers. The storytellers speak from the core of their being about their deep felt need for genuine, responsible love and intimacy within a spiritual context. They share the honesty of explorers who have been there and returned to tell their tale to anyone willing to listen. And listen we must. Their journeys do not promise paradise or instant happiness, as popular magazines do with their guaranteed recipes for marital bliss and lifelong fiery passion. Their answers will not satisfy everyone, but they will strike a sympathetic note for many. These sojourners have much to teach us, even when we decide that this or that path is not for us. Their individual paths are not nearly as important as the shared message that underlies and grounds each journey. The real message of this book is simple: **God and Eros are inseparable**. God and Eros can come together through many varied incarnations. And they must come together, if we are to nourish and fulfill the spark of divinity that lies at the core of our being.

Sex and Spirit? Or Sex or Spirit? Conflict or synergy?

"An oceanic feeling ... the experience of dissolved boundaries and the mingling of self with the cosmos." Could we — in this age of ours — be on the edge of discovering and rediscovering that this classic modern description of spiritual ecstasy from Romain Rolland is equally true of the ecstatic potential in our sexual relationships? Might we discover as Hildegard of Bingen and Teresa of Avila did so long ago that to be fully ourselves and at the same time share the ultimate ecstasy we need communion with self, with another person or persons, with the cosmos that birthed us, and with the transcendent creator, God, or Ultimate Power?

Robert Francoeur, Martha Cornog, & Timothy Perper

Part One
Redefining It All

An Erotic Meditation on God's Orgasm

God's orgasm
of the hot white explosion
from the deep black hole
poured forth primordial love-juice
of quarks and leptons
from which creation was conceived

One are we
with the Body of the Universe.
Evolving and dissolving, our planetary particles of self
melt back into the great white light
and the joyfulness of cosmic energy.

Into what spheres
of creation's particles
shall we be ejaculated again?

Reverend Ron Mazur,
author of *The New Intimacy*

The Full Picture

Annette Covatta

Reading these stories is like walking through an art gallery. Moving from painting to painting, I stand before each picture just enough distance to take in the whole canvas, not pressing closer for a microscopic view. The wonderment of each story lies in the journey as a whole without picking away at the details.

The women and men telling their stories are clearly journeyers seeking lives of connectedness and ultimate union with God or whatever name you call the Transcendent One. A union that enfleshes spirits, draws them irrevocably into exploration. We humans on the journey toward integration and union wake up each day to explore, again and again, the ways we can best live out our time on this earth with meaning and purpose, with joy and delight. The writers of these stories exude this quality of dedication.

Each story is grounded in the belief that a true spiritual life is rooted in following one's inner compass, trusting one's own experience, finding inside one's self the voice of authority. In each story, the primary measures for making choices appear to be clear intentionality, sensitive respect for the other, complete openness, and telling the truth. Commonalities that strike me are the deep longing for intimacy as way of being whole, alive and connected, and making every effort not to cause pain or harm to another.

❖   ❖   ❖

Annette Covatta is a member and former provincial of the Sisters of the Holy Names, former council member of the New York State Council on the Arts, a spiritual drummer, and founder of Fulcrum, a company offering programs in psychospirituality. She recently produced a cassette of guided imagery meditations, *Reflections in the River*.

3

Even though religious and cultural institutions would have us believe that sex and spirit are quite separate, our experience as lived out in daily life reveals just the opposite. Our sexuality is inextricably merged with our very life-breath. If God is "the Breath inside the breath" as the poet Kabir says, then there is no separation between body and spirit. Every day we are challenged to move and breathe "spiritfully, mindfully and bodifully." Every thought, word, and act is an expression of our sexuality. It is our way of being in the world as gendered persons. When our sexual feelings are joined with a love-connection—both love for self and the other—then, we are well on the path to full aliveness. We experience the union of body, mind, and spirit.

These stories exquisitely portray the numinous, luminous—and sometimes painful—love-walk of folding into the Transcendent the full-bodied passion and truth of one's sexuality. At the heart of the stories is the full meaning of "Intimate Friends." One after another, each story weaves the threads of forming relationships that evolve into friendships of trust, disclosure, and acceptance. The physical attraction and lovemaking are part of the weaving: the fiery red that blazes the body-mind into full aliveness and self-transcending bliss. Then, the intimate friends—the beloveds—become one with The Beloved!

The stories also embody what's happening today in the evolution of humanity. I read recently in *The New York Times* that the "baby-boomers" are a generation of seekers rather than belongers. This post-World War II generation has shifted from the paradigm of conformity to one of creativity. They investigate, experiment, and challenge assumptions. They take risks. In the midst of a chaotic world, this particular generation is wrestling with the question: What are the beliefs, values, and ethics that make sense to me, that resonate with meaning and passion inside me?

Not just the "baby-boomers," but all of us living on the threshold of a new millennium are seeking a personal consciousness and awareness to forge a collective new creation. The road is uncharted, without maps or blueprints. Yet, we have a beacon to light the way. It is the felt-sense of when we feel fully ALIVE … when the FIRE of our being is lit by opening to the impulses of our bodies and the movement of Divine Energy inside us … when we passionately embrace all of who-we-are.

Brian Swimme, cosmologist, says that our greatest contribution to this moment in the unfolding story of the universe is to be who we are—fully. The women and men who courageously placed before us in these pages their love-journeys, with all the struggles inherent in their choices, have embarked on this voyage of standing up and saying and being who they are!

The word "sacrament" is used in many of the stories. It is a powerful way of expressing the sex-spirit connection. It is also appropriate. Sacrament is a sign or ritual for manifesting divine grace or a spiritual reality. The use of it in the stories speaks to the experience these writers are having in their quest for a fully integrated life. In their lovemaking, they touch the Holy. In touching the Holy, all life on the planet and in daily living breathes and reveals the Divine Presence. The Transcendent God is unmistakably immanent.

Thus, the "I-Thou" that Martin Buber talks about becomes a reality. No longer is the other regarded as an "it." The creative life-force — Eros! — is set free from its limited confinement, and life that evolves becomes expansive, inclusive, and liberating.

1. A Southern Rural Pastor

Maude's Friend

My snapshot story begins ten years ago, just before my fiftieth birthday. Maude and I had been talking on the phone a good bit, rather intensely sharing our personal search to find meaning in life in the midst of our fragmented culture. Such searches have a particular meaning in the context of the very traditional "southern county culture" Maude and I share.

These conversations began near to Maude's thirty-fourth birthday. She, by the way, is a professional educator and very spiritually and physically attractive to me. At first, I was ashamed of my reaction. The conflicts were obvious: I am a pastor in a rural area near several large cities. I am also married — my second marriage, with three grown children from my first marriage. I had been in this parish for almost twenty years, and knew Maude casually from near the beginning of my work here. At that time, she had just recently married her husband Harold.

I believe it was she who suggested lunch. I readily agreed, and we have since then had lunch, tea, or coffee together for most of the weeks in the last ten years.

Very soon after the lunches began we became physical ... kissing, holding, and light caressing. All of this seemed to be very easy for Maude. I was finding it enjoyable but fraught with — at that point — mild and sometimes strong anxiety. Then, as the relationship heated up, my anxiety turned into panic. For three days I was in that state. I called a meeting with Maude, and told her that I just couldn't handle the physical part of our friendship any more. I remember she said, "I'll have to think about that." But she agreed, and we didn't see each other for a couple of weeks. Then we got together for coffee, and affirmed our friendship for each other, embraced, but didn't really get physical.

It was about that time when I was reading Anna and Robert Francoeur's book *Hot and Cool Sex: Cultures in Conflict*. It helped to give us both a good measure of detachment and perspective in the midst of our involvement. To

7

be able to image our involvement as "cool" or person-oriented instead of "hot" and genital-driven was helpful, particularly in terms of Marshall McLuhan's "hot high definition media and cool low definition media" distinction Bob and Anna Francoeur expanded on in their book.

At that time, Maude had three rather young children, and they had to be the recipients of a great amount of energy, to say nothing of the energy needed in her primary relationship with her husband. I guess what frightened us both was the possibility, perhaps even the reality, of our parallel relationship becoming primary for us both. That was really frightening, given that so much was at stake in terms of our blood families and our vocations, all in our southern rural, conservative context.

Our friendship became physical again, but never involved intercourse. Yet, it soon became clear that we were in a "bonded friendship." I suppose our reason for not having intercourse as such was to imply that neither of us was comfortable with that. Frankly, "the act" itself seemed fraught with the possibility of several things we wanted to avoid: an unwanted pregnancy, disease, sexual failure, and more physical intimacy than we felt we could comfortably assimilate into our respective lives.

After a couple of years the fact that we were more than just "regular friends" became known in one way or another to our respective spouses. That was especially difficult for Heather, my wife. It really bothered her that I was being intimate with someone else. I think she feared that I would leave her, or transfer my basic heart affection to Maude. But, little by little, "over years," she became accepting, and then even friendly with Maude. I can explain that transformation only in terms of the grace of God. And Heather and I are closer than we have ever been. I can only think of one thing that I did that may have helped. Actually, it was something that I did not do: I stopped trying to persuade Heather to accept my "friendship." I just let it be, and took responsibility for that tie without seeking approval or even consent. Actually, it was as if we had reached an unspoken agreement, a major part of which was that I would not leave Heather, that I would love her and be loyal to her. As for my three grown children, they are all aware to varying degrees of my friendship with Maude. They seem to accept it without knowing details. I suspect the fact that I'm comfortable with this friendship spills over into their acceptance of it.

Well, we could end this snapshot story here, but two other storylines need to be shared. Maude's husband is not entirely comfortable with our friendship. In fact, he became very uncomfortable a while back. So, I know he is still struggling with the concept of a "larger family." Really he is struggling with his wife's freedom. Marriage in our culture is so often thought of in terms of "possession" and property rights. I find myself often helped by reading about the emerging new family structures, with their marital diversity, and hope that Harold will become more secure with a larger image of the family. Harold is, in fact, a member of the parish I serve. While he is a person of growing spirituality, he is simply not at the point of being able to accept his wife being intimate with another man. Nevertheless, I believe the fact that she has stayed with him for all these years of our friendship contributes to his growing sense of security with Maude's lifestyle.

The second storyline has to do with my own spiritual path. My relationship with Maude has awakened me to my spiritual depths. I have been really blessed by the Spirit, I believe, in the context of Jungian psychology. I have become much more meditative, and daily seek to be in touch with what Jesus calls "the kingdom within." I find that, if I am in touch with the depth of my own being, I am liberated from trying to find personal validation from people around me. It's not that I don't appreciate that, or feminine affection, but I no longer feel so needy for those external expressions. I have found what Julie Henderson calls "the lover within." Now I find I relate to Maude more out of choice, and less out of "have-to-have," and that's better for everybody.

It's like the song says: "I'm OK without, but you've got something I need." Actually, it's not so much that Maude has something I "need" but rather that Maude serves as a mirror for me. I see some of my undiscovered selves reflected in her. (Of course, Heather also mirrors hidden riches within myself, but they are different riches.) Both Maude and I consider ourselves to be fairly conscious persons, and share a mentality which is out-of-step with the dominant conservative ambience around us in our southern rural church. We find that we are both strengthened spiritually simply by being in each other's presence. Both of us work with groups of people seeking to point them to their inner richness — to the Divine Presence within and around them. We find that we affirm, and confirm each other in our respective vocations. There is most often a wonderful "energy exchange" when Maude and I get together — even if only for lunch or some other occasion which does not include physical intimacy. We would in fact maintain our relationship even if there was no physical intimacy. We would do so because of the "energy exchange" which seems to happen regardless of the level of physical intimacy present. (And, there have been stretches where, because of circumstances, we have not been very intimate physically.)

Finally, from a theological viewpoint, I have come to believe that God's Spirit is present in the energy of human passion ... maybe God's Spirit even is that energy. The *Song of Solomon* suggests that, and so does much of Eastern spirituality, especially the traditions of Tantra and Kundalini. Several years ago, Matthew Fox affirmed that Western spirituality is not complete without Eastern spirituality. I believe that both dancing together can lead us to begin to appreciate the sacredness of our sexuality.

2. Sunglasses and Baseball Caps

Colin Flaherty

The seminary prepared me for life as a celibate Roman Catholic priest by making sure that I was well-grounded in the Way of Self-Denial, or as the Latin scholars among us dignified it, the *Via Negativa*. This brand of spirituality operated on the presumption that the individual was a battleground of two opposing forces—the flesh was at war with the spirit, the body at war with the soul. To suggest a possible complementarity between these presumed opposites would have been the equivalent of sleeping with the enemy, the devil. According to the economics of the Way of Self-Denial, the name-of-the-game was withdrawal. If you wished to secure a niche in the Saints' Hall of Fame, you had to withdraw from "the world and its allurements"—a fanciful way of saying "**NO SEX**."

In keeping with the logic of its own premises, the Way of Self-Denial concluded that perpetual virgins occupied the highest step on the stairway to Paradise. Although I never bought into the Way of Self-Denial completely, it got a foothold in my psyche, where it acted as a wedge separating my sexuality from my spirituality. How this split played out in my life, I'll explain shortly.

But first I must deal with a second force in my life that provided a counterpoint to the Way of Self-Denial. This second force was casuistry, a way of cataloging every sexual thought, word, and deed according to its appropriate degree of moral righteousness. In casuistry, we learned to dissect every sexual thought, word, and deed for its moral/immoral content as though it were a laboratory animal. We used casuistry to divide the human body into zones, above the belt, below the belt, and inside the belt. One could commit a serious sexual sin in any zone—even in the zone of Spiritual Love, in the mind, above the neck, where a lusty thought could equal actual adultery or fornication. French kissing, prolonged kissing, and fondling the breasts were "above the belt" sins. "Below the belt sins," of course, included self abuse, and mutual abuse that included genital fondling—the evil of "oral sex" was unspeakable, actually, unthinkable, inconceivable. Of course, the ultimate

11

sexual sin was inside the belt—intercourse. In the final analysis, we were caught in a sexual morality of belts and pelts, with scarcely any consideration given to one's intentions, interior dispositions, motivations, or any covenant based on love. The deed, not the heart, determined the moral content.

Taken together, the Way of Self-Denial and casuistry led me—and I'm sure most other adolescent want-to-be priests—into some strange behavior with the people who came into our lives as Significant or Quasi-Significant Others, the people who have helped mold me out of biblical clay into the person I am today. While the Way of Self-Denial held me back, casuistry thrust me forward into explorations of my sexuality. It was a schizophrenic dance. The Negative Way, with its emphasis on perpetual virginity defined as the ultimate gift to God and its loss as the ultimate betrayal, led me to protect my invisible male hymen by avoiding penis-in-vagina intercourse at all cost. Casuistry, on the other hand, offered a descending scale of seriousness based on what body parts were employed. Above the neck and outside the brain was serious, between the neck and belt more serious, and below the belt even worse. Inside the belt lurked the ultimate serpent, the worst sin of all sins.

Pursuing the mental gymnastics of casuistry, I argued that I could protect my virginity and remain true to the Negative Way by denying my body its ultimate craving. At least we "technical virgins" could be proud we "never did it." At the same time, I could use casuistry to give myself permission to explore above and below the belt, lesser if still somehow mortal infractions, just as long as I don't hit sin's rock bottom and go inside the belt. This cock-eyed thinking had me robbing Peter—no sexual pun intended—to pay Paul.

People who became significant to me and I to them found themselves confronted with my strange, schizophrenic brand of spirituality. While they were thinking genuine spiritual thoughts—sharing mutual love, comfort, growth, and support, celebrating life, and the like—I was working on how to satisfy and at the same time deny my penis. This I could accomplish as long as I avoided the rock bottom sin of intercourse. If I avoided that ultimate sin, I could still protect my place on the top step of the stairway to Paradise in the company of other perpetual virgins.

The funny thing is I successfully found a way of moving from the Negative Way and casuistry to a Positive Way when I was dealing as a pastor with the spiritual and sexual journeys of others. As a pastor, I can see the big picture, and I can communicate it to others. What inner spirits are striving for is far more important to me than what the genitals are doing. Yet, when it comes to organizing my own spiritual and sexual journey, my early imprinting is still very much with me. The irony is that I have precious thank-you cards and letters in my files from people who came to me for counseling, and discovered new ways to connect their sexuality and spirituality. In my own case, however, it's a matter of "Doctor, heal thyself."

Sometimes all this seems mysterious to me; at other times it is perfectly obvious. The mysterious part is that I have entered into a very important relationship that is sexual in the broad sense, but not genitally focused. And this relationship I have found enriching beyond all my expectations. This is what life has to be all about. And what spells life spells Spirit, "the giver of life." The obvious part is that I needed such a relationship to put an end to my game-playing with the Negative Way and casuistry. I had been trying to play the piano without hitting the black keys. The music was boring. The gift here is that I met someone who wants to make the same journey. I have taken my first baby-step on the Positive Way. It's a strange paradox. I now feel more whole, sexually and spiritually, than when I was slipping and sliding under the burden of a morality dictated by casuistry and the Way of Self-Denial.

One evening some parish staff and myself went to a restaurant for supper. Just a few booths away, I noticed a man who seemed familiar. With him was a woman I didn't know. It was one of those situations where you ask yourself, "Is that him, or isn't it? Where have I seen him before?" Then I remembered. He was a fellow priest. It struck me as strange that he was eating his meal wearing sunglasses and a baseball cap. His clothes looked as if he had taken them from a Salvation Army collection bin. Our eyes met briefly. He looked away quickly and whispered something to his companion. They left in a hurry—his disguise had been blown.

How sad, I thought to myself. Were they also victims of the Negative Way? They were sharing companionship. They were breaking bread. No doubt, they were also sharing stories. If they were also sharing physically, sexually, would that invalidate, or corrupt, their connectedness, if, as one lecturer put it, the Eucharist means "gathering, telling the story, breaking bread"? Followers of the Negative Way would have no doubt about such a situation: if there was sex, there was sin. The Negative Way gives no weight to interior dispositions. It calls us to rise above the flesh, and yet its judgments are centered in and obsessed with what the flesh does. The Negative Way calls us to poverty, yet its approach to sexuality is centered in and obsessed with the materialness of the body. The Negative Way has not come to grips with the Incarnation, which it struggles furiously to limit to the safe confines of a baby born to a virgin and foster-parented by a man with no interest in sex.

I know my fellow priest's pain. I too once wore sunglasses and a baseball cap. Not any more. I'm no longer looking for a clever way, or a sneaky way, or a slippery casuistic way, to rejoin my sexuality and my spirituality.

It's hard work, but I am learning to recognize my spirituality in my sexuality, and experience my sexuality in my spirituality. My thanks to those patient souls who have loved me without understanding me, who may have been hurt by my poorly integrated sexuality and spirituality.

3. The Story of a Single Pastor

Alicia Smith

As a young single pastor in a large city church, I felt a need to learn more pastoral counseling skills, especially in the area of marriage, family and sexual issues. Seeing an announcement in a professional journal of a workshop in my area sponsored by a pastoral counseling center in a neighboring city, I enrolled. There I met the workshop leader, Bill, a minister, and his wife, Beth. I learned a great deal from them about how I could be a more effective pastor with the families in the parish I served. I also attended a second workshop they offered a few months later. In the course of the workshops, I explored some long neglected and underdeveloped areas in my own life as a single adult regarding my thoughts and feelings on sensuality and sexuality.

Later that year, Bill and Beth called to say that they had been invited to do a workshop in an area near where I lived and that Beth was unable to co-lead the workshop with Bill. Since I had attended two prior workshops they had led, they both felt that I could function as a co-facilitator in this new workshop and were inviting me to share in their workshop leadership.

Bill and I did the workshop together and in the process shared many ideas about the future of marriage, family, and sexuality. Bill and Beth had shared with me earlier that after much reading, study, prayer, and discussion they had decided that their marriage to each other could be enriched by allowing each other to include in an occasional friendship an openness to sexual intimacy with another partner, keeping the marriage as the primary commitment and with the full knowledge and agreement of both partners in the marriage. If either partner felt uncomfortable they could say so and the secondary sexual relationship would not take place unless both partners felt comfortable about the satellite relationship of the partner wishing it. Their idea of open marriage did not come as a shock to me, as these ideas had been discussed in previous workshops. The theological rationale for a decision such as this made sense to me.

I had earlier in my life concluded that a traditional, exclusively committed marriage was not for me. I felt called to live my life as a single person, free to pursue any direction that God might lead me, without what appeared to me to be the encumbrance of others—spouse and possible children—to consider. I had been happy in this choice of life style, but had been somewhat unsure of how to deal with my own sexuality, given the choice of the single life.

I believed then, as I do now, that sexuality was and is a gift from God, part of our created nature and as such, good. It was difficult for me to believe that the only valid place in life for acknowledging sexuality would be in marriage. I had looked for answers in Christian books about sexuality, but found few authors ready to tackle the subject head on—only a sentence here and there and many of those scattered sentences were vague and timid. Bill and Beth had read and studied extensively. He had taught in a theological seminary and served as a leader in his denomination in the area of family life, including sexuality. They did not appear to be taking this step into open marriage with any thing but the deepest sense that it was consistent with the Old Testament, the New Testament, the teachings of Jesus Christ, and the love of God. This decision was not out of conflict in their relationship, but an enrichment of their life together. I felt very moved by their willingness to take risks into new territory from a faith that was deep and sure and theologically sound. I wanted to support them in taking this position and I was also strengthened in my own developing beliefs by their views on sexuality, able to accept my own sexuality at a deeper level and to feel somewhat freer in my own sensual and sexual expression than I had previously felt.

Bill and I began to explore the possibilities of being sexually involved together during the week that we taught the workshop together. We saw each other a few times after that as well. After a year or so, I was called to a new job far enough away that I did not see Bill and Beth for five or so years. We kept in touch with occasional correspondence and visits. For different reasons, we both moved to the same city. Bill and Beth invited me to a dinner party at their home. I met their children, now young adults themselves. I met some of their friends and associates, and I felt immediately at home with their other guests. Meals were wonderful and conversation around the dining room table was the most open family conversation I had ever heard. Avid discussions about religion, politics, city, state, national, and worldwide issues, and, yes, sexuality was a frequent topic. Everyone participated and all views were acceptable for discussion. The young people felt free to discuss sexual issues they were facing—homosexuality, AIDS prevention, abortion. Transvestites and transsexuals were occasional topics as well as occasional guests.

Having come from a family where sexuality was never openly discussed, where my mother had been obviously embarrassed even to tell me about my own menstruation, this openness about sexuality was refreshing. My father had once denounced the novel *Lady Chatterly's Lover* as a trashy book — a view with which my mother, who loved books, politely disagreed, and then the subject was quickly closed, never to be reopened. Aside from my mother's answer to my "Why did you get married?" which was "… to have a baby," that was truly all I knew about their views on sexuality. My father once said, "Don't have too much fun," as I left for a high school date. I wasn't even sure then what he meant, but I can now guess that it probably referred to feeling or doing anything sexual.

Bill and Beth's home was a place where sexuality was viewed as natural, normal, and good. The children had been encouraged to ask questions as they grew up. The family hot tub was a place where nudity among adult friends was natural and comfortable.

Over the years, Beth has sent Bill and me off on a good many happy adventures. She would say to Bill, "Why don't you call Alicia," and we would go off for ethnic food (which by the way Beth detests and Bill and I love) or to attend an opera, play, or movie that Beth didn't want to see. Bill always checked in with Beth before making plans with me. I respect him for giving his primary relationship the honor it deserves. Also Beth and I have done things together without Bill — a play, movie, meal, or shopping. I am friends with them both and believe this is a key to the success of our relationships.

I can honestly say I have rarely been jealous of Beth, although there was a time that Bill and Beth went on a fabulous trip (they did invite me to go along) and I spent a fairly miserable and lonely time without them that holiday. I took them to the airport, picked them up, and planned the welcome home party, but it took months to deal honestly with the feelings I had and to understand them.

Bill and I have been to professional conferences together as our work has been in similar areas of counseling. Bill, Beth, and I and other friends have taken vacations together. Beth delighted once in taking me on a shopping trip for clothes, "to change my image," she said. She decided I needed a more updated exterior to match the interior me — rather than looking so ordinary. I think she only partially succeeded in making me into a classy dresser like herself. I'm comfortable in jeans and tennis shoes, while she wears the latest styles, make-up, and jewelry in a style that is all her own.

It is important to me that my relationship with Bill is not my only intimate relationship, nor my primary one. In fact, it would be a mistake for me to make Bill my primary relationship, for then it would not be balanced. This relationship is not his primary relationship. His marriage is primary and it will always be.

Months may go by without seeing or talking to Bill and Beth. We are all busy in our careers and lives and other friendships and family relationships. Then, all of a sudden, one of us will call and we will get together, either at my home or theirs, or go on a trip together, or to some event.

This is a very valuable relationship in my life and has made me a more open person in my other relationships as well. It has validated my feelings from long ago, that I am not by nature a person who can be satisfied with only one intimate relationship per lifetime. I am today meeting more and more people who have come to the same conclusions and do not feel this position inconsistent with basic Christian beliefs. Whether or not Jesus was married, we do know that he had a number of intimate friendships. We don't know if he was sexually active, but he was clearly comfortable with his sexuality.

Marriage is not for everyone. It is more socially accepted now to choose to be single than it was when I first chose to do so, and I am glad. Too many people for too long have felt somewhat abnormal if they weren't married. They have had nowhere to turn for help in self-acceptance and assistance in knowing how from a Christian perspective to have a life that is fully sensual and sexual without feeling guilty.

In more recent years, I am finding many people eager to talk about sensuality, sexuality, and spirituality. I find that I include in my friendships various sensual as well as sexual pursuits such as massage, nude recreation, including hot tub gatherings, yoga, etc.

There is a different feeling altogether in these open encounters than in the old "sneaking around" when relationships were not open. I do not think of my relationship with Bill as an affair. Neither does he. It is an intimate friendship, such as described by James and Betty Ramey in their book, *Intimate Friendships*, published in 1976.

Intimate Friendships is only one of several books published in the 1970s by different authors that all point to the same ideas. Rustum and Della Roy's *Honest Sex*, Anna and Robert Francoeur's *Hot and Cool Sex*, and Ron Mazur's *New Intimacy* are a few. Each of these authors (or pair of authors) is seeking from a sound spiritual background to see what is wrong with the modern American system of serial monogamy (marriage, divorce, remarriage, repeated over and over), and what other patterns of intimacy might work better with less hurt and pain for all concerned, and more joy and sharing.

Perhaps for most people in the Christian church and in the society as a whole, an exclusive monogamous commitment will continue to be the norm and will by far be the most prevalent form of primary relationships. I have no problem with that. I honor and respect those who have found that kind of relationship and are fulfilled in it. However, for those of us who either have not found that option or who have not felt called to that option, perhaps other options could be accepted as not being a threat to Christian values.

To survive, to grow in today's changing world, we need to be aware that some very committed and spiritually concerned men and women are finding ways to meet their spiritual needs and their sensual and erotic needs in a variety of relationships that do not fit the traditional patterns of sexually abstinent single life or sexually exclusive marriage. These options, including sexually open committed relationships and networks of "intimate friends" need further exploration not just by sincerely committed Christian people, but also by the church leaders who, unfortunately, just don't understand that we are living in a radically different world than Christians knew two thousand years ago. Our basic Christian principles still hold true, but applying them today gives us some different answers.

4. This Is My Song, This Is My Sacred Journey

Henry Bullmann

"This is my story, this is my song,
  Praising my Savior, all the day long;
This is my story, this is my song,
  Praising my Savior, all the day long."

We used to sing this old Gospel hymn at the Sunday evening meetings of our Youth Group in an Evangelical Church where I grew up and in the area-wide Youth Conferences. Another hymn, "Blessed Assurance, Jesus Is Mine," expressed our convictions and our commitment to Jesus Christ. I was reared in the church, had most of my early social life related to the church, was later ordained as a minister in the church, and served Christ in that capacity for many, many years.

What snapshots should I share with you? My spiritual journey covers seventy-five years, so choosing is not easy. Obviously, I can't tell my whole story. But I also can't talk about spirit, soul, and spiritual love as good and matter, body, and sexual love as somehow dirty and dangerous, if not outright sinful. For me, they are part and parcel one with the other. I can't and don't accept the neo-platonic view adopted by the Church Fathers that still darkens the Biblical interpretations and ethical teachings of the organized churches when it comes to sex. My rejection of the neo-platonic dualistic view and my integration of my sexual and spiritual life would be condemned by my church—hence my need for anonymity. Names are also changed in my snapshots to protect those I love.

I'm like gays in the military, and many in the churches whose sexual orientations, lifestyles, and family and marriage patterns do not fit the socially accepted traditional norm. Most of us are very circumspect and remain in our "closets." We may experience doubts or inner conflict about our lives. Some of us have heard that what we do and how we live are "of the flesh" and

21

"evil." Some of us now dare to write, although anonymously, of our own journeys, and reflect on our lives, in the hope that our experience may help others in this pluralistic society where marital and familial diversity is a fact, and the much touted "traditional American marriage and family" are a fiction with little basis in reality. Individuals cannot be forced into a single mold, nor should we try.

My own secret is that I have been involved in a sexually open monogamous (one spouse) marriage for the last third of my life. Combining a primary marital relationship with satellite friendships that have also involved sexual love is as much a part of my spiritual journey as my prayers and devotions in the sanctuary. I suspect you're wondering what I mean by a sexually open marriage, and why I chose this form of marriage. "Why be married and pretend to be a Christian if you want to fuck around?" is a good question.

Our society sees marriage as a legal as well social relationship between two consenting adults, one man and one woman, governed by civil law and a matter of public record. In a marriage, a man and woman covenant together, exchanging vows to love, care for, support, cherish, and encourage each other and live together as husband and wife. "Monogamy" means "one marriage," only one spouse, one sexual partner.

This form of monogamy is the only legal marriage pattern in the United States. This relationship is meant to last a lifetime. And there is great value in that expectation. In such a relationship, with its societal support, two people are able to learn to love because each is loved, to trust because each is trusted. They can learn that love must endure problems, warts, running noses, sickness. As Ron Mazur wrote in *The New Intimacy*, "There is much painful learning in the give and take of mutual growth, and the constancy of this relationship is crucial to our evaluation of who and what we are" (page 12). Marriage is intended for mutual growth and happiness of its partners. It is a school for learning to love.

In our society most of us have been conditioned to consider marriage as a license for sex. For most that means sexual intimacy should never under any circumstances occur between a married person and one who is not his/her spouse. We have been conditioned to use terms like "infidelity" and "cheating." And indeed it is infidelity and cheating if one of the marital vows has included a promise to be sexually exclusive. "Infidelity" is unfaithfulness to a vow, any vow. The Episcopal marriage service includes only one statement which may be interpreted as a promise of sexual exclusiveness. These are the words "forsaking all others" in *The Declaration of Consent*. When Sarah and I were married several years ago we studied the Episcopal service and its vows for husband and wife carefully and decided it was right for our wedding, except for those three words. We got the officiating minister to leave them out because we had agreed to a sexually open marriage.

We made this decision because we believed in the value of monogamy. But we had seen so many people smothered in monogamy, prevented from following their own interests and growing, restricted in their friends and companions, held in chains by possessiveness, abused by jealousy, forced into uncomfortable roles, and encouraged to tell lies or to keep silence when afraid of a spouse's reaction. When we agreed to marry, Sarah immediately said, "But I've got to be free!" We both exclaimed, "It's got to be open!" We talked frankly about sex and for the years of our dating together we had gone out with other people. We agreed that if and when either of us was out with another companion, sex would be okay if it were in a context of caring and responsibility — and if we were open with other each other about it.

In our open marriage, Sarah and I have had to deal with the fact that all relationships are partial and no one person can totally satisfy or meet all the other partner's needs. An open marriage is not necessarily sexually inclusive. It is up to the spouses to determine to what degree they want to include others, emotionally and sexually — and who that might include. We did not believe in "fucking around," casual sex for the sake of sex. We did believe that genuine love for another person in some instances might include an erotic component which, when mutually desired, could be morally accepted. A sexually open marriage is simply an open marriage of equal partners in which the spouses have agreed that each may engage in separate, companionable, and sexualove relationships with other partners so long as these are openly discussed and are in conformity with guidelines to which the spouses have agreed.

It was very important for Sarah and me that any relationship she or I might have with someone else not be secret. Whatever you call them, "satellite or comarital relationships," "intimate friendships," they are not "extramarital." Each of us knows of the other's special friends, and often they become our mutual friends. All involved must recognize the marital relationship itself is always primary.

Sarah and I have had an open primary relationship for over twenty-five years and we remain deeply committed to each other and to our relationship. We have each had other sexualove relationships and certain comarital partners have enriched our lives and brought greater joy into our own relationship. Our expanded family is a web, a network of intimate friends, comarital partners, former lovers, friends of friends who have grown close to us, some "blood" relatives, associates with whom we have become close because we share some common values and goals. This wonderfully supportive group, any one of whom we can call on when needed, is the joy of our lives. And in various groups, we party, play, travel, pray, and have fun together.

I only arrived at this inclusiveness in loving after many years of steps and missteps. It was and is a spiritual journey, a sacred journey, because it has always been grounded in love of my Creator, love for Jesus and a commitment to his Way as I understand it, and love for myself and others. It was St. Paul who said love is life's highest and greatest value (I Corinthians 13:13). Paul used the Greek word *agape* for love, a love that focuses on concern for and service to the welfare of others. There were other Greek words that emphasized various subjects or objects of love if you will, eros, philia, etc. But *agape* emphasizes the universality of love and the caring quality that must be part of any connectedness that we may identify as true love.

Early in my life journey I learned that *agape* alone was pure and good. *Eros* was banished to regions below the belt and hidden. At best erotic love was suspect; at worst it was the wicked means whereby original sin was transmitted from generation to generation. In carnal lust lurked the seed of all sin. Somewhere early on, I had to learn that just as matter and spirit, body and soul, are joined in one and blessed as good, so are sex and spirituality joined in one and blessed as good by the Creator. *Eros,* the erotic, needs *agape* and *agape* needs *eros* for balance. Erotic desire without respect for the personhood and well-being of another can be brutish. This is the "lust" which Jesus called adultery (even in thought). To treat another as an object, to deny or denigrate their personhood and use them for one's own pleasure adulterates and pollutes the alleged relationship (Matthew 5:38). This lust is in contrast with the concerned love of Matthew 5:43-48. Sex coupled with violence, abuse of another, and disregard of the other's wishes is heinous sin, in or outside a marriage.

Erotic love has had a bad reputation in Christian thought ever since and before Augustine of Hippo. *Eros/Agape* together are what some today are calling "sexualove"—a good term. It is not *gamos,* marriage, that sanctifies sex if you will, but *Agape,* a caring love.

We come to what we call the spirit only through the flesh. Is this not the message of the incarnation of Jesus Christ? Is this not in the very symbolism of any sacramental observance where physical elements are used to facilitate the experience of communion with deity and with one another? In sharing sexualove, woman has been for me a priestess, leading me through the gate of ecstasy to a sense of community and spiritual reality that transcends the physical and in which self is absorbed or lost or transcended. I remember how this awesome experience once terrified Sarah. Experiencing orgasm, she jumped from the bed and said, "I've lost myself. I don't even know who I am. I've got to get myself together." Needless to say, I was mystified by her reaction at the moment. Now I understand better. I hope that in sexualove I have sometimes been priest to woman.

I should hasten to add that I do not believe what I have been talking about applies only to heterosexual relationships. There was an old view that as male and as female we are all half persons and need the other half to be whole. Psychiatrist Carl Jung has helped us to see that we are whole persons and that within each of us, whether we have male or female reproductive/sexual organs, we include what he calls *anima* and *animus* (in varying degrees and intensities). To put it simplistically, this femininity and masculinity makes us whole. In gay and lesbian lovemaking, may it not be that the *anima* of one and the *animus* of the other find each other and connect? I believe that gay lovers and lesbian lovers can be as truly priests or priestesses to each other just as heterosexual couples can be. Sex in sexualove should never be reduced to a genital function and considered antithetical to spirituality. I must admit that I have traveled a long road coming to this place.

Enough theorizing! What of the road I've traveled and my significant experiences along the way?

I was only nine or ten years old when I was confirmed in the church, publicly expressing my faith in Jesus Christ. I remember it as a meaningful spiritual experience. I was about sixteen years old when, at a Youth Conference, I heard a stirring sermon on Isaiah 6:8. "And I heard the voice of the Lord saying, 'Whom shall I send, and who will go for us?' Then I said, 'Here I am! Send me.'" I was awake most of that night pondering what I had heard. I could only find peace and fall asleep after I said in my heart, "Lord, I don't know how I can do it, don't know how I'll find the money for years of college and seminary, but I'll be a minister if you want me to be and open a way." College and seminary would take seven years.

I pondered and prayed, and ended by choosing life-verses for my journey. These verses have guided my life ever since:

"We know that in everything God works for good with those who love Him, who are called according to His purpose." (Romans 8:28)

"If I speak in the tongues of men and angels, but have not love, I am a noisy gong or a clanging cymbal.... Love is patient and kind; love is not jealous or boastful.... So faith, hope, and love abide, these three; but the greatest of these is love. Make love your aim...." (I Corinthians 13:1,4,13 and 14:1)

"And above all these put on love, which binds everything together in perfect harmony." (Colossians 3:14)

"Come, my beloved, let us go forth into the fields, and lodge in the villages; let us go out early to the vineyards, and see whether the vines have budded, whether the grape blossoms have opened and the pomegranates are in bloom. There I will give you my love." (Song of Songs 7:11-12)

"Set me as a seal upon your heart, as a seal upon your arm; for love is strong as death, jealousy is cruel as the grave. Its flashes are flashes of fire, a most vehement flame. Many waters cannot quench love, neither can floods drown it. If a man offered for love all the wealth of his house, it would be utterly scorned." (Song of Songs 8:6-7)

At age sixteen I knew my Bible quite well. I had just graduated from high school near the top of my class, also having engaged in many extracurricular activities, from band and orchestra to the school paper, student government, ROTC officers' club, chess club, honor society, Spanish club, and Bible club. I had studied the Bible in depth in Sunday School for years and was program chairman in the church Youth Group. I was serious and bookish, but people person enough to run for student body president at school. I was shy around girls, but dated a few from our church Youth Group. My sex drive was plenty high and I wasn't convinced that premarital sex was really sinful even though I admit to some inner conflict as that stage. My dates, however, were "good girls" and I was more afraid of rejection than anything else.

The Bible had not convinced me that sex must be saved for one person and one person only, what with all the wives and concubines of the Patriarchs and people like King David and the "wise" King Solomon. And even Rahab, the harlot of Jericho who befriended Joshua's spies, was commended in the New Testament, accepted among the blessed faithful, and was listed in the genealogy of Jesus. Indeed, Jesus said to the chief priests and elders of the people, the pious religious leaders of his day, "Truly, I say to you, the tax collectors and the harlots go into the kingdom of God before you" (Matthew 21:31).

And what of the Song of Solomon? And its poetic, sensual invitation to loveplay?

> "Come! Be swift, my lover!
> Be like a gazelle or a wild young stag!
> Come! Play on my twin mountains of myrrh!
> The fountain in my garden is a spring of running water,
> blowing down from Lebanon.
> Arise, north wind!
> O south wind, come!
> Blow upon my garden, let its alluring perfumes pour
> forth.
> Then will my lover come to his garden and enjoy its
> choice fruits.
> And the lover's response? ...
> You are a pleasure ground filled with flowers....
> You are an enclosed garden, my sister, my bride,
> a garden close-locked, with a secret fountain.

Does not this message praise erotic love while many in the church still imply that sex is dirty, an enemy of the spirit? Claiming that only marriage can purify it?

But I did not experience any sexual involvement apart from hugs, holding hands, and rather chaste kisses until one month after my eighteenth birthday. The day after I enlisted in the army I became "sexually active" as the saying goes, and left home for a tour of three years in the U.S. military.

Our country had been drawn into World War II with the attack from Japan in the Pacific and the German U-boats taking American lives with the sinking of ships in the Atlantic. I enlisted. The induction station was not far from where I lived and while still there I secured a weekend pass to visit home. On Saturday night I went to choir practice at our church. When it was over I walked a lovely soprano—four years my senior—home. We were well acquainted but had never dated. She invited me in and we talked for a long time there in the living room. No one else was home. We began "fooling around" and before long a few garments came off. We were both very turned on and I'm sure the factor of my going away in service played through both our minds. She introduced me to French-kissing, oral-genital sex, and everything they used to call "heavy petting." We were about to fuck when we heard a car come up in front of the house and we scrambled madly to pull on our clothes. We just made it. This was my first sexual experience. I shall always remember Anne with affection and appreciation.

We soon lost contact, what with my being sent away and with her moving to another city. I look back on that experience as a spiritual and deeply meaningful experience. With the caring and concern we shared the physical closeness seemed very special. In this, God, who works all things for good to those who love him, used Anne as a priestess to bring enrichment, new knowledge, and greater maturity to my life. She mediated love to me as surely as those who preach sermons.

During my many months in the military there were significant events and experiences: sexual, in church, in illness being saved from death while my comrades were killed in combat, wondering why I was left alive while my friends perished. In the midst of it all, I committed my life as a follower of Jesus to a life of service in the church. Yes, I would be a minister one day. But I did not question the impropriety of nonmarital sexualove. During my service in the army, I had intimate friendships that included sexualove with five or six women.

When I was out of the service and in college, I married Lucy whom I had known for some years. I began studies in a theological seminary.

Lucy did not ask me about my sex life in the years before our wedding and I did not volunteer any information. Perhaps I should have, but I was afraid that she, a virgin, might feel hurt. (In today's age of AIDS I would surely have shared my sex history with her.) Lucy and I never even talked about our expectations in regard to extramarital sex and as I look back at the wedding service and the vows we exchanged, there was nothing explicitly requiring that we be sexually exclusive. I am very sure, however, that both of us assumed that sex would be restricted to our marital relationship.

I had several extramarital relationships of a loving nature with caring, responsibility, and always respect for the primacy of my marital relationship. I felt no guilt over the companionship and sharing of sexualove, but I did feel guilt in violating an assumption Lucy and I shared in regard to the sexual exclusiveness of our own relationship. I felt guilt in regard to the pain I believed she would feel if she knew of these relationships.

Increasingly I came to believe that fidelity meant being faithful to one's vows. When the Saducees asked Jesus about a woman who was married successively to seven brothers, one after the other, from the oldest to the youngest. Each husband died without producing a male heir, and so as each died, the next youngest brother took the widow to fulfill the levirate law. "Whose husband will she be in the resurrection?" Jesus had the perfect opportunity to speak out against this levirate law and against polygamy itself. Not only did he not condemn either, he did not even mention them. Jesus indicated that God intended for marriage to last so long as its partners should live; but he did not indicate any limit to the number of partners. Moreover, in his reply to the Sadducees he indicated that marriage was not forever and the relational pattern in the ideal life. "In the resurrection they neither marry nor are given in marriage, but are like the angels in heaven" (Matthew 22:30).

The concept of resurrection was one of a perfected state of bodily existence in the "afterlife" where perfect love, universal love, unlimited love, would exist. Marriage, as a school for learning to love, would no longer be needed. Marriage, with its rules and "safeguards," throws a wall around spouses, but the wall intended as protection also prevents the expansion of love to others. Love is that which draws all together. Many biblical commentators, tacitly accepting the "sex is sin" dictum, rejoice that there will be no sex in the "afterlife." There could be none if there is no marriage and sex cannot occur outside marriage they reason. They look at the words, "like the angels in heaven," and assume that angels are sexless beings. But the Bible only tells us that angels are God's messengers. They are communicators. This means that we will be perfect communicators in the ideal or perfected life. "Resurrection life" is a way of speaking of what ideal human life should be. Given our limitations in this age, we cannot achieve perfection here ... but Jesus sets it before his followers as he does in the Beatitudes of Matthew 5. No person ever claimed that we should not strive after such a life, and do what can be done here in this life. It seems to me, therefore, that a deeply committed marriage that remains a primary relationship might well be open to other responsible, sincere sexualove relationships in which openness, honesty, and caring are the rule. The school of love opens itself to expanded love — and this is part of our journey towards that which is perfect.

It would be many years before Lucy and I renegotiated our marriage covenant so as to explicitly allow and approve of separate companionable and sexualove relationships with other partners. Many experiences and influences, and much study and reflection, led up to that decision. So far as I know, Lucy remained sexually exclusive within our marriage during those early years. I did not.

Just before Lucy and I reshaped our marriage we met two Methodist ministers and their wives (each couple had a sexually open marriage). They helped facilitate our decision. A third Methodist minister had led us in a workshop that also helped us open up sexually to each other and talk honestly with each other. We visited Sandstone Retreat just north of Los Angeles and talked with John and Barbara Williamson, its founders, about the Community they had established seeking to break down the walls of separation and foster expanding love among people. We lingered there to experience the open sexualove shared among the members. We traveled to a huge conference in Colorado where we made the decision to open our marriage. This was over two decades ago. My first comarital partner was the wife of one of those Methodist ministers, the second was a divorced social worker I met at the Colorado conference, and the third was a close friend of the minister's wife. Although none of us live in the same city and we are separated by many miles, we continue as good friends after all these years. My third mentioned partner had been in a sexually open marriage for a number of years. Her husband was a university professor and they and their lovely children were active in both church and community affairs. He had been a comarital partner with the Methodist minister's wife and she with the minister. With my own relationships with Rose, Emma, and Bobbi, we became very close in an intimate network.

That network actually was the beginning of the expanded family which means so much to me today. Emma and Bobbi are even now good friends with my wife Sarah to whom I have been married for at least twenty years. Both Emma and Bobbi have visited us and Sarah has visited Bobbi, and we all stay in touch.

Before I met Sarah there were several other comarital partners of great significance in my life. At one point, Lucy had gone with me to another city to help with a workshop I was leading. One of the participants was a minister named Libby, single and into counseling work. She had a rich and varied background, had once lived in the city where I now resided, and was very interested in my work. I'm sure we both felt some attraction from the beginning. A few months later I was leading another event in the city where I lived and Libby came as one of the participants. Lucy was again involved. We welcomed Libby and were happy to see her. No sooner was the workshop over than Libby and I were making love. Lucy knew and was very accepting. During that visit I recall our meeting Libby's parents and going out to dinner with them. Later on, when I would visit the city where Libby lived, I would stay over at her house. On one occasion she went with me to another city to lead a workshop. After a time, however, Libby completed what she was doing where she lived and decided to move to a distant place where she remained for fully ten years. We lost contact. Her life went on with other work and relationships as did mine. But we would meet again and remain close, caring comarital partners to this day. We now live in the same city where Sarah, Libby, and I are good friends and share in a very supportive relationship.

Neither my first wife, Lucy, nor Sarah, nor I are into the swinging lifestyle. Sex that is not an aspect of sexualove is just not our cup of tea.

After years of evolving from a traditional to an open marriage, Lucy and I separated. I moved to the Midwest where I found work in a well-established and highly respected agency. I helped coordinate and teach in their educational program. I was happy in my work and was getting my whole being integrated and feelings dealt with. I rejoiced in my comfortable bachelor apartment and single life. I remembered what Emma had told me about "kicking my butt if I got married within two years of Lucy and I separating." During the many months that I lived alone there I had several significant relationships, one of which came to be most important—a very deep and genuine love and a person with whom I feel sure I might have most happily some day married. I spent more time with her, and often with her two lovely daughters (she was recently divorced), than everybody else put together. Ours certainly was a primary sexualove relationship.

When my time had come to settle permanently in that city or move on, Joan and I looked at every aspect of potential work for the two of us there and elsewhere. I suppose we had both grown old enough not to be adventurous and we looked for financial security. I couldn't find the right thing there. I would move. We wept. And after my move we visited a number of times, ran up huge telephone bills, even wrote endless letters. Joan is one of the very significant people with whom I shared a bit of space and time on my life journey. I still love her very much in spite of time and distance. She has remarried and we are no longer in contact.

About a year after I resettled I met Sarah and it was love and lust at first sight. I introduced Lucy to Sarah and to Sarah's husband from whom she was planning to separate regardless of my being on the scene. They loved each other but had enough differences to feel that happiness and growth meant going it alone.

Sarah's husband and I became warm friends and we have since come to call ourselves "husbands-in-law" and "brothers we each never had." John is as much a member of my family today as anyone. I love him deeply. He and Sarah and I do many things together, and together with their children who are now grown and on their own in their own relationships. We have always all been very open and honest with each other about our lives and relationships and I have never seen a better adjusted "crew."

For two and a half years or so Sarah and I had our separate apartments and "dated" other people. But we were growing to be partners in a very special primary relationship through many ups and downs and crises in the relationship. We both consistently fought for our "space" and sense of freedom — but coupled with the togetherness we wanted. During this time we both were periodically sexually involved with other people. There were certain other sexualove relationships that were very important — and some that remain so, especially as friends no longer sexually involved.

About a year before Sarah and I decided to marry, we met Kerry, a psychiatrist, and Mary, his sociologist wife, who had for some years had a sexually open marriage. I developed an intimate relationship with them both and when they moved 150 miles to another city, Mary drove back for two days of classes at the university where I was teaching. She was an older graduate student finishing up her residency and course requirements. She arranged to stay overnight once each week in my apartment. We slept together and often enjoyed sex. On one occasion when Kerry came with Mary, we enjoyed a fantastic and very loving threesome. A bit later on, after the school year and the regular visits ended, Sarah and I visited them for a weekend. At this point, Sarah and Kerry became quite involved.

Sarah's sexual relationships were far fewer and usually much briefer than mine. There was always caring and a context of friendship, but long-term intimacy was not usually involved. One was with a Roman Catholic priest for whom she cared a great deal and whom she had met before meeting me.

In truth, Sarah never cared too much for straight men. There were a few exceptions. A physician friend of Sarah's in the "old days" always held a special place in her heart and fantasies, but there was never any sexual involvement. She loved John very much and he loved her. Four years after John married, his wife — and Sarah — learned that he was gay, but the marriage continued and held them together for years. One of their lovely children, a well put together person if I have ever known one, is homosexual. John has a first cousin who is gay — and a priest. He has an uncle, now deceased, who was gay.

I have a host of gay and lesbian friends. As a very straight male I can but weep at the ignorance and homophobia I see in our heterosexist society. I become angry with much that I see. Some who are the subject of intolerance, bigotry, and injustice are part of my expanded family. As for sexual orientation, Sarah is very straight. Apart from sex, however, she has always related intimately with other women more readily than men. Two of her highest compliments to me were, "Henry, you're straight, but you're the next best thing" and "Henry, you're the only straight man I've truly loved."

Sarah loves me. There were times in the first years when I doubted it. That's because she often would not let me into her space as I wanted. She cherished her freedom and independence. By the same token, she holds my freedom to be sacred. And she has less jealousy in her make-up than anyone I have ever known. We all must learn that genuine love is not jealous and that it is freeing. It turns loose. It does not clutch and grasp.

There was one time when I saw Sarah's jealousy erupt, break forth; in contrast, I could tell you a dozen times when jealousy has been a pain in my life and a thing I hated in myself. Six months before Sarah finally said to me, "Henry, I'll marry you" (to which she quickly added, "But it's got to be open and I've got to feel free"), I met her friend Betina, then a student in an Episcopal theological seminary. Betina was an even more ardent feminist than Sarah. She was bisexual—and very sexual. An exciting, bright, articulate woman, we had much in common, and were very erotically pulled to each other. At the time I felt Sarah was pushing me away and I was in a relationship simply going in circles. Perhaps, I was feeling "needy." Whatever the case, Betina and I, to use well worn words, "fell madly in love with each other." I know now after all these years that it was more than that. I still love her very, very much although our paths rarely cross. When she came to visit for a week, Sarah was so uncomfortable she went out of town. Later Betina sent me a huge floral arrangement. A few days later I got one from Sarah. Betina and I grew very serious about each other. I let her know that I had a prior commitment to Sarah, and had, in fact, asked her to marry me—even though at the time I did not expect her to accept. For six months Betina and I shared visits, scores of letters and cards, and telephone calls.

Suddenly, to my surprise, Sarah, whom I still loved so very much announced, "Henry, I'll marry you." A wedding date was set about six months in the future. Betina was crushed and angry. We might well have married each other if it had not been for Sarah. At this point Betina was not ready to be a comarital partner. Our contact began to break off. I think her own therapist encouraged it. Also, a very dear Episcopal priest whom we all knew very well—and who knew us—must have encouraged it as best for all concerned. This priest, whom I had known for several years, was a priest and pastor to John and his wife. He also officiated at our wedding. A fun-loving person, and one of the most loving individuals I have ever known, a great saint of God!

Our wedding was a wonderful event. No one thought it odd or strange that "forsaking all others" was omitted from our vows. A good number of our comarital partners, past and present, were with us. We had many Afro-American friends and gay and lesbian friends on hand with a large contingent of straights. I rather think that heaven or the resurrection life will be quite as inclusive.

The clergy leading our ceremony were just as inclusive. Along with the chief celebrant were two women clerics, one from the Episcopal Church of the U.S.A. and the other from the Church of Wales, also an Anglican. We had two Presbyterians, one of whom was a seminary professor and the other in parish ministry. An Episcopal priest and his wife read as the Old Testament lesson some of the most erotic and sexually explicit parts of the Song of Songs. After the wedding, a dear, devout lady was heard to remark that what was read was really obscene. Someone explained, "But it's in the Bible!" Her reply rather illustrates a feeling about eroticism and sex fostered by the church itself: "Well, it oughtn't to be!"

So began a sexually open marriage that has been one of great joy and happiness, great commitment and mutual supportiveness, remarkable role flexibility, pleasure in a host of mutual friends, and freedom to pursue separate interests and relationships.

This story of my sexually open marriage journey with Sarah touched on a few vignettes. Some of our intimate friends now live far away. Our expanded family is spread across the United States, with a few in Britain. This did not just happen. Our intimate network has flourished because Sarah and I were quite prepared and ready at the time of our wedding. We freely and mutually chose this lifestyle at the beginning. We had already worked through a lot of potential problems and had grown in our own sense of personal worth and security so that we were ready for what many perceive as threats to marriage. We have been rewarded not only by mutual stimulation from each other but by the stimulation of other relationships which our freedom has afforded us.

When I look back across the years and think of those life-verses I chose when I was only sixteen years old, I marvel at how appropriate they have been for my journey. I have not always been happy with the lack of love I perceive in the organized church, but I have always felt very close to that great, self-giving man of love, Jesus Christ. In many varied ways I have tried to serve his cause. When sexualove has been truly love, I believe he has been present. I have made many mistakes and have some regrets. But I love God and still believe that "in everything God works for good with those who love him." I have also found that love is that which "binds everything together in perfect harmony." I have learned, too, that sex is not sanctified by marriage, but as with everything else it is sanctified only by a genuine caring love which yearns for and works for the welfare of the beloved. So my journey has been very much a spiritual journey.

This is my story, this is my song—a sacred journey! And God isn't through with me yet.

5. The Body Sacred

A Modern Teresa

It was a hot summer afternoon. I had just returned from my long day of piano practice. It was just one week before my first doctoral recital. I went straight up to my room, opened the window, and removed my religious garb called "the habit." I threw myself over my bed. A cool breeze was brushing over my body as I lay on my back. I let my brain chill out, simply being in blankness, not thinking of anything at all. I gradually became aware of my breath and belly. How my belly swelled and flattened with the rise and fall of each breath. When my awareness moved inward, I felt a sensation of being alive, alive just by being. No thoughts. No judgments. I was inside my breath.

Then it happened. I felt a tingling, quivering sensation in my genitals. It was delicious and, oh, so pleasurable! I gently touched myself, letting my hands dance with the wonder of body-energy I had never known before. My response was spontaneous and seemed genuinely natural. I felt I had received a gift from God. At some intuitive level, I knew that the quickening of the spirit—familiar and energizing to me in my relationship with God—and this quickening of the body were the two impulses creating the core vibration of that which moves toward wholeness, the deep-down longing of the soul.

When things quieted down, the Church's strong dichotomy between body and spirit and the tightly woven fabric of the Church's rigid sexual dogma which were chiseled into my early tender years loomed before me. Floods of doubt, guilt, and fear engulfed me. The bridge which carried me out of this storm was a priest whose wise counsel widened my vision of passion, ecstasy, and eros as inherent in both the sacred and the sexual. He helped me see that my lifelong yearning and longing for union with God and my passionate embrace of the sensual and the erotic in music, art, poetry, dance, nature, and, yes!, in my body were like the ball and socket joints in my shoulders and hips. The two together have movement and meaning to the whole of me with the body as the central vortex stimulating, empowering, and radiating who-I-am.

Since then, I have journeyed from orthodox, patriarchal religious beliefs to the path of listening to and following the nudges of the multitudinous Holy Guides within and around me. I am on this earth to attend the Universal School of Learning how to grow, expand, create, and be in relationship with other humans, the earth, my body, and the Beloved of my soul—Pure Presence, Light Energy, Primal Sound.

I am on this earth as an embodied spirit, a sexual being. My sexuality embraces the full range of my feelings, perceptions, dreams, behaviors, and sensual responses. I feel my body alive when I smell flowers, taste kiwi, touch skin, listen to the birds, play the *Appassionata Sonata*, and dance with the primal rhythms of my drums.

The dynamic life force of living the fullness of my humanity, my womanhood, and my divinity is relationships. This is especially so for keeping my sexuality fertile and integrated with Spirit. I express my relationships with self and others through touch, look, speech, emotion, and action, and hopefully, with honesty, integrity, and reverence. It is in the cycles and rhythms of relationships with the giving and receiving, the risking and the trusting that sex and spirit merge and blossom as one. For too long sexual energy has been fixated solely on intercourse. As one author put it, "It is time to rescue eros from the genitals."

"How do you reconcile these views with your choice of religious celibacy?" This question frequently comes up whenever I am in a group talking about sex and spirit. First of all, I cannot imagine embracing any lifestyle that is not strongly connected to being whole and alive. "I have come that you may have life and have it to the full!" These words of Jesus became the central theme of my Christian life since childhood. Secondly, if sexuality is a way of being—and I believe it is—then, being celibate cannot rule out being sexual.

I continue to explore the ways I can tap the energies within my body to empower and enliven my life. There are times when I feel deep pulls and experience passionate drives around issues, situations, and events. When I do not deny these attractions, but channel them into some creative outlet, the embodied energies of my being shoot through me like a fountain!

My celibate life is rooted in and flows in a wide sphere of loving. My affective life embraces many persons in intimacy rather than committing exclusively to one other. I feel amazing liberation in giving and receiving love generatively and generously. For me, loving knows no limits and there are as many expressions and manifestations of loving as there are diversity and uniqueness of humans.

Like every other life stance, religious celibacy has both an external and internal side. The external profile of the celibate is one who chooses not to "marry." As a member of a vibrant religious community, I grow in the company and with the support of empowered women who affirm, challenge, and speak the truth to me. My inner life is illumined by the radiant Fire-energy of Divina, my name for the Passionate Presence of God. I know that I am the Beloved of Divina. There are times when I experience divine love as a fire in my body, an ecstatic flame of energy that sears, purifies, and transforms me. An orgasm of spirit not unlike physical orgasm.

I take great delight in the writings of mystics such as Teresa of Avila, Hildegard of Bingen, and John of the Cross. In describing their ecstatic visions and all-consuming desire for blissful union with their God, I am struck by the erotic imagery and sexual symbolism of their language. In one of Teresa's prayers, she addressed God as her Beloved "from whose divine breasts there flow streams of milk bringing comfort to all people...."

Hildegard hears God's Voice: "In the shaking out of my mantle you are drenched, watered, with thousands upon thousands of drops of precious dew." John of the Cross speaks of being wounded by love as being penetrated by God. Then, there is Solomon who, in the Old Testament, speaks to God: "Kiss me with the kisses of your mouth, for that love is better than wine."

One of the stunning memories of my visit to India is the erotic imagery etched on the walls of the Hindu temples at Khajuraho and Konarak. The copulation of the lovers exudes joy, playfulness, and rapture. Sri Ramakrishna, the 19th Indian mystic, seems to capture this sacred/sexual celebration when he said: "God cannot be seen with these physical eyes. In the course of spiritual discipline one gets a 'lovebody', endowed with 'love eyes', 'love ears' and so on. One sees God with those 'love eyes'. One hears the Voice of God with those 'love ears'. One even gets a sexual organ made of love. With this 'love body' the soul communes with God."

When I meet these mystics in their imagery, I am affirmed, loud and clear, that there is no separation between sex and spirit when I open myself to warmth, desire, depth, expansion, and trust. Then, I am connected.

It is a glorious time to be alive in spite of all the suffering and chaos; an unprecedented period in human history when boundaries are thinning and margins are leaking. Forces about us are in a dizzying movement toward convergence and synthesis. We see it everywhere! Bio-eco-psycho-spirituality in the cosmos and in our bodies. Perhaps the work that best expresses this current wave is connectivity. At last, the Light is dawning in our consciousness of the electromagnetic dance going on all the time in the universe where everything is constantly vibrating back and forth between spirit and matter.

This bioenergetic phenomenon is electric in my body. I intend to nurture this dynamism in as many ways as I can. I am drawn to a deeper knowledge and experience of the body chakras and the practice of Yoga. Yoga is a marriage of spirit and body. Its aim is union with the Infinite and Ultimate Truth and Light. Supreme Consciousness. Awesome Mystery. Such, too, is my aim.

6. A Nun's Transformation

Teresa's Daughter, Not Maria's

I must admit I struggled a long time with writing this piece, reluctant to tell a story I share with almost no one. Then this morning at Mass, the first reading from Paul (1 Corinthians 6:13-15) for the feast of St. Maria Goretti, who died a virgin martyr at the age of 12, was like a clarion call: "The body is not for lust; it is for the Lord.... Shun fornication. Every other sin that a man can commit is outside the body; but the fornicator sins against his own body."

Overlooking the obvious sexist language, I wondered what Paul's words mean today, and what it meant that Maria Goretti in 1902 took 14 knife wounds rather than allow a farmland to rape her. And what it meant that my Church canonized her for this in 1950 with her aged mother in attendance.

I recalled how the story had once made a deep impression on me. I was eleven years of age when she was canonized, but I never understood the "crime" for years afterwards. *The Scarlet Lily*, a biography of Maria, simply said, "He wanted to have his way with her." Rape was not a common noun in my home or in the Catholic schools I attended for twelve years. Sex education was simple: "Avoid until marriage." What we were supposed to avoid was not explained. I distinctly remember one of my elementary teachers telling us that "there are no venial sins against the sixth and ninth commandments." And if Sister said it, it must be true.

I became one of those Sisters in 1959, the day after my twentieth birthday. The oldest of six children, I came to religious life having dated several young men, one seriously; but my inclination to service, to reflection, to teaching, to a Gospel-centered lifestyle proved too strong. Two years of secretarial work drove me to consider what I had felt called to from childhood: the convent. I entered with my virginity intact—and was sure I would go to my grave that way.

Three years after entrance and the sort of novitiate one makes movies of, I was sent to teach fifth grade at a Catholic grammar school—and found chastity would be a tougher vow to keep than I had anticipated. The other

41

fifth grade was taught by a young man close to my age, who was also the church organist. As I ended up choir director, our paths crossed six days a week. The convent was rife with personality conflicts. I, being the youngest in the house, felt isolated — and my teaching partner and I developed a genuinely innocent friendship. June and the close of the school year brought much soul-searching. I was transferred to more healthy living situations over the next few years, completed my bachelor's degree, and began teaching high school.

In 1967, I professed my final vows and promised to live chastely until death. I meant the words, but I would not understand the cost of the promise for five more years.

By 1972, change was the order of the day. Vatican II had altered religious life irrevocably. My entrance class numbering fifty had dwindled to sixteen. (Today six remain.) We had doffed habits, modified the Rule, changed our lifestyle, taken back our baptismal names, giving up the religious names we took when we became novices. I had begun graduate work, was deliriously happy in my teaching career at a diocesan high school, had just passed a driver's test, and was elected president of the Sisters' Council, which I had almost single-handedly established. Celibacy had not been a serious problem for me after that first year of teaching. Living in a convent with Sisters from eight other religious communities, I felt "free" for the first time in my life.

In February of 1972 I was organizing a day of recollection for Sisters in the diocese and needed a priest to deliver a talk and say Mass. The Vicar for Religious suggested that I contact one of the members of his community — and the rest is my story of trying to unite sex and spirit.

I met the priest I would eventually fall in love with when he was very vulnerable. (I was also vulnerable, but didn't know it then.) Having just ended a relationship with a nun who left her community the previous summer, he was trying to get his life back together (which is why, I'm sure, the Vicar had given me his name.)

We were (and are) very different people. My inclination is towards books, art, music, conversation, and theater. He prefers solitude, enjoys reading, and is passionate about sports. What we had in common was a long-term religious commitment, a love of teaching, a propensity for serious conversation (often about the nature of God and Church), a love of Baroque and Renaissance music, and a mutual sense of humor.

By the summer of 1972, I was among the most conflicted people on earth. Words like *temptation* and *broken vows* took on ominous meaning. But I prayed harder that I ever had, and we spent time together trying to work out a "non-threatening" relationship.

Within six months it was very threatening. Sex outside marriage was something that one read about in novels. Sexual intimacy between two religious doomed them ... period.

Looking back, I don't honestly know how I survived trying to meld body and soul two decades ago. A Sister from my community with whom I lived made an appointment with our major superior in 1973 to discuss my "relationship," which she saw as disruptive of community life. To be fair, she was right. I did prefer being with him to being with her. But for the first time in my religious life, I held my ground against authority. I demanded the space to work out my own life—and miraculously, it was given to me.

It's probably significant that the priest I loved was also a clinical psychologist. We have supported each other through our mutual Ph.D. journeys, through family deaths, major and minor surgeries. But I think in retrospect, that I simply learned to trust my experience, to listen to the Spirit that I believed dwelt in both of us. I read not only Paul but John, whose phrase, "God is Love," summarizes the Law and the Prophets. I never rejected prayer. I never gave up on God or myself—but I changed my idea of who God is and what it means to be human. In phenomenological terms, love transformed my way of "being in the world."

Sexuality had been for me just another word in the dictionary. I had never learned to accept my sexuality at home, at school, in Church, or in the convent. Ultimately, acceptance came at a great price. I had to break down walls built around me for three decades. It was painful beyond words, but it was liberating as well. I cried often, sometimes far into the night, and usually alone. The guilt I felt in those early years was oppressive, but gradually I became whole—more integrated, better able to counsel students and understand the pain of opening oneself to another person, of becoming vulnerable through love.

When one falls in love with a priest, the added burden is not being able to share that love with others. Discretion can almost turn into paranoia. The wonderfully funny, relaxing overnight "vacations" that we shared on rare occasions over the years could be discussed only with one another. My family and friends knew him. He was eventually invited to my family celebrations and I to his, and, admittedly, in the early years I would have left the community to marry him—if he had asked. But he told me from Day One that he believed the monastery was where he belonged, and I eventually had to decide whether friendship, a committed sexual relationship, had to culminate in marriage. Again, my experience told me it did not. Ultimately, I decided that I really did not want to enter marriage either; I had come to treasure my freedom and independence.

My life has changed radically over the past twenty-five years, and I never doubt that falling in love—and growing in that love—had a great influence on choices I have made. In 1988, I left my traditional religious community and joined a non-canonical community, one not affiliated with Rome and its regulations. Self-supporting, I still teach at a Catholic liberal arts college, where I began my seventeenth year as department chair last September. I own a small home, live alone, and feel blessed that I share such a rich friendship with such an extraordinarily dedicated, good man. I have learned at a level I never could have imagined what the mystics wrote of when they tried to express spiritual union with the divine. Bernini's sensual, ecstatic sculpture of Teresa of Avila in the Vatican is closer to me in spirit than Maria Goretti! I have few regrets. I am never lonely. My life is rich with friends and family and work. Prayer and the Eucharist enrich my daily life. While I have not been to confession for many years, I no longer feel "doomed"—although St. Paul occasionally leads me to reflect on sex and spirit. Today he prompted me to write my story.

Who Says There Is Only One Way to Experience the Divine?

Marilyn Fithian

"Oh God" is an exclamation I and my associate, Bill Hartman, have often heard men and women utter as we monitored their sexual arousal and orgasm by masturbatory and/or coital activities during a therapy or research session in our laboratory at the Center for Marital and Sexual Studies.

While women were more likely than men to utter this joyous exclamation as they reached orgasm, we have heard it from both sexes often enough to ask what they meant by it. "Why that expression? What do those two words mean?"

The answers have come from men and women in all walks of life, from high school drop-outs on welfare, a former nun, and three children of missionaries, from people from nineteen different countries and a variety of religious beliefs. Whatever their cultural and religious backgrounds, the explanations shared a common thread. "Sex is a spiritual experience." "Orgasm brings the sense of being at one with God, one with the Creator, one with the

❖   ❖   ❖

Marilyn A. Fithian has been co-founder, associate director, instructor, researcher, and counselor-therapist at the Center for Marital and Sexual Studies in Long Beach, California, since its inception in 1968. She is coauthor with William Hartman, her life partner, of *Treatment of Sexual Dysfunction: A Bio-Psycho-Social Approach* and *Any Man Can: The Multiple Orgasmic Technique for Every Loving Man.* She has also held several offices in the Society for the Scientific Study of Sexuality.

45

universe." "It's an expression of passion, emotion, a deep sense of being." For these women and men, orgasm is indeed a spiritual experience. This is not so strange since religion and sex have been linked since earliest times. Only in the last two thousand years or so have sex and religion been split apart, separated, and certainly not on a par with one another.

Early religious groups in Europe recognized the relationship between sex and spirit—some of their religious rituals involved sexual intercourse and/or masturbation. Ritual intercourse in a freshly plowed field to ensure the fertility of the crops was not just a copulatory act; it was a joining with the deity. Sacred prostitution and May Day rites, where sex occurred with others than one's own partner, embodied a deep sense of spirituality. The Dionysian rites that allowed sexual license to the participants were likewise part of a religious ritual.

Although early Christian sects condemned these sexual rites as lascivious, immoral behavior and elevated the spiritual life far above the domain of sexual passion and pleasure, the early links between sex and the spiritual dimension have never completely died out, even among conservative Christians. One only needs to recognize contemporary expressions of religious and sexual ecstasy to realize that the intimate connection between sex and spirit is still alive. The ecstasies of religion and orgasm, alone or together, can bring a oneness with God, with the divine, the transcendent other, with another person, and the universe.

Over the years, I have attended a number of African-American church services. Sometimes, I was very moved by the sermon, the ritual, or the congregation; sometimes, it was a combination of two or more. One such Christian church I found particularly interesting. During the very emotion-rousing sermon, a group of female parishioners moved to an open space up front and began dancing and swaying. They went into a state of ecstasy that transformed them into a trance-like state. Their faces looked like those of women I had observed having orgasm in the research laboratory. Their dancing was certainly erotic. Their behavior was obviously seen as sexual, because females dressed in uniforms quickly encircled the dancing women and prevented any males who might be tempted from entering the circle. Some of the women became so aroused they lost consciousness and fell to the floor. While a loss of consciousness is rarely seen during orgasm in a research setting, men and women do occasionally experience a short period of unconsciousness with intense sexual arousal in private encounters.

As we watched, I commented to Bill, my partner, that I wish we could have had them all hooked up to our research equipment to measure their orgasmic response. Having observed several thousand people have orgasms during our years of research and recording orgasmic responses enabled us to easily identify what was happening to many of the people in this group.

Several of our research subjects over the years have talked to us about having orgasm during church services. I relate to that very well. For me it was usually the music, although I have heard some very arousing sermons. (When talking about a religious service, people usually leave the "a" off because church is not supposed to be arousing, just rousing.)

Many of the stories in this book express these spiritual feelings. As sex has become less a procreative act and much more a pleasurable sharing, an expression of love, caring, and intimacy, it is easier to find in sexual pleasure and release a feeling, if you will, of being one with God and the universe.

Spirituality and a oneness with God are important aspects of many people's lives. The vignettes in this book tell how some people find this dimension of their lives in a sexual context. Who are we to make value judgments on their behavior? This is meaningful for them as humans first, and as spiritual leaders second. It is the humanness of the behavior that makes these stories important. When we make our spiritual leaders more than human by our expectations, we deny them their humanity and their ability to understand, nurture, and cherish those they serve.

It is also important to realize that even though current marriages have a fifty percent divorce rate, this is only for those married less than ten years. Marriages that last beyond this initial period tend to become much more stable. In earlier times, men often died young through illness and accident while women suffered from the added death risk of childbirth. As a result of this higher death rate for both men and women in earlier times, marriages were often short-lived and men and women frequently had several spouses in their lifetime. My grandfather was married eight times. All of his wives died before him even though he married younger women as he became older.

Faced with much longer life expectancies and much less time spent in child-rearing, some couples in long-term marriages look for the connection between sex and spirit by expanding their primary relationship so it cannot just survive, but also thrive. Some of the people in these vignettes have tried some "unorthodox" ways to keep viable a relationship that is meaningful to them. They have been able to share with us their spiritual journey through their sexuality and by doing so have come closer to God. In some cases it worked out. In other cases the experiment did not last.

Where there is a fear of loss, jealousy occurs. Where there is no fear, jealousy is less of a problem. Currently, when I see married couples where both work and are not financially dependent on the other, there is much less concern about a fear of losing the partner to another person than there is about fear of the risk of AIDS. Where there is a committed secondary relationship, this fear is reduced.

The insights in these stories may very well help others who are trying to reconnect their sexuality and their spirituality. Many more might ... would take up this question, were it not for the lack of support they find in their religious communities. For some men and women today, like those in these stories, traditional religious morality is too rigidly black and white for today's world in flux, too uncomfortable with sexual pleasure, and too biased in relaxing the "until death do us part" marital bond while flatly refusing to discuss any adaptation in "forsaking all others."

Who says there is only one way to experience the union of sex and spirit?

7. The Creative Fire of Knowing and Loving

Peter Declan

Several years ago a special friend asked me a question that left me scrambling for an answer. "Why did you to go straight from a Catholic elementary school to spend a dozen years in an all-male seminary to become a celibate priest, when all the time you were so curious about sex?" Somehow that question connected me with another question I had just encountered in a lightweight but provocative utopian mystery novel about the quest for an ancient Mayan manuscript guide to living a fuller life. One step to living a fuller life, the author of *The Celestine Prophecy* suggests, is to find out "What basic life questions were my parents not able to answer in their own lives and thus left to me to solve in my life?"

My parents were thrilled that I would ride my bike a mile to church on dark winter mornings to be the altar boy for the 6 AM Mass, but they were not happy with my insisting, wanting to enter the seminary when I graduated from eighth grade. My parents were then and still are today devout Catholics, loving parents who seldom expressed in public their emotions for each other or their children although it was always obvious to all they loved each other and us very deeply. I learned it was nicer not to express my emotions. My parents never mentioned "that," meaning sex. Nor did the seminary priests. I was left to find my own way in the dark confusing tide of adolescent emotions, hormones, fantasies, and erotic urges.

In my seminary years I was a very puzzled but driven adolescent, with conflicting romantic fantasies. At times I yearned to become a Trappist monk. At night, novels and films about *Captain Blood*, *Scaramouche*, and the *Phantom of the Opera* inspired quite different fantasies in which I was the irresistible male rescuing some beautiful sexy maiden. There were endless struggles with fantasies about the naked women I discovered in the magazines my atheist uncle hid any time we visited. Weekly, sometimes daily confessions of "self-abuse" followed by rededication to the Virgin Mary. The only other thing our Spiritual Director told us about sex was that we had to avoid at all

49

costs the "particular friendships." With very little information about boy-girl sex, homosexuality was a total blank.

Eight years in a Prussian-type high school and college seminary passed in a totally male, sex-denying environment, framed with the rich rituals of Gregorian chant and vibrant stained glass. At times, my passionate side found temporary relief playing the pipe organ in the dark, empty chapel.

I realize now there was always the unresolved dilemma of rejoining sex and spirit in a religious world that denied totally anything sexual. Looking back, I realize I inherited this question from my parents who could not answer it. "How can I connect my sensual and erotic nature with my quest for the transcendent, the spiritual and God?" That question sharpened after I graduated from college and started four years of theological studies. The "major seminary" atmosphere was the exact opposite of my rigid guilt-focused life in the minor seminary. The priests encouraged creativity, and individuality, within limits of course. I reveled in the new theological currents coming out from European biblical scholars, taught myself French and read as much as I could of "the new theology." Knowing I would have to teach high school after ordination, I spent my free time in the college psychology lab, talking with the professors, overtly developing my counseling skills to help the parishioners and students, but also reading everything about sex I could get my hands on.

In scripture class I encountered the mystery of *yadah*, the Hebrew word for sexual union and "knowing" another person, for finding the universe and transcendent in and through that person. I thought about the ignorance of the man who has read only one book, and wondered whether someone could really find the spiritual in sex if they limited themselves to "knowing" only one person in their life. Of course, as a priest, I would not be allowed to "know" anyone in this intimate way.

I wondered about a popular quote floating around at the time—I still do not know who said it, but I found the quote interesting enough to jot it down back then: "Someday, after we have mastered the winds, the rains, the tides and gravity, we will harness the energy of love, and then, for the second time in human history, man will discover FIRE." Instinctively I added "and through woman," through "knowing." Celibacy, I somehow knew, would not work for me, but that thought I shoved into shadows even as my conflicting fantasies continued.

Ordination came and went with the usual celebrations, followed by parish work and teaching in the parish high school. Then my bishop decided to send me off to earn a graduate degree in psychology.

A very human, smiling, even jovial Pope John XXIII was throwing the Vatican windows wide open. Changes of all kinds including optional celibacy filled the air. Nuns gave up their habits and went off to college for teacher education. The local Jesuit and Marymount colleges were fermenting cauldrons where liberals gathered at every opportunity to discuss it all. Giants of Vatican II, like Gustave Weigel and John Courtney Murray, dropped by to share their fire. Sister Coretta Kent's inspiring and bold graphics jolted us with their bold primary colors.

My quest for a way to integrate, celebrate, and experience my erotic and intellectual passions increasingly occupied my mind. But I still knew nothing about what an intimate relationship might involve. I wanted a relationship that would be mutually self-enhancing (whatever that might mean) and filled at once with a sense of ever-expanding horizons and simultaneous fulfillment. I also wanted all my sexual fantasies fulfilled, even though I never dated, kissed, or held a woman close.

In graduate school I met Rosemary, a practical, down-to-earth woman headed for success in the corporate world. We dated, got serious despite my naivete, and decided to marry. That meant leaving my secure clerical womb. Fortunately, my limited training and some experience in counseling opened into a career as a psychologist with a rewarding private practice. We started a marriage and our family with all the traditional stereotypes and unspoken monogamous expectations of our parents, with my question about the ignorance of a man or woman who knows only one book tucked away in the closet. For a dozen years, Rosemary and I shared a mutual, fairly open-ended interest in exploring where our marriage might go.

In the late 1960s, the Essalen Institute was the "in place" to explore self-actualization. But I took another road, when I met Barbara and John Williamson, the founders of Sandstone, a community of professionals and educators exploring the frontiers of sexually open relationships on the edge of Topanga Canyon north of Los Angeles, and down the road from Essalen. My first—our first—experience with public, optional nudity followed. Sexual intimacy was also optional and open at Sandstone. Mind-blowing, exciting, scary as hell! Rosemary asked all the nitty-gritty questions about jealousy and sexual diseases. Sometimes we went together for the Wednesday evening rap sessions at Sandstone where we debated new perspectives we discovered in

George and Nena O'Neill's *Open Marriage*, Carl Roger's *Becoming Partners: Marriage and Its Alternatives*, Alex Comfort's *Joy of Sex*, Tofler's *Future Shock*, the Roy's *Honest Sex*, the Francoeur's *Hot and Cool Sex*, Gerry Neubeck's *Extramarital Relations*, and Ron Mazur's *New Intimacy*. We never knew when one of these folks might show up at Sandstone.

We met Bob and Irma Rimmer at one of the alternative lifestyle conferences we attended in those years. Bob was the guru who wrote that underground bestseller, *The Harrad Experient*. Irma matched Rosemary's skepticism and down-to-earth realism. I devoured Bob's aggravatingly philosophical but irresistible novels and tried every way I could to get into discussions with him. I was particularly drawn to his novel *Thursday, My Love* because it deals with the spiritual dimensions of sex, and even has a Jesuit presiding at a sensual ritual celebrating Adam and Angela's intimate, comarital love. The union of sex and spirit was still driving my intellectual and experiential quest.

Early on, Rosemary and I struggled with jealousy and our changing conception of marital fidelity. A lot of people we met, especially those with some religious background, were wrestling with the meaning of fidelity, trying to redefine it in some way that allowed for both a loving long-term commitment and space for personal growth. Somehow the model of marriage we grew up with seemed suffocating in its demands that this one spouse would completely and totally meet all my needs for all my life, and I in turn was bound to satisfy all her needs—an inseparable "twin-pack." Terms like "comarital," "primary and secondary or satellite relationships," "open and closed marriages," "intimate friend and intimate networks" helped—and didn't help. Those of us who came out of the ministry struggled with the idea of a covenant between two or more persons that allowed for changing and renegotiable responsibilities and commitments. Later on, "polyfidelity" was suggested, with different interpretations.

For a dozen years, Rosemary and I evolved through the ups and downs of monogamy, into an open marriage, and then drifted into a fairly comfortable kind of Compartment 4 marriage that has lasted 30 years. Rosemary concentrated on parenting before our children went off to school, and then added a career, hobbies, and for a while some intimate friendships. I've combined a couple of important intimate friendships with parenting and the fun of guiding college students through the intricacies of love, sex, and intimate relationships.

Early on, I met Katie at a business convention. She lived and worked near us, on the same side of town. Living with her parents after divorcing a man who thought sex was disgusting and animalistic, she had a steady, not too pressured management position. With our fairly flexible work schedules we could arrange an occasional movie, dinner, and evening together, an overnight now and then, and even an occasional short vacation in the mountains. In eight years, Katie and I explored elementary aspects of sex and spirit that complemented and went beyond what Rosemary and I were exploring. The two women were very different, and I learned important lessons from each. Meanwhile, Rosemary explored a few friendships of her own, getting together with a special friend for a day, an evening, or even a few days when I was away on business or otherwise occupied.

From the start Katie and I acknowledged her need for a primary relationship. I supported and encouraged her search. After eight years, she found a serious friend, and we parted at a quite painful dinner. Katie called a couple of times after that to ask my advice on a problem her new partner had, but then silence, softened by occasional recollections of special times and my concern for her happiness.

Then, for several years, it was traditionally exclusive monogamy, Rosemary, the children, and me. Until I met Betty, an intense woman, 20 years my junior. In her childhood, Betty's doctor had told her mother Betty would be a bed-ridden invalid by her teens. Betty's wild, free spirit rejected this fate. She pursued yoga and dance, and became incredibly in tune with her body. Before we ever met, she had already decided from conversations with people who knew me that she wanted to explore some kind of relationship with me beyond the usual friendship. She had always been faithful in a rather rocky marriage, but this seemed to her the right time to explore. It was also, I learned, the ripe time for me to take another major step in my exploring the union of sex and spirit.

Early on Betty and I were caught up in the meaning of myths, in Mircea Eliade, Joseph Campbell's *Power of Myth*, and Tantric views of sex and spirit. Two years later Betty and her family moved twenty miles away, and she stopped calling, and seldom returned my calls. We never had closure or said "God bless." That pain was intense, as I tried to handle the unexplained end of a friendship in which I had learned many new things about myself and about sex and spirit.

My special friendships with Katie and Betty involved me as a male learning about the feminine and the ways male and female body/souls can relate. I was focusing on my own sexual potential and on discovering the power of female sexuality, pretty much in the traditional view of coital sex. Each taught me something unique about myself.

After Betty, I was wounded and depressed about where life's "chance coincidences" might take me next. I passed the "double nickel," and figured my exploring new challenges was over. Time to settle down and relax in "old age." I decided to concentrate on my marriage and relate better with my children now on their own and pursuing their own quests.

Four years of exclusive monogamy followed. Then, without premonition, one day, a colleague in her mid forties confronted me with a couple of totally oxymoronic questions that told me in hind sight, she had targeted me for an intimate friendship I could not escape. That not so subtle encounter would open doors of understanding and sensual experience I never dreamed in my wildest fantasy could exist between a man and woman.

Diana approached me at a business conference and we moved quickly into an intense friendship and loving sensual intimacy that has brought both of us many delightful surprises and ever new ecstatic hours together. During our second lunch together, in the midst of business talk, I inexplicably shifted the casual conversation 180 degrees and gave Diana a three-minute sketch of my personal quest with Rosemary, Katie, and Betty. Why, I don't know; I just blurted it out. Instead of being blown away by my sudden revelation, she calmly told me in equal brevity that she was similarly happily married but also had a concurrent twelve-year intimate friendship with a man from her church. Having blurted this out, she couldn't believe she had just shared a secret she had never shared with anyone else. We both knew what that meant.

Back home, since we were within driving distance, our friendship grew. Despite the problems and frustrations of arranging our private time, we managed to share intense hours together. At one point the intensity of our sensual sharing seemed to lessen her sexual desire with her friend and we decided to concentrate all our sensual energies on non-coital paths to orgasmic ecstasies. We shared occasional lunches, visits to a local coffee bar, workouts at the gym, and frequent phone calls to get advice and critique ideas about some current project at work, or just relax and talk.

Diana has brought the delight of experiencing a changed world, a universe suddenly transfigured with a new light, an attention to the hushed, delicate beauties we tend to ignore in the rush of life. I think it providential that Diana's name can be linked with the idea that another person can be the diaphanous window that let's me see the world in a new way and connect with the inexpressible transcendent Being/Energy with an incredible intensity and ecstatic joy I never dreamed even existed.

Our friendship meant sensing the energies of a world womb that bathes our senses constantly. Although I, and she, remained incredibly intense in everything we did including our many family and professional commitments, we both were more relaxed, more laid back, less tense and stressed. Sure, our special love and friendship complicated our lives. It's difficult enough keeping a primary relationship vibrant and healthy. Add a special friendship like Diana and I enjoyed and one has to wonder about our sanity. But my doubts about the wisdom of my path evaporated when I realized the treasures Diane brought me and the ecstasies she repeatedly assured me I brought her in our friendship. I think the reasons I am now so comfortable with myself is that my friendship with Diana gave me a new sense of fulfillment—completeness, a sense that after more than five decades of searching for a way to join sex and spirit, I am closer to answering that question my parents left me about the union of sex and spirit.

I now sense the world around me very differently because of the incredible intensity of our sensual sharings. The same morning fog shrouds the road as I take my morning walk, but somehow it is now different, more sensual, more intense. I've always been sensitive to nature, but now more so to the varieties of the dawn, the coolness or warmth of the air, the brightness of the sky, and fullness of the moon. The unexpected glory of bright cool sunlight on dish-sized pink and white hibiscus by the roadside can bring our car to a quick halt and an intense shared experience of the beauty of our cosmos. A storm with gorgeous lightning and thunder rumbling over the desert, the view from a mountain top, an eerie walk past waterfalls in a redwood forest.

My latest adventure in joining sex and the spirit has brought a very new and unexpected comfort in expressing my playful side. This has been an experience and gift beyond measure for a compulsive workaholic, treasured more because it takes me back to my youth, to my seminary days and my question about "knowing." The Genesis image of an all-powerful Creator shaping this universe out of nothing and then withdrawing to Heaven above has been replaced by the image of a playful Creator, a dancing God (in Sam Kean's vision), the dancing Light/Energy of Tantric and Taoist visions that works with us to create this universe—and ourselves—in many playful, laughing ways.

Some may follow an ascetic, celibate path. Some pray, some meditate, some practice yoga, some go to church regularly, some care for others in hospitals or social agencies. There are many paths of self-transcendence and union with others in today's world. My path was not planned, nor anticipated. I have to confess, at first sight, my path seems unexpected, serendipitous. On reflection, however, I believe the twists and turns in my path were not coincidences but foreordained synchronicities — each twist came at a critical time when I was ready for a new opportunity to develop more fully. At opportune moments, Rosemary, Katie, Betty, and Diana appeared in my path. Because our needs matched, my path took an unexpected twist, somehow fated.

Looking back over my life I see myself following a path I did not choose. Through the years, I have been fortunate to know and love four women, each in a unique and individual way. Each has led me deeper into my forest and closer to understanding and experiencing what it means to be more fully human, more fully sexual, more spiritual. The years have mixed moralistic conflicts and painful struggles with times of sensual/emotional body-mind ecstasies and the delights of unexpected twists. In the process, I am still learning to know what it means to explore and experience the presence of a loved one inside my mind and skin, and at the same time explore and experience myself inside the mind and skin of another. Yin/Yang are one, two sides of a coin. The too common distinction between lusty and saintly loves, above and below the belt, destroys humans. It tries in vain to split the human by celebrating our safe spiritual side and repressing our unpredictable, passionate emotional side. But this is a deadly split. Our spiritual nature requires that we integrate our multidimensional potential for LOVE.

Looking back on my early religious training I could spin my wheels in anger that my church gave me such a negative, and yes, distorted picture of my sexuality — my sensual and erotic side. Augustine's conviction that "Nothing so casts down the manly mind from its [noble, rational, spiritual] heights as the fondling of women and those bodily contacts which belong to the married state, that are part of marriage" ran though practically everything I read on sexuality and spirituality.

Christian males endorsed the neo-Platonic split of body and soul. Terrified of females and their chaotic creative powers, Christian males have pictured women as dangerously sensual, emotional, and sexual. Their solution has been to enthrone themselves in hierarchies of power. Males in the churches have tried to reduce the cosmic mystery of our sexuality to phallic power so they could carefully measure and control their coital performances, and define their masculinity by their performance. Unfortunately all the great religions have more or less bought into this limited, negative view of sex as the enemy of spirituality. Christianity—and Roman Catholicism in particular—baptized this patriarchal virus. How sad that the male enthronement of reason and our male fear of the sensual, emotional, passionate, and feminine replaced the prehistoric celebration of woman as the teacher of sensual-erotic-ecstatic union and the eternal human quest for the divine/transcendent hidden within the playfulness of eros and Venus. How sad that we bought into the belief of Augustine, Jerome, and other early Christians that reason is the "superior faculty" that makes us human, and their belief that reason is meant to control all our appetites, emotions, and passions. Augustine's message that our erotic and sensual nature "clashes inevitably and permanently with reason," diverting us from our spiritual vocation, has wreaked havoc by dehumanizing us.

Sometimes I wonder how much better off we would be if Christians had celebrated the body sacred as Jesus did. But then I, and others, would not experience the joys, the pain, and delights, of discovering for ourselves the cosmic energy/spirit immanent within ourselves, in a loved one, and the transcendent Spirit that breathes life into the physical womb from which we draw our nurturance and sustenance. Nor would I have to wrestle as I create the whole bodiedness of my sexuality that challenges me and my lovers to grow. How else could I have exchanged my adolescent genital focus for the experience of whole bodiedness in my body sacred over the years? Nor would I be able to thank the Divine Energy that guides our universe for my parents, Rosemary and our children, Katie, Betty, and Diana, and the many friends, casual and deep, who have guided me, taught me, and continue to challenge me to grow. Without this negative starting point, I might not appreciate how important it is to feel—as well as think, to become more comfortable with blurred boundaries, to release my sexuality from its phallic-coital box and see it as many women do as the unruly creative beast that it is.

Being an analytical male, there are a couple of facets in my friendship with Diana that I feel compelled to at least acknowledge because they are probably shared by other males who are in or have explored comarital relations.

Because the air of "traditional values" that we breath maintains that sexual and emotional exclusivity is the prime, inviolably sacred value of any marriage, I think anyone who breaks with this value is bound to experience guilt. For some, it may be the sinful guilt of "I'll burn in hell for all eternity for 'cheating' and violating the monogamous 'forsaking all others' rule." For others, the guilt may revolve around the risk of a negative reaction from children or friends should they discover their "secret."

Diana and I faced a different kind of guilt because we are both very competitive, driven, creative, work-oriented persons. We have a wide variety of interests and commitments in our work. Our time is limited; we never seem to have enough time for all we want to do. Maybe we qualify as workaholics. And yet we both feel we need time to play and relax, together, and individually with others. The time we spend together can take away from the time we spend with our spouses unless we can be together when both of our spouses are otherwise occupied. Sometimes an hour or two playing and relaxing together, away from our many work and family commitments, can trigger some strong guilt feelings.

Another facet is harder to label or pigeonhole. Terms like confusion, conundrum, puzzle, or a just plain perplexing question come to mind. Frankly I do not know which fits best. Whatever the feeling, it troubles us every now and then. I am conscious of this puzzle sometimes when I am with Diana, sometimes when I am alone watching a ruddy sunrise over black trees, or while driving along and a passing thought of some time we have shared causes me to smile. With me it is an unsettling question I do not feel compelled to answer, maybe because it has no real answer.

My conundrum has several versions ...

> "Why am I feeling so intensely passionate with Diana when I don't feel this intensity with Rosemary any more—if I ever did, even when Rosemary and I first fell in love?"

> "How can I spend hours of sensual intimacy with Diana, and not share this same time and intensity with Rosemary?"

> "Why do I have such totally unique and fiery reactions and sensual feelings with Diana? No other woman has triggered such sensual delights. I admit I had some uniquely different feelings with Katie and Betty, but I do not recall feeling this guilt with them."

> "Why are there subtle walls that keep me from sharing a similar intensity with Rosemary? Am I not open enough, willing enough to try, to work at it? What am I doing wrong that I don't experience this same cosmic wholeness, a similar openness to the energy of the universe and the earth womb that nourishes me through Diana, but not apparently in my marriage?"

> "Is the openness and sensual intensity I share with Diana sparked by the sporadic togetherness we share, and dulled or blocked by the comfortable daily routine Rosemary and I have shared for many years?"

Or one last version:

> "Do the intensity and uniqueness of my love for and fierce passions I experience with Diana violate my love for and commitment to Rosemary?"

Rosemary accepts my "compartment 4," my private space where no matter what I do my marriage remains primary. But she would be threatened by the fierceness of the passion Diana and I have experienced from our first encounter on.

Two years ago, Diana and I passed through the phase of adjustment every couple has to pass through as the brain gets accustomed to the passion of "being in love." A few months of lunches, occasional walks in the woods, and celibacy convinced her that indeed we have the basis for a long-term, more relaxed intimate friendship we both continue to want. For the past two years we have kept in touch but without any physical intimacy. Where will our path lead? No one can say.

Beyond the occasional twinges of guilt and unanswered questions I wonder why I am not satisfied being exclusively monogamous like everyone else? Why do I NEED to be intimate with more than one person at a time? What needs is it meeting, and are these valid needs?

I can't speak for anyone else, and I know Diana has a very different take on this. Each of our views has its own validity. I can only try to appreciate and share in fumbling words what I semiconsciously feel with her. Talking with understanding, supportive friends helps me, but Diana has no friend to talk with about our friendship. Of course, we talk about these feelings when they prompt her to pull back for a while, but we still have not put them to rest. They remain—as I suspect they do in many comarital relations—yet-to-be-resolved, perhaps unavoidable perplexities.

There is no growth without some birth pains, and the joy of birthing something new far exceeds the birth pains. Those who decide to explore the union of sexuality and spirituality in ways society and the churches do not recognize in today's world have to deal with the pain of living more or less in a closet. We lead a dual life, not being able to share with others some of our most vibrant joys. Doubts, questions, and frustrations are a constant companion for anyone who decides on an "unorthodox" lifestyle.

Which brings me to a closing thought, another quote a friend shared with me years ago whose author I do not know: "Think of play as a preview of Paradise, time disappears, self-consciousness shrinks, and fulfillment prevails …!" Looking back over human history, I see us on the verge of a new global consciousness and a new human being. Soon, it seems to me, more and more men and women will discover for the second time in human history, a cosmic fire that transforms the human spirit and joins us with the energies of the cosmos. Happily, we're now redefining our visions of love and sexuality. Sometimes I feel like Abraham must have felt when Yahweh told him to "Go forth from the land of your kinsfolk and from your father's house to a land that I will show you" (Genesis 12:1). Paul's comment to the Hebrews about Abraham's subsequent wandering through the desert fits my situation perfectly: "He went forth, moreover, not knowing where he was going" but trusting in the Divine Energy (Hebrews 11:8). Maybe that is why I sometimes feel more ecstasy in passion than in prayer.

8. Tantric Unions–A Quest for Ecstasy, and Agony

Ed Palmers

For ten years Cheryl and I maintained a relationship that included an eight-year marriage based on an open marriage model. We both committed ourselves to an open marriage from the beginning. Despite our basic agreement, some differences existed on each side of the equation. Cheryl requested that she know about anyone with whom I was involved. On the other side, I did not want to know anything she was doing alongside our marriage. We agreed that any relationships Cheryl had would be kept secret, and that I would let her know about anyone with whom I planned to be involved with. We broke both sides of the contract. As our relationship evolved, we amended our contract and changed it several times. There was even one attempt to close our marriage and return to a traditional standard pattern.

As you might expect, we had very little support for our marriage contract from other people, including friends. I don't recall discussing it with anyone except when someone asked me after my wife told them of our agreement and left them with some questions. Many of these people were outright hostile toward me. Almost none were supportive. Similarly, when Cheryl discussed our arrangement with her friends and associates, for one reason or another even they found it unconscionable. They attacked either her, myself, or our marriage. The only ones who could even listen to a full description or explanation of our marriage were people in a similar relationship.

During our marriage Cheryl worked for the federal government and was being considered for a new position which required a security clearance. I was not privileged to the investigation report, remembering that our contract required that her sexual activities be kept secret. I know that there were a considerable number of questions asked and even a request for a polygraph test concerning her sexual activities. Cheryl did not get the job and eventually left the government service.

I can't really say why Cheryl, from whom I am now divorced, entered into such a relationship. I believe she longed for a deeply caring and honest relationship with another female although she masked this by presenting it as one of my needs rather than one of hers. She believed that men were "never" faithful in relationships, so she felt sure I would cheat if asked to be faithful. I had never cheated at any marriage in my life with the exception of the last two weeks of my first marriage. In my earlier marriages I remained faithful because I could never imagine myself being able to manage my wife's having sex with another man. Hence, my request for secrecy.

As for myself, after two previous marriages, I had been in a series of short-term, intense relationships which no matter how hard I tried, never seemed to last more than a year or two. Also, I was at an early stage in my exploration and discovery of the link between sex and spirit. I had just begun the practice of Tantra when Cheryl and I became sexually involved. Tantra introduced me to the idea that Goddess resides in every woman. This made perfect sense to me. Why shouldn't everyone understand that the two most wonderful experiences of the human existence, communion with the divine and sex, should at least reside next to each other, if not in the same place?

Tantra also brought me to the realization that being inside a woman during sex was the thing that I wanted to do most in life. My career, my possessions, everything I did, was in order that I might appear more attractive and acceptable to a woman who then might allow me to come closer to her soul and share her body. I was, in fact, doing the things about which I had been warned by the conservative Christian church during my upbringing. I had begun to worship the flesh. I had placed another God — Goddess — before my devotion to their Father God who was in heaven.

As a child, in our Bible-belt Methodist church, I wondered why I was not experiencing God as other people I heard talk about, with joy and fervor. What I heard was that I was a sinner and that the second greatest sin, next to murder, was to have sex. As a young adult I was very sexual and could not reconcile the disparity between my early religious teaching and the "rightness" or "righteousness" of sex/love with another human being. This left me with two options: to reject either my spiritual/religious life or my sexual life. Usually the sexual part won out. The initial answer to my dilemma came when I discovered that God would accept sex as a part of loving. A deeper answer came from the Tantra belief that each person held the God/Goddess within their being, when I learned that I could combine my experience of the divine and my intense pleasure of sex.

I was sure that I wanted to experience the divine in each person. I soon realized that there is no more profound way to do that than in sexual union. At the same time I was realizing that my partner Cheryl was a very fine human being with easy access to her unconscious spiritual side. I wanted her to be my "soul mate." Having had several committed, significant relations of no more than a year in length, I knew that if I made that major commitment to a single individual that the eventual end was not far away. I wanted to keep my primary relationship and growing edge with her, and still have my sexual edge with the high energy from the other women. This is not intended to suggest that she was not a highly energetic, sexual person. I had experienced the intense consuming fire of a new sexual relationship several times during my adult life. I wanted to use those short-term relationships to increase the power of the ever-heightening spiritual flight of our souls. The way I intended to use this high intensity was to fuel my own sex drive. I had found that when I was feeling sexual and powerful, I not only felt that with one woman but in all aspects of my entire life, including my marriage. I wanted to draw sexual energy from these exciting new women and bring in that energy to my marriage.

This may sound like I planned to use—some might think exploit—the women in short-term relationships, but remember I had already learned that they don't last anyway. In the final analysis I was drawing sexual energy from Cheryl in order to maintain sexual relations with some of the women she brought into our marriage. Additionally, I can honestly say that I loved and honored each one of them. I still do.

In the beginning, there was a lot of sexual energy between the two of us. I had decided that I was going to enjoy as much of that energy as possible and that I was going to intentionally love her. I did not "fall in love" with her until three or four years into our marriage. This marked a significant change between this and all of my previous relationships which began by "falling in love" and then "falling out" one and a half to two years later. I am convinced that the reason for this intense loving and later "falling in love" with Cheryl was the depth of honesty in our relationship about sex. Specifically, I was offered other committed relationships during our marriage, but I knew that no other primary relationship would allow me the freedom that the marriage did. No other woman would commit to being my primary partner and tolerate the "other women" the way Cheryl did.

I had a very good deal, and I knew it. I had a partner who appeared committed to me, and she accepted and allowed me to form other relationships.

I was even allowed to share those relationships with my wife. When I felt "jilted" by another woman, I could talk about it with Cheryl. When I was excited about the prospect of a new relationship, I could talk about it with Cheryl. When we saw an exciting and pretty woman in public, we could discuss her beauty and appeal together; we were like a couple of "buddies."

Cheryl, I think, wanted to be in relationship with me and possibly agreed to some things which she shouldn't have. For instance, I think it was a mistake for me to ask her to keep her relationships secret. The biggest mistake of all was that I assumed that her relationships were with other men. Some were, I think, but her energy and most of her acceptance came from other women. She had been in a previous marriage where her husband's lover was also her friend. These relationships between her and the other women were more love and less sex than my relationship, which was based on sex and became love.

It took me several years before I could trust that the gift Cheryl was offering me was for real. Part of my mistrust was that it was damned difficult for her to deliver with the gift which she had offered without becoming angry. At times she plainly denied that she had even made the offer.

There was a time in our marriage I call the fantasy years. It was when Cheryl really wanted a relationship in which I could be sexual with another woman with whom she could also be friends, and possibly lover. I also operated with a fantasy which I believed might never come true. The fantasy was so powerful that it kept me interested in our sex life far longer than any I had ever known previously. The mere suggestion that I might have two women together kept me interested in and devoted to her far longer. I was so interested that I entered into a practice which could only take me deeper into her soul, where I found the truth about her offer.

The combination of this fantasy and Tantric sex rituals created some mighty powerful worship services. About once a month we took a day for what we called "worship." On those days we stayed home from work and arranged for the children's care after school. Then we committed the day to the practice of Tantra. Each event was planned, often a week or more in advance and a lot of energy, thought, and preparation went into the creation of a sacred space and time.

Our master suite became a temple and we always referred to it as such and treated it as such. No infidel was ever allowed into it. Most of those days the temple was decorated with flowers and incense. Gem stones, opals, amethyst, garnets, emeralds, and rubies provided energy. Sometimes they were laid in a circle around the altar. The altar was the mattress or blanket on which we made love. Food was prepared and brought to the temple in order that we did not have to leave the sacred space once it was created. Circles were cast to cleanse impurities and provide protection for the lovers. Often gifts were exchanged and always the chakras were anointed with oil and opened in a ritual.

After everything was made ready, we began the rituals of Tantric sex. Usually lasting from six to ten hours, these were highly spiritual and mystical times. They were times when two souls intertwined and flew through the universe and across time. There are no secrets that one can keep from another during times like this. I came to realize that I could trust that she would accept another woman in our marriage. We continued this practice for several years until the last year of our marriage.

After I realized that she was honest about allowing another woman into our marriage the real work began. That was of finding a lover for me who would also be friend and lover to her. I knew that it would not be difficult for me to love a woman who I was having sex with, but that it would be difficult for my primary partner to form a deep relationship with a woman I had chosen. Our solution was for her to choose the woman. I would then focus my attention on both of them equally. This sounded good in theory. However, every time she chose a woman, the other woman wanted me out of the picture. Needless to say it was difficult for me to bond with the women she chose. Similarly, then the women that I chose would be frightened by the idea of involving Cheryl or Cheryl would have no attraction to the woman I chose. The other women also did not trust that such a gift could be offered. The two who did trust it did not make much of a commitment to the relationship with my primary partner and myself. Instead they would either bond to myself and separate from Cheryl, or visa versa. I was prepared to search for a long time. Indefinitely, perhaps, if necessary! The fantasy alone was enough to provide me with much of the energy for which I was searching.

Eventually, a woman who was very important to Cheryl ended a long-term committed relationship and wanted to become a part of our marriage. This woman was both mentor and primary support for Cheryl. She had been one of the few people who had known about our relationship and did not try to destroy it. This was a very powerful attraction for my wife. It was an attraction to which I could not say no. I loved them both and knew that I could not come between them. In retrospect I should have. Cheryl immediately fell deeply in love with this woman. There were days of Tantra, powerful days when the three of us really bonded, our souls intertwined at once. I was delighted to make love to both of them and to watch them make love to each other. I felt no threat at all. At first I was uncertain that I would be allowed to truly enter the bond of these two women, so I held back for a while. I reserved the right to form other relationships, just in case.

Then slowly I began to give myself over to them. I was ready to commit everything to the two of them. I finally made that commitment. I offered the two of them everything. Everything. I ended a twenty-seven year career as a reserve officer because I did not want it to interfere with my commitment of time and energy to the two women in my life. At that moment, there was nothing which I would have held back. I believed I had found perfection and was in heaven. It seemed that as soon as I made that commitment the whole universe turned against me. Then, true to form, the other woman began playing out her anger toward men against me and trying to exclude me from the relationship. I had dealt with the anger of my wife but with two women together their destructiveness was multiplied. Just as the ecstasy was multiplied, so was the agony. When I could take no more I ended the sexual part of the relationship with the other woman, hoping to salvage something of my marriage.

For the first time in my life I had told a woman "No." Big mistake! When I ended the sexual relationship with my wife's chosen lover, I also ended my marriage. Although we stayed married for another year and a half, we were never soul mates again. Later there was a brief and wonderful relationship (as far as I was concerned it was wonderful) with a woman whom I had chosen, but my wife would not give her soul to that relationship as it already belonged to someone else.

I have learned and continue to learn from these experiences. When more people are added to a relationship the complexity does not just increase, it multiplies. I have learned that I can trust a woman's gift, even if there are costs included. I have learned the shear ecstasy of having my soul wrapped around another and it around mine. I have learned that one quantum leap from that ecstasy is a place where my soul is woven between two other souls who are also woven together.

I learned that there truly is another side of our human existence. There is a world or place where there are no egos, where there is no time. I have learned that there really is a heaven and there really is eternity. I learned how vulnerable a man can be in the presence of Goddess. And I learned that if one considers the divine to be feminine, they should also be aware that Satan might also be feminine.

I have learned that I will probably never be satisfied in a traditional relationship again.

The Tantric Sex Path to Spirit

David Schnarch

Several of our storytellers mention their discovery of India's ancient Tantric yoga tradition and its teaching that sexual passion and intercourse can be a direct path to nirvana and the transcendent divine. There is nothing in our Western Judeo-Christian religious traditions that even hints at the beauty and power of this Eastern celebration of the connection between sex and spirit. Perhaps that is why several others who tell their stories here also mention the help they gained from their Tantric encounters as a remedy to the Judeo-Christian separation of sex and spirit, body and soul.

Several years ago I had the good fortune to experience this view of sex and spirit when I visited the "erotic" temples of Khajuraho in northern India. These ancient temples date back to the eleventh century, constructed about the time that the Roman Catholic Church was building monasteries in Europe to solidify its program of clerical celibacy. These temples rise some hundred feet in the air, completely covered with exquisitely detailed sculptures providing an almost unimaginable education in the anatomical possibilities of human coupling and an appreciation of the beauty of the human body. One coupling depicted a man and woman engaging in rear-entry coitus; the man's

❖   ❖   ❖

David Schnarch, a well-known clinical psychologist, has spent twenty years exploring the relevance of spirituality and morality to sexuality. He has described his integration of sexual, marital, family, and relationship therapies in the highly acclaimed *Constructing the Sexual Crucible: An Integration of Sexual and Marital Therapy*, and *Passionate Marriage: Sex, Love and Intimacy in Emotionally Committed Relationships*.

index finger touching the sacral section of his partner's spinal column. This coupling actually displayed a highly evolved form of "sensate focus": channeling "psychic" energy to stimulate physical energy in the woman's *chakra* (center of energy located in the spinal synapses)! Clearly, this society had evolved its own notion of a sexual quantum model, well integrated with their prevailing understanding of human physical functioning.

Hindu Tantric Yoga stresses a view of physiology and spirituality in which one attempts to arouse the *kundalini* (sexual energy) located at the base of the spine-brain, and unite it with the *lotus* (highest and most powerful psychic power) located in the head. The purpose is to gain spiritual energy and salvation. Ritual intercourse, preceded by careful preparation, prayers, and meditation, is seen as a cosmic experience. The fullness of human consciousness is thought to occur in the profoundly absorbing experience of an aroused *kundalini*, developed through the activation of sexual energies. Merging of sexual energies with another individual is considered as the most intense awakenings of consciousness. This is quite a contrast from a Western dogma that states that full human consciousness is achieved by suppression of these same erotic energies.

However, the full impact of the temples lay both within their walls and in the bustling village surrounding them. While the exterior of the walls depicted every conceivable manifestation of erotic behavior, the interior chamber was unadorned. At the center of this circular chamber, some 15 feet in diameter, was a simple ceremonial bed platform, around which one could barely walk without brushing the plain stone walls. Inside the chamber, there was nothing to suggest it represented the culmination of a society that had developed sexuality as its religious core and as a means of spiritual worship and transcendence.

And yet, the *aroma* of the eight or ten sexually aroused visitors within the temple was striking. It was as if there were a sexual radiance, such as people experience during embarrassing adolescent arousal, coming from each of us; each of us vibrated in harmony with a sexual energy that seemed to come out of nowhere and everywhere. There were simple, knowing, friendly smiles between the men and women tourists who resonated with the moment; we probably would not have truly looked at each other if we had passed in a hotel lobby earlier that day. It was a very unusual experience, being highly aroused *for nothing or anyone in particular*. There was no impulse to start an orgy or even to pair up. There was this peculiar sense of eroticism and sexual desire emanating from each of us, in the context of an intense spirituality. It was not that any of us became more attractive at that moment; we simply became *desirous without an apparent object of that desire.*

To my Westerner eyes, the cultural contrast of sexual values was stunning. Here was a religion that fully demonstrated acceptance of sexuality as part of men's and women's spiritual life; it brought eroticism right into the tabernacle. How very different from the more austere and chaste presence in the altars of our churches and temples. Indian Hindu temples have a stone effigy of a penis *(lingam)* and a vagina *(yoni)* prominently displayed on the floor. In contrast it was with great trepidation that I even mentioned the formal names for male and female genitalia when I was given the honor of presenting a sermon at a Unitarian Church recently.

I wonder why Christianity has never been able to bring eros into the tabernacle? I wonder whether it ever will be able to. I wonder what could help our religious traditions find the union of sex and spirit.

Part Two

Reinventing Marriage and Intimacy

An Erotic Meditation on Ecstatic Connection

I sip the nectar
of your lips,
tongue exploring
hidden tongue,

While you
in magic warmth
enfold with ecstasy
the rosebud of my garden.

And when
with joyful force
it releases
its fluid fragrance,

I, too, spring the source
of your sweet abandon
as we connect
in a flicker of eternity.

Reverend Ron Mazur,
author of *The New Intimacy*

The Reality of Eros

James B. Nelson

It strikes me that the theme of *eros* fills more pages of this book than any other. What is *eros*? Though deeply connected to our sexuality, *eros* is not simply genital urges and feelings—a common mistake. More fundamentally, *eros* is, as Paul Tillich, one of the greatest American theologians of this century, reminded us, the moving power of life, the hunger for connection, the passion for reunion.

Eros, fundamentally, is that dimension of our love born of desire. It is the yearning for fulfillment. It is sensual and bodily in its energy, open to feeling and passion. It is a divine-human energy, a drive toward health—and toward union with that to which we belong. Eros seeks the integration of body and spirit, of human and divine. Indeed, the true erotic dynamism of the human self is something that aims not primarily at the momentary satisfaction of the senses but at the deeper pleasure of connection with persons as persons, the connection with life, the connection with God. Eros, perhaps most profoundly, is the passionate love of life in all of its fullness, and if eros does not infuse the other dimensions of our loving, they are diminished and distorted.

❖   ❖   ❖

James B. Nelson, professor emeritus of Christian Ethics at United Theological Seminary of the Twin Cities in Minnesota, has been a pioneer in the quest to reunite sexuality and spirituality in a holistic Christian perspective. Among his many important books are *Embodiment: An Approach to Sexuality and Christian Theology* (1978), *Between Two Gardens: Reflections on Sexuality and Religious Experience* (1983), *The Intimate Connection: Male Sexuality and Masculine Spirituality* (1991), *Body Theology* (1992), and *Sexuality and the Sacred: Sources for Theological Reflection* (1994).

So, as Augustine, in one of his better moments, taught us, the problem is not to uproot or transcend our desires, for desire is an essential mark of our humanity and of our belonging to God. Rather, the challenge is to order all objects of our desire in accord with their true relation to God, the Spirit in whom alone our restless hearts will find satisfaction and fulfillment.

Culturally defined, however, eros is simply raw sex. A catalog of video films I received recently had some predictable descriptions in the section labeled "Late Night Video … Uninhibited erotic encounters … See uncensored erotic action … Live out your erotic fantasies … Erotic antics abound … High voltage eroticism." This is what eros has been reduced to in popular culture.

Theologically, the picture has been different, but no less confusing. The dominant Christian interpretation has elevated *agape* love to a normative position and has denigrated *eros*. *Agape* has been seen as the divine, spiritual love Christians are to emulate. It is self-giving, sacrificial, other-directed, epitomized in God's self-giving in Christ on the cross. *Eros* by contrast has too often been portrayed as a love that is egocentric, narcissistic, and self-seeking. The spiritual life then becomes a constant warfare between *agape* and *eros*. I was reared on that kind of theology and piety, and I suspect I have plenty of company. As a youngster I was taught that if you just sat real still and didn't wiggle, *eros* would go away.

But, enormous problems — both theological and practical — have flowed in the wake of such denigration of *eros*. The integration of sexuality and spirituality becomes forever problematic, for sexual energy participates deeply in the erotic. Self-love continues to be confused with egoistic narcissism, and self-effacing behavior is baptized, especially for marginalized persons. In spite of an incarnational faith, the body remains theologically suspect and hence so does passion — passion for anything, including justice.

The denial of the erotic is also closely linked to the confused state of sexual pleasure in religious, especially Christian, ethics. Two dominant historic positions, the Augustinian and the Thomistic, are still the most common. Augustine found sexual pleasure dangerous because it is virtually irresistible and it threatens grave sin. Thomas Aquinas argued, typically more moderately, that sexual pleasure is not evil. Neither, however, is it truly a human good, hence not a proper end for human activity. Rather, sexual pleasure is justified insofar as it is a means to higher human ends, particularly procreation.

Out of fear of *eros*, most of contemporary Christian ethics harbors a strong suspicion of sexual pleasure as a good in its own right. Fearing the social chaos of rampant hedonism and individualism, which our sexual culture has in abundance, contemporary ethicists are still inclined to bless sexual pleasure only as a means to a "higher" end—primarily that of strengthening the relational bond. The argument about sexual pleasure is parallel to common religious arguments about self-love: self-love is justified derivatively. It is justified only as a means to neighborly love, but it is never a good in itself. However, I believe that authentic sexual pleasure is one of the most persuasive life experiences that teach us that the deepest interests of the self and of the other are not naturally opposed. They are finally linked together.

In a variety of ways, then, the recovery of eros constitutes a major issue in religious sexual ethics. But I must say that resistance to the erotic has been heavily the province of straight white male theologians. On the other side, the call for erotic blessing most often has come from those whose very body-selves have been branded in patriarchy as dangerously erotic: women in general, lesbian women, gay men, and persons of color. Such persons are teaching some of the rest of us that even though our erotic capacities are often distorted by the abusive power relations of domination and control, they remain the sacred basis of our capacity to be involved in mutually fulfilling and empowering relationships.

Granted, the Christian tradition often has feared the erotic. I think of the Church Fathers of the early centuries. Tertullian called women "the gate of hell" because he saw them as essentially erotic, bodily and sexual. And Origen, who counseled Christians against reading the Song of Solomon until they were at least sixty years of age. I think of the harsh suppression of the beautiful erotic theology written by the women of certain medieval religious orders—Hildegaard, Dame Julian, Teresa of Avila—who all felt in their bodies the sensual love of the divine Lover.

Erotic fear also makes me ponder our continued anxieties about body pleasure—for example, why so much of our homophobia is grounded in the fear of sexual pleasure as a good in itself. Or, why the clitoris has been so overlooked as divine revelation, when we know that it has no other function whatever than to give pleasure. Yes, I fear that traditionally men in religious power have often found more pleasure in controlling other people's bodies than they have found God's pleasure revealed in the body itself. We do well to remember W. H. Auden's astute observation that it is the pleasure haters who become unjust. This matter of loving our own flesh and loving God in our flesh is not easy, and we know it. But the stories in this book amply show that the quest for such love is alive.

9. New Marital Patterns Work–
If Lived with Principles and Patience

Eleanor and John Sharp

Background

When Bob Francoeur's letter arrived inviting people to contribute to a book about sexuality and spirituality, we were reminded of how one's life is changed by chance events. Back in the fifties and sixties, John had been to Kirkridge, an ecumenical retreat in the Pocono Mountains of eastern Pennsylvania a few times, and came to admire its director, Jack Nelson, for his vision and courage. But it was only by chance that Jack, not knowing anything of John's personal situation, mentioned that Rusty Roy had persuaded Bob Rimmer to come to Kirkridge to be part of a retreat on contemporary sexuality. Of course Bob Rimmer's novels, especially *The Harrad Experiment* and *The Rebellion of Yale Marratt*, had been seminal in shaping John's thinking almost as much as avant garde theologians from Tillich and Bonhoeffer to John Robinson and Rusty and Della Roy's *Honest Sex*.

So it was that the two of us, John and Eleanor Sharp, husband and wife, went to that rainy, cloudy weekend which eventually became known as K-Sex I in 1968 or 1969. We were there by chance, but it also shaped our lives.

Although Francoeur's letter asked us to recount the story of one or two nontraditional relationships we have had in our quest to connect our sexuality and our spirituality, we decided to deviate from his instructions, and in a very short essay have John speak for both of us and tell about a nontraditional lifestyle we have lived for thirty-five years, without going into details but rather as an overview.

So let me, John, start with the theological roots Francoeur asked us to comment on.

At the time of K-Sex I, I was employed by the OEO (often called the Office of Ecclesiastical Opportunity) in New Jersey. I was a former pastor, a true WASP, with traditional but liberal Protestant roots in Connecticut Wesleyan and Yale Divinity School. It is not relevant to the story, but in between we moved to the West Coast and back to the Virginia suburbs. By every measure, Eleanor and I were active, if atypical, Christian laity. We were what became known as peace and justice types, pushing all the causes in civil rights, labor, the boycott of Nestle baby formulas, antinuclear campaign, Nicaragua, gay and lesbian rights, etc., etc. All these causes were part of our faith commitments, as was our commitment to a nontraditional sexual lifestyle which also started by chance.

Our connection between a nontraditional sexual lifestyle and our spirituality began in the early sixties in our clean upper middle class suburban New Jersey town, where several of the very active Church families became involved in small groups of one sort or another. Eleanor and I became very close to Wally and Jackie, a very dedicated, active couple. He was an engineer at Bell Labs, she a housewife with five children. We, and others, did everything together, not least, discussing theology, politics, and sex. Premarital sex was the issue then: was it always to be prohibited by the Church? But homosexuality and even wife-swapping, swinging, or genuine "open marriages" were all thoroughly discussed in the context of a Christian Commitment. Out of all of this came an Augustinian stance, "Love God, and then do as you please," but also a Pauline, "All things are possible, but not all things edify." What follows is our report of living with these twin guidelines for thirty-five years.

The Passage to Openness

Our living the connection between sex and spirit in a faith commitment that has involved a nontraditional lifestyle started with Wally's sudden death, killed by a passing motorist, in town while loading groceries into his station wagon. Long after the grief subsides, the reality surfaces. What are the limits to a loving, caring, friendship, between two families? How does a thirty-seven year old widow in her sexual prime, sublimate her friendship, affection, and gratitude for her best friend? How does a wife claim 100 percent of her husband's bodily affection, dropping off their strangely quiet, mutual widowed friend after every concert, or picnic, or evening out? Jackie did not need financial help, but we all knew that we would have shared totally equally had it been needed. What then should we not share? Surely the Christ of the New Testament could not have recommended monogamous sexuality on some legalist grounds. "Never!" we all said.

That's how Eleanor, my wife, and I had entered into what would be called by others an "open marriage." We prefer the term "co-marital" friendships.

The basis for any deeper involvement for us always lay in a solid friendship. One could, if everything else was right, add more or less in the way of intimacy. That was the pattern that worked: friendship first—then add warmth. And there really has been a full range of such warm expression in what became an erotic friendship. Looking back, and talking with dozens of others, one can identify at least four (or five) clusters of behaviors which enhance sexual intimacy with one's friends. At the first level is sharing saunas, skinny-dipping, nude beaches, and shared nudity, which creates a pleasant, warm bonding.

Next add touch via nude group massages. We made a regular practice of this among appropriate groups. This is definitely one step higher in intensity of connection. (For an accurate report, we must add that a very uncomfortable fact of American life makes nudity divisive; small or flat-breasted women and overweight women, most of all, tend to stay home and make excuses to avoid such events.)

A third level of intimacy was one-on-one personal massage, with explicit prior agreement that while it could become genital and orgasmic, it would definitely not lead to intercourse. Some now refer to this level as "outer-course." In the post-AIDS era, and even before, we found this a very valuable way of giving reality to Friendship Plus. This level is, in our experience, more acceptable to many persons with their present value systems. Biologically, psychologically, and spiritually, many today make a clean, and in our view, valid distinction between this level and intercourse.

For the really experienced, there is another sublevel of sexual intimacy we found very helpful in our quest to link our sexuality and spirituality. Translations of the *Kama Sutra, Kama Shastra,* and *Ananga Ranga* (*The Theater of God*), ancient Hindu sacred texts, led us into discussions of the Tantric spiritual tradition of erotic love. We meditated on pictures of Hindu temple art in Khajuraho and Konarak showing *mithuna,* bas-relief sculptures of loving couples, in sensitive, emotionally warm, and intensely spiritual embraces celebrating all forms of sexual intimacy (except adultery and violence). Unlike Christian and Jewish scriptures, these Hindu scriptures and sculptures deal openly and naturally with the spiritual aspects of our sexuality, as well as with advice on positions and techniques for increasing the sexual enjoyment of sexual intercourse as a path to the divine and transcendent. In the Taoist and yoga tradition of ancient China we found the idea of a ritual lovemaking that involves prolonged vaginal intromission with no movement and no ejaculation. The only "Christian" community to experiment with this specific level of spirit—embodied sharing—was the "Perfectionist Methodists" of the Oneida Community who practiced a form of group marriage for fifty years in the 1800s. Learning to channel our sexual energies in this Indian mystic view, the *kundalini* or serpent power, from the base of the spine to the heart and head gave us another way of sharing a quiet, spiritual, and bodily communion with a co-marital friend while reserving the special intimacy of full intercourse for our spouses.

The Record

In 1962, I was chosen by some computer in some university survey, probably because of my Yale Divinity connection, to be one of the guinea pigs to keep a detailed record of my sexual activities and report them to the sociologists conducting this survey. We found the results so intriguing and partly surprising, since memory plays such terrible tricks on us all, that after the two-year survey, I continued that record-keeping for nearly thirty-five years. What is described below is therefore about as reliable as such records get.

I start by saying that, at least for us, this nontraditional "co-marital friendships plus" pattern has worked very well. We feel we have lived out our Christian faith and call to love: we feel enormously enriched with friendships, of all kinds.

Over the years, the numbers of friendships have proved to be about even with the two of us each having some ten or eleven co-marital friends. Over the years, however, the amount of contact has been quite different, because John's relationships with widowed friends continued for decades. Nearly all these persons continue to be good friends—with only one mysterious exception, albeit the level of intimacy has changed in many cases with circumstance—getting married, moving away, age, and sex drive.

The Learnings

Perhaps the most helpful way to look at our experience is to answer the questions that most often occur—as they did to us—when anyone is entering such non-traditional relationships.

Out of the Closet or In

This is of course totally determined by one's circumstances. In our case, while we were very clear where our values and our "theoretical" commitments were, our government jobs made it absolutely impractical to be public. Moreover, in all our personal experiences we have found that discretion, not secretiveness, is invaluable. A wise friend gave us a guideline: "On all personal matters, do not lay any information on someone else UNLESS you believe it can do some good." While it does help our ego, and gives us warm fuzzies in a group, we have not shared our private lives, except in anonymous impersonal situations such as this. Our experience has completely confirmed the wisdom of our choice for us. That does not mean, in any way, that others may make quite different choices.

- **Does "co-marital friendship plus" help or hurt the marital relationship and marital sex life?**

Not only in our own, but in the three or four other married couples with whom we've been involved, all are convinced that such involvement has helped on both fronts. In every case, it has sharply increased sexual knowledge, experience, and enjoyment. Sexual intimacy is not a zero-sum game: our ability to love is not limited to one person, although the constraints on our leisure time and energy are quite real and unavoidable. Careful planning and setting priorities are always important.

- **Uniqueness, Territoriality, Timing**

For long-term relationships, we have found it is wiser for a woman to maintain a kind of ownership over certain space—this town or this house. Likewise, any areas of unique overlap of interests—Bach or baseball or whatever—can help define a particular friendship. It always intrigued those in our generation as to how much time would have to elapse between two sexual episodes with two different partners. Everyone we know, including a Catholic nun, has found that this is not at all significant: half an hour, fifteen minutes, or even five!!

And as the younger generation, and the more venturesome in ours, who have experienced group sexual intimacy (i.e., with more than two) have found, this factor is insignificant.

- **Longevity**

Since one of the reasons most of the moral philosophers and theologians give for supporting co-marital sex is that longevity of a relationship is more important than exclusivity, one can well ask whether such relationships really last? The short answer in our experience is: about the same length as most American marriages.

Four relationships, two with singles and two with couples, have been going on for, or lasted, between fifteen and twenty-five years. In a half dozen others, the friendships are of like duration, although the sexual intimacy may have been practiced only over a period of a few years.

- **Sexual Practice**

There is a substantial gain in quality and quantity of sexual activity. There is a real transfer of "skill," of "technique"—everybody wins. There is very little transfer of disease—once or twice yeast infections **may** have been transmitted—among middle-class, non-urban, non-drug using, non-promiscuous Americans. Sexual activity for over twenty-five years ranged from three to five times a week, and even in one year, six times a week. One of the very definite benefits of co-marital sex is that everybody gets more of it. In a normal professional life, one can relate to two or three partners including one's spouse—one to two times a week each. Friends in different cities, or attendees at the same professional meetings in far-away cities, fit very comfortably and easily into the **"friendship-plus"** patterns, whatever the particular level of intimacy.

The Don'ts

Our don'ts have become very clear. Do not get involved with strangers or casual acquaintances. Perhaps a short intense shared retreat experience could lay an appropriate base, but learning and sharing about each other is essential.

- Do not blab unnecessarily about one's relationships.
- Do not act in secrecy from those with whom one has prior commitments. *Honest Sex*, the title of Della and Rustum's key book, became our byword.

EPILOGUE

It was chance, I said, that brought us to Kirkridge. In the twenty-first century, most of the middle-class, educated persons who read this book will have "situations" so radically different from any for which ANY religious tradition provides guidelines, that for all intents and purposes, they have been tossed into turbulent seas with no compass. This book cries out for each of the writers, who, according to the editor's instructions, have lived an alternative sexual lifestyle and held on to their values, to share their wisdom on how to navigate in these new times and unexplored territories.

Here is our "wisdom" of translating our Christian background into sexual ethics for today.

1. Pursue friendship (love) as the greatest good of human existence.

2. Focus on the good of the other (or others) to the maximum extent possible. A small part of this is to focus on the pleasure of the other during all intimacy.

3. Slow down in getting more involved, physically. Build the relationship; add intimacy later.

4. Add intimacy step-wise, and slowly.

5. Longevity is much more important than exclusivity in friendships, and in sexual intimacy.

6. All kinds of nontraditional intimate partnerships work quite well; with the same amount of energy and commitment, they can be as lasting and fulfilling as marriage.

10. Forty-Two Years of Sexually Open Relating

Atwood Henderson

I guess I was always a free spirit. I grew up a non-conformist, the eldest child in a very fundamentalist Protestant family. Almost everything was forbidden, yet my father smoked a pack of cigarettes a day. This was against his religion but no one ever spoke of it. This was the first, but certainly not the last religious paradox in my life. Early on I was aware that vaginal intercourse outside marriage was a no-no. Fortunately I had the good sense not to ask about other forms of sexual involvement. In my teens, my friends and associates tended to be much older than I, and my early sexual relationships were with much older women who were concerned about pregnancy, so everything worked out just fine for me.

I went from one brand of religion to another, looking for one that was based in reality. They all preached love, but actually condemned love except in carefully delineated terms in very restrictive relationships, one per person for life! I have little patience with any authoritarian religion that has upheld the status quo while promising better luck in the afterlife, treating the female half of the population as second-class citizens, or worse. While preaching love they have fueled a thousand wars and killed millions of innocent people. Love is not a weapon and should not be used as one. Neither is it a zero-sum game. On the contrary, the more you love, the more your capacity for love grows. What can be holier, more of a mountain peak experience, than making love? The goddess religions understood this and practiced physical love-making as the epitome of union with universal truth and spirit.

I was always very skittish about revealing my feelings and thoughts to clergy or established religious groups, because even as a child I saw the disasters that occurred when people confided in their church. Established religion has no more claim to spirituality than I do. Men make gods in their own image. Monogamy may have served a purpose in a male-dominant society in which inheritance was the issue and a woman didn't even have a right to her own name. Today women have options. A woman can control her own biology and be self-sufficient. Monogamy has become an option, not a moral imperative.

I have always been relatively open about my lifestyle. I do not shout it from the housetops, but I do not hide it either. My friends are aware of it, as are my children, my parents, and siblings. My mother, a devout Christian, said, "I love you anyway." My first sexually open relationship began in 1952 when I became part of a circle of intimate friends who shared several common interests, including geology, photography, travel, music, and sex. The people in this group were all career professionals. They did not think of themselves as an intimate friendship group, and it has been my observation over the years that most intimate groups and networks do not think of themselves as such until someone points it out to them. Some see themselves as swingers, but generally it is just "our crowd," and "our friends in x city or x country." Soon after joining the group I entered into a live-in relationship with one of the women members of this group. Several months later we married.

A few years later we moved to a university town where we both were successful Ph.D. candidates. Fortunately some members of our group had ties to people in the new location so that we soon had a new circle of intimate friends. After graduation our careers took us to a different location and we left behind our intimate support group. During that time, both my wife and I each developed a single intimate friendship that was very supportive throughout the rest of our marriage, which lasted until she died of cancer a few years after our graduation. Her intimate friend was my oldest male friend. He and his wife remain our friends to this day. My intimate friend was a professional colleague. The story I have to tell is about my relationship with this colleague.

We first met in the luncheon line at a professional conference. By the time we returned to the conference room we were holding hands and that evening when I took her out to dinner, I told her I wanted to make love with her. We had already spent several hours before dinner sitting in a cemetery discussing sexually open marriage and intimate friendships. This friendship quickly grew as she and her husband visited us and we visited them. The relationship grew, with the full knowledge of our spouses, although they did not become sexually intimate with each other. Soon we named her and her husband legal guardians to our son in case we should both die. Her husband and our son became great buddies.

She and I talked about everything, especially career things, primary-relationship things, and family things. She was concerned about making more than her husband, and about whether to accept a pending promotion that would have increased her income substantially. She had an aversion to writing, but was in a publish-or-perish profession, and we worked on that too. She saw me through a problem period with my son and helped my wife deal with a phobia. We were very involved emotionally but we emphatically agreed that we wouldn't last a week in a primary relationship with each other, because we each had personality characteristics the other would not have put up with in a primary partner. Our relationship worked well over a period of several days to a week, but would not have survived on a day in and day out basis. Still, we were deeply involved in each other's households. For example, when my wife and I were contemplating a move, my intimate friend and I spent as much time house hunting as my wife and I did. Once when her husband was making a trip on his firm's Lear jet, he took my son along to Toronto and back because they had an extra seat available.

One day my wife came home from a routine doctor visit and announced that she had cancer. I immediately contacted my intimate friend, who is a psychiatrist, and from that day until my wife died six months later, they were in daily telephone or personal contact. The very positive support of our intimate friends during this trying time reinforced my resolve never to get involved in a relationship that was not sexually open. The crisis in our household became their crisis as well. The particular friend about whom I am writing indicated her willingness to come and stay with us if we wished. Within a few days of my wife's death, my employer ceased operation, so I was bereft of a job as well as a wife. After my wife's death, my intimate friend and her husband insisted that my son and I come to their home for an extended healing visit. Their place was familiar territory to us. We stayed with them for a week of hanging out and talking through the way life takes unexpected turns. Her husband took me down to his office where he and his boss talked to me seriously about becoming a vice president in the firm.

During that week, she, he, and I had a long discussion about my spending more time with her and being in the same firm with him, in the light of our relationship. He and I also discussed this alone, and he reassured me that he found my relationship with his wife supportive and felt that it had contributed to her growth and development. I felt the same way about it having motivated me professionally as well as having broadened my awareness of some facets of my life that I had never explored in depth before. Up until then my intimate friendships had not been as close as this one, even though I had shared social, intellectual, and career intimacy as well as sexual intimacy with several people. Ultimately I decided not to take the job with his firm because a unique career opportunity developed that I couldn't resist.

While becoming involved in this new career activity I became reacquainted with an old friend who had also lost a mate to cancer. We didn't plan to become primary partners. Neither was at all anxious to get married again. As old friends, we felt we could safely discuss what was wrong with marriage as a way of clarifying why we were each avoiding primary relating. She had been married to a man who had outside relationships which he denied. She was unwilling to get into a relationship unless she could be assured there was a way of being honest and maintaining mutual trust. I was determined to continue my intimate friendships.

The more we talked, the more we realized that we saw many relationship issues from similar perspectives, that we respected each other's career patterns, and that we each firmly believed in truth as the basis for relating. Eventually we realized that we were consulting one another more and more frequently and spending more time together although we lived in different cities. My intimate friend encouraged the new relationship, and I valued her insight.

My potential partner and I agreed that entering into a primary relationship need not force the participants to couple-front, e.g., they could still function as individuals in a partnership that not only allowed but encouraged individual growth and thereby strengthened the peer aspects of the relationship. We also agreed that love is not a zero-sum game. She was interested in exploring sexually open relating when I described how well it had worked in my previous marriage. Having had this extended feeling-out conversation before, I recognized where it was leading. We eventually agreed to explore such a relationship together, feeling we had nothing to lose because if it wasn't comfortable, we wouldn't pursue it.

Spending time together merged into living together. The day the moving van brought my furniture to her place, it was drizzling. As they were bringing in my grand piano, the phone rang. It was my intimate friend, calling from a hospital bed, telling me that she had kept back a bunch of pills and was on the verge of taking them. For the next two hours, I talked her through the crisis that had brought her to that point. Eventually I got her promise to talk to a mutual friend on staff there at the University Hospital, which she did. As I sat on the bare floor with moving men coming to and fro, I was oblivious to everything except that tenuous link with a loved one who was hurting. That call began a process of working through a problem that had exploded into her life. She was attracted to a woman and was considering entering into a relationship with her. We worked on the problem together until she felt able to talk to her husband about it. He suggested that her friend move in with them, but that presented problems that her friend could not handle, so he ultimately moved out and the two women lived together. The impact of her new relationship on her career became unbearable, although we continued to work on it. Finally she and her husband agreed to divorce, she resigned from the university, and she and her friend moved to another city. Their lesbian relationship has survived for the past twenty-six years.

Her ex-husband, who soon married a friend we all knew, has remained a firm friend who has been there whenever she needed him. Our relationship continued, perhaps even closer than it had ever been, and after some hesitation on her new partner's part, they came to visit us for several days, after moving out of state. There have been many visits back and forth since then, the most recent in August of this year. Her current relationship has been sexually open from the beginning and our intimate relationship continues. However, since we have been 2,000 miles apart for fifteen years now, it is no longer the kind of close interactive relationship it once was, and it has not been sexual for the past eight years. Letters and phone calls are no substitute for in-person relating.

How has my current marriage worked in practice? Beautifully. Over the years we have followed different paths because we are individuals with different needs, interests, and desires. We can certainly affirm that the grass is not greener on the other side of the fence if there is no fence! We have each tended to have more than one intimate friendship at the same time. I seldom see an intimate friend more frequently than once a month, whereas my wife has stayed overnight with intimate friends every two or three weeks for the past seventeen years. We have each sustained intimate friendships for as long as twenty-plus years. Unfortunately as time has passed, some of these friends have died, and it has not been easy to sustain those deaths. Over the years we find that we are becoming intimately involved with new friends much less frequently and we attribute this to AIDS in particular but also to getting older. We share information about our intimate friendships just as we do about our non-intimate friendships, no more, no less. We have felt free to share concerns that troubled us about an intimate relationship or about the other's intimate relationship so that we could help each other work though such concerns. On occasion we have respected the wish of an intimate friend not to share something, but this has been a rare occurrence. Neither of us is interested in pursuing an intimate friendship that would have a negative impact on our own relationship.

I love to travel and have attended conferences or driven across country, and traveled abroad with several different intimate friends. These trips have lasted from a weekend to over a month, so even though I generally see friends less frequently, spending concentrated time on a trip tends to even out the time spent outside the primary relationship. My wife doesn't enjoy travel as much as I do and she has seldom spent longer than a weekend with an intimate friend. We have attended parties with our intimate friends, including sleepover and weekend or longer events, together and separately.

There have certainly been occasions when an intimate friend needed lots of time and psychic energy because of a problem he or she was experiencing, and on occasion both of us have pitched in to help him or her. This has not taken away from our primary commitment. If anything, being there for intimate friends has strengthened it. Sharing our love with friends somehow intensifies our commitment to each other. Our intimate friends have been closer than family and we have tended to call them our "real" family over the years. These relationships have not always continued to involve sexual intimacy, nor were they ever sexual at every single meeting. But having been sexual at some stage, these individuals became part of that charmed circle of intimates, those who had made themselves vulnerable with one or the other of us and with whom we could therefore be open about who we really are and what we really think about anything and everything. With other friends, the sharing has always been more superficial because there hasn't been the same degree of shared vulnerability. We don't feel free to discuss our lifestyle or to share concerns and problems at nearly the same level of intimacy.

Our children have known from childhood about our lifestyle. Two of them have been in intimate friendship groups and still are, although I am not sure that they are still sexually intimate. We did not push them in this direction and were, in fact, surprised when each volunteered that they were in such an intimate circle. The other child has also had a philosophy of sexually open relating until the AIDS crisis came along. I feel that I am much healthier emotionally because of my lifestyle. I do not have to deal with many of the problems that face monogamous couple-fronting people. I am free to individually develop different facets of myself with different people and bring those new insights, skills, and interests back to my primary relationship.

I believe Americans in particular have gone much too far down the path of going it alone. We are gregarious creatures, who tend to be happiest when solving problems together, or simply hanging out together. To restrict one's self to a single partner for life, or even for the length of a relationship, unable to connect with others except as a couple, is to cut one's self off from much that is good, satisfying, and fun. Denying sexual attraction, excitement, and fruition as a part of relating to others seems strange to me. I believe my openness to the possibility of sexual intimacy in a relationship has helped me to be more open to people in general and has attracted people to me that I might not otherwise have met. Many people are put off by a willingness to make one's self vulnerable in a friendship, and so this becomes a litmus test for finding people with a strong sense of self, and these are exactly the people that interest me.

Various studies have found that at least one member of most so-called monogamous couples cheat at some time during the marriage, and it appears that the more recent the marriage, the more likely the involvement in extramarital sexual relationships. Although we tend to think of these outside relationships as cheating, many of them are actually consensual, and this consensual extramarital sex falls into two categories. The first is consensual sexually open relating and the second is swinging. Swinging is often condemned as an unemotional, compartmentalized couple-front activity, but as many as half of all swingers, according to some studies, have followed a path from cheating to couple-front swinging to sexually open relationships that include not only sexual involvement, but social, emotional, and other types of intimacy as well. Several of the people with whom I have had relationships went through this growing process.

My wife and I find ourselves more and more committed and in love as the years go by. We wouldn't change a thing in our sexually open relationship, but we have changed our sexual behavior. Safe sex is the name of the game since the advent of AIDS!

In my early years I rejected the dogmatic pronouncements of the fundamentalist Protestant church in which I grew up. Early on, I questioned and rejected the limitations the preachers placed on loving and their anti-sexual values. Today a Unitarian-Universalist church group, guided by a woman minister and nestled in a lovely rural woods, is our spiritual home. This friendly community promotes healing and communion with the earth that births us. Although most are not aware of our lifestyle, those who do know are comfortable with our open-ended pilgrimage in a way most church folk could never be, given their ambivalence about sex, and their myopic view of love and its potential, both sexual and spiritual.

11. Growing in Synergy

Valerie Triumph

My husband, Del, and I have had an open marriage for twenty-four years. We have been core members of an open lifestyles social club for twenty years. We have never had difficulties with jealousy or other conflicts from our lifestyle choice.

I am very fortunate to have a partner capable of open-handed, generous love. Once we lived in a house converted to three apartments. We were friendly with the young man, Sam, who lived upstairs. One night after Del had gone to bed early, I went upstairs to borrow a cup of sugar or something. Sam and I found ourselves attracted, and we drifted into involvement. Four hours later, I came down to find Del awake and concerned about my disappearance. He was upset because I had gone away without leaving a note. After we had dealt with the problem, and I had resolved to be more considerate, it occurred to me to mention that I had fallen in love with Sam. Del smiled and said, "Oh, I knew that the minute I saw your face, when you came down the stairs."

I cannot explain how Del came to be the man he is, but I can relate my own entry into polyamory. My spiritual journey came from asking questions, seeking hard evidence, needing to be whole, and needing to be honest with myself. In elementary school, high school, and early college, I explored religions. Raised as a Lutheran, I investigated a range of religious experience: from Christian fundamentalism through Catholicism, to Reform Judaism. During this period, I sang in a choir, read a lot, and discussed. The link between spirituality and sexuality began when I felt the spiritual dimension of the mundane world. The immanence of God in all matter came, as a college freshman, from the transcendental concept of God as the Ground of Being. By labeling a consecrated wafer "divine" we held God within an arm's length. He manifested Himself in every molecule of our bodies, and in everything around us.

I moved away from divine creation meaning a completed act, static and fully defined, which people merely interpreted. People create meaning in an

95

ongoing dynamic process. Every human activity—art, music, literature, humor, entertainment, business practice, defense, government, law—generates meaning. We create powerful meaning through sexual intimacy, ranging from soul-destroying devaluation to direct personal validation. To my eyes the claims of religion to spiritual privilege dwindled. Soon Occam's razor cut the final thread.

One morning in the beginning of my junior year in college, I woke up and realized that I had not believed in God for some time. For two years I was a Unitarian/Universalist, then an Ethical Society member for another two years. Finally I abandoned organized religion when the minister refused to marry my fiancé and me without extensive counseling, just because we were an interracial couple.

My spiritual journey moved into areas not traditionally called "spiritual." For example, I studied interpersonal control, dominance and submission, traumatic bonding, and the Stockholm Syndrome. At a sexual party with people I loved and friends, I was subtly ridiculed by a new member of our group. I'd opened up when I made love. My defenses were still down. When the others supported his ridicule, I couldn't face the pain. I felt turned inside out, and lost touch with my anger. A while later, I massaged the attacker's shoulders to distract him, so a friend could get acquainted with the man's wife. Eight hours later I awoke from a nightmare in which I felt hatred for men, and myself, for the first time. Only then did I realize how dishonest that manipulative massage had been. I'd tossed away a lifetime of ethics without noticing. In that moment of pain I had betrayed myself and undergone a form of traumatic bonding. How could I respect myself? How do we free ourselves from the limitations of instinctive survival responses? Eventually I understood my weakness—that others might sometimes control who I am—as the down side of the greatest human strength, the capacity for self-transformation and transcendence. Mutual respect among equals, in my opinion, not only evades our instinct for mindless submission, it's the social foundation for the greatest spiritual adventure.

Humanity is reinventing itself by self-analysis and personal growth. We have begun to free our spirits from the bonds of instinct. Many areas of study contribute to such growth, such as psychology, the study of bias in communication and culture, and the study of bias in language itself. Michel Foucault leads us to deeper levels which shape our perceptions, in what he calls the archaeology of knowledge. Many leaders have shown us how to free ourselves, Frederick Douglas, Susan B. Anthony, Mahatma Ghandi, Malcolm X, and Gloria Jean Watkins (Bell Hooks) to name a few. My polyamorous community participates in this recreation of the human spirit.

Life churns with chaos. Intimate friendships center me. Amidst the turmoil of politics, unstable stock markets, the spread of new diseases, disintegration of Earth's exosphere, the death of relatives, and sudden physical handicaps, joy wells from my intimate community. For me, spirituality isn't about ghosts or deities. It's about the very meaning of life. It arises, not from submission to mysterious powerful entities but from people who care about each other.

Some months ago, I met a middle-aged man who grew up in Red China. He was almost a virgin, and was bright, articulate, and well educated. We made love, then stroked one another, and talked. He shared his fears and lack of experience. He wanted to know what was possible, how could you love someone that you did not intend to marry. I described the kind of personal validation that can be shared. Then he did the most amazing thing; he changed himself, instantly. He made himself vulnerable to me. His eye contact and body language reached out. He shared his deepest secret, an early childhood experience, with me. I had not known that kind of conscious control was possible for a human being. Within two hours, we had formed a lasting, personal bond. Polyamory constantly presents me with marvelous surprises. He later said that his life had been changed. We care for each other as whole people through sex, and support one another in our journeys of discovery.

12. Faithfulness in Marriage

Art Rosenblum

I am the child of reform Jewish parents who were more involved with the Ethical Society than with formal religion. My parents probably had a perfectly faithful monogamous marriage, but never ever said a word about sex. At twelve, I sensed all adults shared a conspiracy to withhold some great secret from children. Sex was never even joked about in our family. Schoolmates hushed up when I approached because they saw me as "innocent." I was very lonely.

When I started to masturbate, I felt extreme guilt, the more so because no one ever mentioned stains on my sheets, letting me know it was something too terrible to talk about. For years, my greatest fear was that some day another boy might point to me and say: "I bet he masturbates!"

At fourteen and fifteen, I had visions of community. First I saw myself in a subtropical commune where we lived and worked together without money; six years later that proved to be totally precognitive. At fifteen, I saw myself as older, about twenty-five, sharing a loving community with age-mates who were totally intimate with one another. By then, I had notions of sex as something dirty the boys made rude jokes about, but also something beautifully intimate when shared by lovers. Yet, I still had no idea what it was.

At seventeen, I feared being drafted and decided to travel free by motorcycle across the country. As I rode, I pondered why adultery was — in 1945 — the only legal ground for divorce in New York State, and I wondered why, if I loved a wife, I would have to divorce her just because she shared sex with another. I decided I would not do that.

In a college dorm, my masturbation was discovered by my roommate who told me it was much better to have sex with a girl even if I had to go to a prostitute — I had thought sex was only for marriage. Perplexed, I finally asked my mother if it was right to have sex before marriage and she said, "it was good for a young man to have some experience." I was amazed.

In college I became a pacifist, a student of Gandhi, and was led to Quakers from whom I learned of a community of six hundred people in Paraguay who did not use money and did not go to war. The dean encouraged me to visit them, so at twenty I left college for the Bruderhof community, which I then joined. The Bruderhof is a Christian community that began in Germany in 1920. They believe sex outside of marriage is akin to murder since it could result in abortion which is murder. Those who remained true to the community never divorce, and all their marriages appear to work well. I believe that is because they have a clear method of settling small disagreements quickly, lest they be forgotten and lead to unconscious resentment later on.

I became a Christian and remained with the Bruderhof for almost seventeen years, during which time, with the help of the brothers and through prayer, I overcame the sinful habit of masturbation. I was celibate all during that time, but did not find it easy.

I was often depressed in the community, but not as much as before I came there. At twelve, I considered suicide because I had failed to do what I could to prevent the war in Europe. I never thought of suicide in the community, but felt sad that marriage was not given. After a very long struggle against masturbation, I found Soren Kierkegaard's words: "Melancholy comes when the Spirit wants to change something in a person's life and that person is resisting the change." A translator's note followed: "On this particular point Kierkegaard really knew what he was talking about."

When I was depressed again I asked: "What does the Spirit want to change in my life, or what change am I resisting?" I soon sensed I had to make an embarrassing apology, and as soon as I decided to do it, I felt much relieved. After several similar experiences, I knew I'd found the answer to my depression and became very open to changes.

But I was still lonely and longed for a mate. One day I fantasized living in a community where everyone was free to make love with any of the others because in a communal society all children are loved regardless of whom the father might be. I was deeply ashamed and confessed the fantasy to a leader who said: "Free love is neither loving, nor free, and extramarital sex destroys a person's spirituality." I was sure he was right and refused to let myself dwell on that concept again.

Shortly after solving my problem of depression, I became severely depressed again. It took two days to accept the Spirit's leading: that I was to leave the Bruderhof to see if I had some other calling. That was very hard. The community was my entire security and my promise as a member was to remain with it all my life. Surprisingly, though, the brothers declared that while they knew I was called to the life of community, they also thought it would be good for me to leave for a time to become more certain of that calling. They asked me how much money I wanted to take with me and then gave me twice as much—even so, it was still only a modest sum.

From the Bruderhof, I was led to several other, less dogmatic Christian communities but became dissatisfied when none of them wanted to do anything to stop the Vietnam war. A leader of the Reba Place Fellowship (1967) asked me to leave if I wanted to be a printer for Students for a Democratic Society (SDS), which he regarded as "Communist." I couldn't bear to spend weekends helping brothers paint our nice houses knowing that at that very moment napalm was being dropped on helpless Asian villagers.

At SDS, I clung to my Christian celibacy and was troubled by the "free love" approach of most students. I could not effectively demonstrate that it destroyed their spirituality. In fact, those who shared love and sex often seemed more spiritual than those who did not, but I remained firm. Suddenly, at a national council meeting in Berkeley, I was asked to become National Secretary for Education for the group; to give up the printing and travel from college to college preaching what I knew about communal living or any other insights. I longed to take on the task as I saw communal living to be a major answer to the problems of humanity, which has always lived communally until a few thousand years ago when we began to overpopulate and destroy the planet.

But I feared that none of the students would listen to me because they would ridicule my views on sex and the need for celibacy till marriage, so I turned down the position without honestly declaring the nature of my problem. The person who filled the position was not very competent. Within a year, the whole organization collapsed. The Weathermen faction became violent and committed murders, some died in bombings, some went to prison. Later the head of the Weathermen wrote that the violence was wrong, "the military error," and that they should have started communal groups instead. I came to feel that if I had been open and honest about my sexual views, I could have been corrected and become National Secretary for Education. SDS might have flourished in greater love, communal peace movements might have bloomed, and the world might already be a different place. From then on, I began to see sex as holy and that it was absolutely essential to share about it honestly, even if I am frequently accused of speaking much too freely. In those days, I saw the horror of hiding the truth.

Now I see the truest purpose of sex as neither reproduction nor pleasure, but as communication of the most honest, intimate kind.

After ten months as printer for SDS, I was replaced so that I could travel around and set up printing presses for any group that opposed the war. I worked without pay because wherever I went I found communities of all kinds willing to give me free lodging to support my work. In New York, eight students living in a two-room apartment told me they were a group marriage and so they could easily put up one more. The four men and four women were open and intimate with each other and made love just as naturally as they ate together. I could observe no lack of spirituality, but a deep concern for the need of the poor and the suffering of the Vietnamese. They worked with humor and love at very creative consciousness-raising among other students. Among all the communities I visited while setting up twelve printing presses in two years, I was convinced that the group marriages were by far the most loving and honest relationships I had shared.

By then I had also dropped my own celibacy, finding to my surprise and delight that in a community where abortion would never be needed, I felt no guilt at all about sharing honest sex with a woman I did not intend to marry. I also realized that premarital sex destroys spirituality only because it is almost always secret or dishonest.

When younger folks began setting up their own printing equipment, I went to Philadelphia to spend my full time researching the future to find out how a rulership of love could come to this planet. Finally, after eight years of poverty and excitement, I met Judy who had the same concern. After one date, a trip to a "Towards Tomorrow Fair" at the University of Massachusetts in Amherst, I asked her to marry me. Her greatest fear was that I had a whole harem of women somewhere, but twenty-eight days of complete honesty and a few miracles were enough; so we got married. It turned out that Judy was expecting me to marry her from the day we first met at an alternative book fair. She had come there looking for a husband and a new career because the astrological signs were just right for that to happen.

Judy and I were married by a rabbi, and again by a Catholic priest. The priest told us that the best time for prayer, for closeness to God, was the deep relaxation immediately following orgasm. I sensed the depth of his experience more than his commitment to celibacy. Our ability to listen to and follow leadings of the Spirit depends on deep relaxation. Knowing the joy of a partner openly sharing love with another without fear or jealousy is a gift of God, a unifying experience of true love.

Part of the marriage agreement Judy and I made with each other was to have no one else live with us for at least six months, but two weeks later she met an old friend of mine from the Bruderhof and asked her to move right in with us. The friend saw how nice it was to be married and asked us to find a man for her. Within a few weeks that happened, and since then we've brought about a dozen couples together. We find it far easier to find partners for others than it ever has been to find someone for ourselves. That is because we have less tension, less emotional involvement when looking for another, and in that more relaxed state, we are always much more intuitive. So, if anyone needs a good partner, just find that rare, happily married couple and ask them to do the intuitive part for you. You will make the final decision yourself.

A year later we had a visit from Andy, a young woman from Canada who wished to stay the night. While Judy made supper, I was telling Andy about a kind of shared therapy called "Reevaluation Counseling" (R.C.) and I showed her how we held hands while we shared whatever we needed to talk about with each other. We might have hugged a bit also, as the R.C. folks do, and I asked her if she wanted to sleep in a room by herself or if she would prefer to cuddle in with us. She really preferred to cuddle in with us and so I asked Judy if that was OK and she agreed. It was great fun in bed with two women and I felt pretty turned on and tempted. I wanted to make love with Andy right there, but didn't know whether to ask Andy first, or Judy, as I couldn't help both of them hearing the question. I finally asked Andy and she said she would prefer not as we didn't really know one another well enough. Judy then complained that I should not have asked that of Andy without her permission; I explained my dilemma and was forgiven. We had a great night, but no sex.

A short time later, I attended a meeting where I met an older man, Robert, although that was not his name. At the meeting, I invited Robert to visit us any time and a few days later, without a phone call, there he was at the door. A practical fellow, ten years older than myself—I'm twenty years older than Judy—he seemed to get on with us very harmoniously. Our bedroom was pretty large and had another mattress next to ours so, with Judy's agreement, I invited him to share our room.

In a very short time, Judy took quite a liking to Robert and asked if I had any objection to their sharing a little more intimacy. He was alone at the time, and I remembered so well my Bruderhof years of loneliness, and the times I wished I could just tell the community that I needed a wife, and leave it to them to find me someone. That was done sometimes in the old days of the Hutterite Brethren when brothers were out on mission and a sister would be sent out to them by the community to be their mate. Having already experienced the joy of honest group marriage relationships, I really felt good about Judy sharing her love with Robert. In fact, it also improved our marriage a lot from the sexual standpoint.

Judy and I married because we saw a common task for the world, not because we had that very special sexual chemistry called "falling in love." I had also been in the Community Farm of the Brethren in Bright, Ontario, Canada, for a few weeks and learned how well the arranged marriages of their young people also worked out. The parents usually arranged a marriage for the young people when a boy declared himself ready to marry and seemed to have the spiritual clarity to remain with the communal lifestyle. Parents met to talk about who would be best suited for the boy and then they would ask the girl if she was willing. When she agreed, the boy, who was expected to accept the parents' choice as a gift of God, was asked, and if he was willing, the two married at once.

I was shocked when I first heard of that from the community leader. I said: "But what about falling in love?" He confidently replied, "Oh, that comes afterwards." It was like a revelation. I had no proof that we had to "fall in love" *before* we could marry. And the marriages in that community seemed to work far better than most marriages I had seen outside.

When Judy and Robert became lovers, her sexual desire for me did not diminish at all. In fact, she would get all turned on with him and after she enjoyed his love and he was finished, she would turn to me. By that time, I would be really ready, having been turned on by the beauty of their lovemaking. We had better sex that way than we ever did before Robert came, and it was all so open and intimate that I wondered why everyone didn't enjoy sharing love as a group instead of alone as separate couples. That went quite nicely for about four months until Robert said he would like to go back to California to get some of his stuff and that he would like to take Judy with him for a month. That was a tough decision. I feared she might prefer to remain there with him, while I felt called to work in the East.

But Judy pointed out that I had traveled for years, and she hadn't. This was the chance she didn't want to miss. Since we had signed that we would settle all disagreements the day they arose, or seek help from a third party, I knew we couldn't put this one off. After meditating, I saw Judy was right. I had to risk losing her. But I also feared the loneliness I would feel when, after only a few months of marriage, she would be gone.

So, I told her the truth and she promised to return, and I admitted how lonely I would be without her. I said: "I'd find it much easier if I had a lover to sleep with me while she was away, and that if she could arrange that, I would feel good about her traveling with Robert." She said, "Fine, whom do you want?" I quickly thought of a few women I would love to sleep with, if they were willing and Andy was the first I thought of. So Judy called and told Andy what was going on, and asked if Andy would spend a month with me while she was away. Andy agreed at once and got here soon enough to also share love with Robert before they left.

As I recall, however, Andy was not that sexually excited by me and we only had intercourse once or twice during the month, but it was comforting to be with her and to feel that Judy cared enough to find me a companion while she was away. I knew that if I had called any of the women on my list and asked them to spend a month with me while Judy traveled, they would have feared our marriage was breaking up and would have refused involvement. But since it was Judy who called, Andy knew it was a totally honest invitation and she was not doing anything that would hurt another.

As the end of the month approached, Judy called asking that we all move to California because Robert did not want to return East and she really loved the West. I explained my feeling that I could be far more effective against the war spirit close to D.C. than I could be out there and I asked her to return. Without an argument, she agreed to get on a plane and come right back and we have remained in a faithful, open marriage ever since. I feel that experience cemented our marriage for life, and jealousy has no part in it. I remember it whenever I see the large poster inside the door of our bedroom. It shows a woman in the mist of dawn releasing a bird into the air and says: "If you love something, set it free. If it comes back to you, it is yours. If it doesn't, it never was."

Now we have both agreed to seek together for a group marriage community for ourselves and our children which will also share our primary concern for a positive, loving future for the planet Earth and we plan trips this summer to make that search a fruitful reality.

Sex and Spirituality as the Ultimate Communication

If spirituality is communication with and following the promptings of the divine, then sex is a deep form of communication between humans who, to my thinking, are all part of the divine. If any one of us did not exist, God herself would be incomplete.

For a long time I have realized that the superficiality of our culture makes it seem as if sex is for pleasure alone, and mostly, selfish pleasure at that. Three years ago I confronted the prevalence of that superficial view when four boys and four girls, age sixteen, shared with me an in-depth view into their special and unusual friendship. Instead of yielding to the peer pressure to get rid of their virginity and prove their budding sexuality with multiple intercourse partners they had formed what they called a "teen lovegroup," in which they refrained from intercourse but shared other sensual pleasure including orgasms through group massage. This let them feel so safe that they could freely discuss all their most intimate physical and spiritual experiences. For the two years before they communicated with me on the Internet these eight young people had found their own solution to the problem of having intercourse before one develops the appropriate communications skills. One boy, "proven" to be "learning disabled," soon became a total mystery to his teachers when he suddenly began doing excellent schoolwork. One of the girls experienced the reunification of her family and a new closeness to her father with whom she could now share her thoughts, and even non-erotic massage. For these teenagers, loving freely with total security dissolved the tensions of their moving through the turmoil and change of adolescence in a frightening world. Risk-free erotic pleasuring with clear boundaries brought these teenagers a deep unity they had never experienced before. And that is "holy," a truly unifying "wholeness."

Personally, I have had a hard time learning to share intimacy in ways that satisfy my partner as much as myself, but that is the challenge of love and we find that the more openly we share honest, responsible intimacy with others, the deeper our contact with one another and the God of whom we are all a part.

Before joining a well-known historic peace church, I shared the facts of my open marriage with the minister to be sure that it would not be considered sinful. "I don't think it would work in my marriage, but if it works for you, that's fine—only don't preach it in the church."

Our particular church has enough problems with the larger body over our equal acceptance of gays and lesbians, so I can understand they are not yet able to handle the issue of open marriage as well.

Some time later, I attended a conference on "Sexuality and Nurturing" at a very conservative church of the same denomination. After the main speaker had spoken a long time, he left ten minutes for questions and answers. The silence was embarrassing. No one of about two hundred in the audience dared to ask a question. So, sitting right in front, I stood up to ask: "Each time you referred to extramarital relationships, it was always related to dishonesty or secrecy. What do you think of open love relationships which are agreed on by all concerned?"

I can't recall his response, but then he came and sat next to me and asked: "Did I really answer your question?" I said he'd done the best he could under the circumstances. I then told him of a time when Judy had a young lover, a man who at twenty-six had never had a relationship with anyone. While with us over ten months, he blossomed out and we discovered his amazing gifts as a writer. After moving on, he wrote Judy that she had saved his life. He had been contemplating suicide until his experience of love with Judy. "Was that relationship a sin?" I asked, fully expecting he would throw the Bible at me, or at least ten verses. Instead, he was silent for a long time. Finally he said, "I would say it was not a sin."

I now feel the evidence is so clear that even very religious people can accept it with careful consideration. Faithfulness in marriage is a matter of long-term commitment and total honesty, but it does not necessarily require limiting the sharing of God's love to the intimacy of the married couple. In fact, a committed marriage makes it far easier to share love and intimacy with others. Especially, I believe, with those in greatest need whose current life precludes the luxury of a secure, long-term relationship, but also, because they are sensitive, might have devastating feelings of guilt for sharing sexual pleasure with another who enjoys the luxury of a secure and permanent relationship.

Love is only love when it is shared. And I believe it is the ultimate will of God for us all to "love one another."

Intimacy and the New Humans

Ron Mazur

Once upon the future, there are going to be growing numbers of women and men whose evolved human consciousness will create a global pathway for other intimacy seekers to follow. This small group, connected chiefly in cyberspace, are free body-spirits who will not be intimidated by the shaming of religious orthodoxies or by the public health hysterics paralyzed by fear of microbes. With awareness and therapeutic self/group work, these relationship pioneers will have freed themselves from the bondages of homoprejudice, homophobia, jealousy and possessiveness, male supremacy, gender equality, erotophobia, and pleasure-phobia.

In the present time, the multitudes are amazingly unaware that the human species has taken a quantum jump in sexual evolution: sex is no longer primarily connected to reproduction. Indeed, that equation is now a menace to a sustainable future. In this post-procreation age, sex functions essentially to provide intimacy, fun, communication, pleasure, and comfort—all those marvelous experiences which bless relationships. Persons may choose from many relationship models the style of expressing their sexuality, including open marriage and/or sexual freedom, as a valid, ethical lifestyle choice.

Once upon the now, we know that the future pathway toward the joys of inclusive intimacy will be littered by pilgrims in pain and anguish. We will be ❖   ❖   ❖

Ron Mazur, author of *The New Intimacy: Open-Ended Marriages and Alternative Lifestyles,* (1973) and *Commonsense Sex* (1968), is pastor of the Unitarian-Universalist Fellowship in Daytona, Florida.

bruised, even victimized by the vision. Some of us will be persecuted (shades of the catacombs) with loss of jobs, loss of family and friends, and threats of antiquated and modern legislative ignorance. Some relationships will endure and grow, some fade, but all will encounter, even crash into unforeseen obstacles. Will all of us be there to offer solace, support, and healing? Or do we fearfully creep along in our paradoxical isolation? In short, what plans do we have to organize and keep the alternative lifestyle community from anni-hilation?

13. Searching for Three-in-One Body/Spirit

Susan Robins

Although I went to Catholic school, worked for a Catholic college, and have many clothes I call my "nun clothes," I feel it is demeaning to say someone is a "nun." I much prefer to call them "sister." I once considered becoming a nun, but could not commit to the philosophy of celibacy. But I was born a sister, soon had three more, and many more since then. I never joined a convent, but there are still nights I lay awake considering the possibility of going to live on women's land; imagining women who live in community and have interesting discussions about diverse interesting topics. The fantasy of living with a group of women has been real for me since I was twelve years old wondering how to blend my feelings of *sexuality* with my thoughts about *spirituality*. At that time the convent was the only choice, even though I knew sex was forbidden there.

"Holy Ghost" is another term I never liked. In high school, in the sixties, we began to speak of the "Holy Spirit." Even then, I recognized it as a feminine aspect of the Trinity, knowing it was necessary to have a female presence with the concepts of Father and Son. Growing up, I looked for more of that aspect, wanting to experience the feminine presence in all aspects of my life. I found it in conversations with my sisters and girl friends, and with the nuns who were my teachers. (Maybe I can refer to them as the "someones" who were my teachers.) I continue to find sisters who are teachers for me. Here I use the term broadly. I'm close with my siblings as well as many women friends I call sister, the "someones" I meet in many of my activities, most recently teaching in public school. Another place I have encountered sisters recently is in twelve-step programs.

"I am powerless OVER (fill in the blank) *and my life is unmanageable."* Many twelve-step programs use this admission to help someone name whatever it is that keeps her/him from living more fully. For me, I feel powerless when I give myself away in a relationship, and my life is unmanageable when I neglect the spiritual dimension. Relationships without spirit would be as

111

empty as relationships without sex. Of course, we all have friendships and other kinds of relational experiences where sex is not an issue. But, in both sexual and nonsexual relationships, I am left feeling powerless if I lose my identity. As I approach fifty, I am looking for relationships where I can find power WITH others. This struggle is not mine alone: churches, businesses, and other institutions are looking for ways to empower people. Fortunately, I have found some tools to achieve empowerment that are part of my search to join sex and spirit.

Spirituality and "higher power" are realities I use to manage my life, and perhaps gain a measure of control over powerlessness. Control and power are interesting concepts, as is the combination of sex and spirit. How can anyone be sexual without a spiritual connection? For me, sex is the most direct way to contact the divinity within myself and others. If I feel powerful when I am in control of my life, does that mean I am powerless when I am out of control? Of course. But there is another choice: letting go of control without being OUT of control, and feeling my power without trying to control others or giving myself away. When I surrender, new possibilities open up, new opportunities to share my power WITH others rather than feeling they have power over me OR that I have power over them. Another way to describe what happens is that I find new power and a balanced sense of control in new ways of relating. Building relationships is the most important work of my life. Relationships offer many opportunities for surrender. Because I want to love both men and women, both sexually and nonsexually, surrender is important to love unconditionally.

As a female brought up in a matriarchal family, I learned to love women from the beginning. My two grandmothers were a central focus. Their husbands were dead, and they each had sisters who never married. The entire extended family was important, all of the sons and daughters, and brothers and sisters remained close to one another, both geographically and socially. The focal point remains with the women, particularly my mother.

Prestige in our Roman Catholic family was based on babies. Babies were, and still are the center of attention. The highest accomplishment is to bring new babies into the world. My mother was an excellent role model. She had six. My father's two sisters never had children, a spinster aunt and female cousin were also part of our frequent family gatherings, in addition to three aunts on my mother's side who never married. Being good Catholics, never married surely means never having sex. These seven women indulged in nothing more than church rituals, an occasional glass of wine, and my mother's children.

Even as my mother had more babies, there were plenty of warm bosoms for snuggling. My single aunts taught us about the Bible, took us to church and introduced us to novenas, talking about the Blessed Virgin, marveling at the purity of the mother of Christ, holding her up as a role model—as if somehow we too could have babies without having sex. I struggled with the sexual stirring I felt toward my girl friends, but in my town in the fifties there was no one to talk to about sex. Sex wasn't the only forbidden topic: politics and other people's religion were high on the list.

We didn't have particularly important discussions with these aunts, but I have fond memories of being stroked and snuggled by the one who was my godmother. When her younger sister went off to join the army, we exchanged letters, but never about anything more than the weather and who attended the most recent christening, birthday party, first communion, or confirmation. In the sixties and seventies, as babies were born to the other aunts and uncles, we all had much to celebrate. As part of a big family, there was always plenty of food, drink, and activity. Playing cards or board games, discussing a movie or TV show, or watching a sporting event were all choices when we were together, which was at least once a week. I longed to be closer to my mother, but she was busy with the other babies. We were all in denial about my father's drinking. He constantly told his five daughters, "Girls should be seen and not heard." At last a son was born!

In our house, the revolutionary changes in the Catholic Church taking place in the sixties got more attention than the protest against the Vietnam war. These changes were as important to us as the rebellions on the college campuses, and later demands for reform in the prison systems, were to families who had an interest in those issues. Our focus was always on a loving God; Mary, as Jesus' mother; the Church representing the "body of Christ"; and the Holy Spirit. Even though not one of us joined the convent, it was certainly a calling I considered as I reached puberty.

One reason for not answering the call to be a nun was I enjoyed the loving touch from my boyfriend. We did not have sexual intercourse because we were "saving ourselves for marriage," but we developed a mutual masturbation that was satisfying at the time. I certainly had no desire to give it up. He and I met when we were eleven years old and dated until I married someone else at twenty-one. Because not thinking "dirty thoughts" was part of the Catholic taboo, I pushed my desire for girls out of my mind. Doing this kind of thing with boys was forbidden, but with girls it was UNSPEAKABLE. This is verified by my sister's daughters who attend the same Catholic girls' school we did. I have taken a vow to be a different kind of mother and aunt, as I attempt to open the space for my nieces and daughter where sexual questions can be asked and discussed.

At least boys were willing to talk about sex, and what sex education I picked up I received from them in the eighth grade. Walking to and from catechism classes, we talked about confession, heaven and hell, the idea that life can be either heaven or hell. Our small group developed a moral code we could live with; it included a lot of gentle touching, kissing, and stroking, but no penetration. Once I experienced being touched in this way, I never questioned that marriage and babies would be my path. My teenage years focused on dancing, friendships, and wanting to get good grades. I applied for and was accepted to college, but my boyfriend had no interest in going. None of our parents, nor our aunts or uncles had degrees. I didn't want to stay in my hometown, and my parents were not supportive of my going away to school. The choices near home were nurse or teacher, and I wasn't truly interested in anything more than dancing, homemaking, and waiting to have sex.

The late-sixties marked the beginnings of "women's liberation." My father spoke vehemently about these things: "Woman's place was in the home, and students should not question authority." He felt college was a place for lazy non-workers, for people who were different from us. The work ethic was what was important. The safety of civil service and an hourly wage was what he understood. He really did not want his daughters to leave home; we never discussed our options in any logical way. He and my mom were focused on buying their first house and he worked long, hard hours in construction. Often out of work in the winter, he enjoyed drinking more than eating.

My father and mother fought constantly; once she confided in me that most of their arguments were about birth control. She wanted to completely abstain from sex which she saw as her "duty and obligation." She did not really have any other choice than being a full time homemaker. Babies kept coming. This was encouraged and valued, not saving to attend college or take a trip. Getting married seemed the easy way for me to leave home. I never questioned my designated sexual role aloud. I knew I wanted to have children, I knew being a mother was valued. I also knew I loved my girlfriends in a different way than they loved me. We never talked about it; I just knew. I also knew it wasn't right. Just as sex before marriage was forbidden, this attraction to women was even more despicable. In my hometown, lesbians still keep a low profile.

Necking and petting were what I liked best. My boyfriend and I had plenty of "sex play" but never "went all the way." For years, I prided myself on not having intercourse before marriage, never realizing it was so easy to wait because I was more satisfied with the external stimulation. My boyfriend joined the National Guard, and unfortunately right after graduation his company was sent to Vietnam. Soon after he left, I met Joe, who was also a Catholic. We went to Mass the morning after our first night together. We had kissed and touched all night long, but still no penetration. Without knowing it, we were practicing the ancient art of Tantric sexual ecstasy and prolonged pleasure. After a passionately short romance, we married.

When I became pregnant with my first baby I wasn't ready, but did not question it. We never considered using any method of birth control; this was another thing we did not discuss. There was no acceptable pill, only the rhythm method was allowed by the Catholic Church. My stance about birth control was, "If God wants us to have a baby, the means to take care of it will also be provided." In the premarital classes at church, we were instructed never to waste a sperm. What that meant was never clear. Abstinence could have been discussed more broadly, and good feelings without "going all the way" allowed and encouraged. Even today safe sex alternatives need to be described in more detail. Currently, many of my friends are willing to discuss the details of sexual encounters, and share options we didn't know were available back then. I want to hear about sex and talk about it as much as I enjoy doing it. I have always liked both definitions of intercourse, the verbal and the sexual. The true meaning of the English *intercourse* goes back to the early Hebrew *yadah,* or "knowing." The Hebrews didn't split humans into body and soul, or sexual organs and mind. "And Abraham *knew* Sarah" — in the depth of her mind and her sexual passion. When we try to split sex and spirit, we dehumanize people.

As my own babies arrived — three before I was twenty-six — I read everything I could find about natural childbirth and good parenting practices. I also searched the local libraries trying to find *something* about my feelings of being attracted to women. But at this time, little was written from a woman's point of view about anything, including childbirth or even breast-feeding. This didn't seem so absurd to me then, it was just the way things were. All I could find about homosexuality was about men being promiscuous with many other men, as "proof" of deviant behavior which needed to be treated and cured. There was no hint of meaningful relationships between people of the same sex, or with more than two people.

Sex between men and women became more openly discussed in the freedom of the seventies. Lots of talk about performance and multiple orgasms, but still nothing about alternatives. I took classes at adult school and joined church groups discussing relationships, but my questions were never addressed. Even serving on a Sunday school committee to research sex education for the children, I found more questions than answers.

Through that experience, I met another mother who was attracted to me. We both knew there was something different about the quality of our friendship, and eventually we were able to talk about our feelings. She advised me not to ask, but I wouldn't go farther than talking about sex without permission from our husbands. My husband, who was a heavy drinker like my Dad, threatened to take the children away and reveal to everyone that I was a lesbian. In 1978, the courts of West Virginia would not have been in favor of women loving women. I went to counseling and was told I was a "castrating female." A lawyer confirmed I was my husband's property, and he had the right to take the children if I was going to defy "human nature" and talk about being attracted to a woman.

Although I was a charter member of NOW, the newly formed National Organization of Women, I didn't participate much. Consciousness raising groups had begun, and *MS.* magazine appeared, but I was afraid to have a subscription. I once again chose to be seen and not heard, surrendering to the mores of the times. My husband was supportive of my interest in alternative spirituality, and together we began the practice of Transcendental Meditation (TM). The calming effect of meditating helped take my mind off the kind of sex I wasn't supposed to be thinking about, and instead renewed interest in our marriage. The benefit of this relaxed focus was that after ten years of marriage, I had my first real orgasm. This release then allowed me to concentrate on the important work of my life: to be the best wife and mother I could possibly be.

We moved three thousand miles away from my friend, determined to maintain the sacredness of our marriage. I prayed the feelings would subside and that I would be more "normal." I did not talk to anyone in my family about what was going on with me. I asked God the Father, his son Jesus, the Holy Spirit, and the Blessed Virgin Mother to deliver me from these "evil" feelings. In California we began to attend a New Thought church, and in my usual way I served on various committees and got involved with the children's programs. One important difference from the Catholic Church was that the ministers were married and their wives had active roles. There was no hint of celibacy, but also no discussion about the sacredness of sex, nor any alternative to the standard heterosexual monogamy.

At the urging of our female minister, I began college when my youngest began kindergarten. I started in a local community college, and then in 1983 chose a women's college in the San Francisco Bay area to complete my bachelor's degree. I was still looking for answers to why I felt different from other women who were my friends. As part of the Mills Feminist Alliance, I met lesbians for the first time. Some preferred female companionship because they didn't have many women around when growing up, or they were not close to their mothers or sisters; for others sexual preference was a result of being abused by a man or even several men in their families. As I learned more about the lesbian community, I discovered women who love women because they enjoy everything feminine. Others desire women because inside they feel more like men. When I confessed my attraction to women, all of them insisted I leave my husband and celebrate my gayness. But I wanted both.

Again a brick wall, silence. No one to support that idea. Ridiculous, crazy, go back and rethink, don't talk about sex. Religion okay. Politics okay. But still not sex. My spiritual search continued, and I met women who were practicing rituals from the ancient Goddess and Native American traditions. Many were becoming ministers in the Unitarian church. Most were married, some were lesbian. "You must choose," they told me. "You cannot stay with a man and love a woman at the same time."

But I did. And I even loved more than one woman, the same as when I was a child surrounded by my aunts and sisters. Many nuns were my colleagues when I took a position at a Catholic college. The book *Lesbian Nuns: Breaking Silence* shed some light and gave me the insight into my own feelings I had been seeking. Now we could read about women becoming priests, even "out" lesbians becoming ministers. About gay and straight women being both spiritual and sexual. But still never a word about loving both a man and women, or the spiritual dimensions of this lifestyle.

During this period of blossoming women's spirituality, I fell in love again and again listening to the warmth of women's music and their stories long into the night. One friend was a minister in a church where she was not allowed to be gay. From her I learned the true meaning of being in the closet. In her life so many things had to be a lie. Hers was a familiar story of an abusive father and neglectful mother. Her first lover was coach of the little league; unfortunately this older woman not only took advantage of her sexually, she also physically abused her.

Another told of incest and a supposedly loving mother who still ignores her daughter's pleas for acceptance and understanding. These women shared the intimate details of their lives with me, but not sex. We held each other and cried together, giving foot massages and back rubs. They suffered from their injustices, and I suffered patiently and silently with mine. It was easier for me to attend to their pain and problems than my own. This was a difficult time of growing. I truly loved them and wanted to hold them even closer, and share on a deeper and more intimate level, but none of us were ready. My children were getting older, and I was spending more and more time away, because my husband and I still didn't talk about our feelings.

Feelings were never discussed as a child, so this was nothing new. I seldom knew what I felt before meeting these women. I was so used to burying and hiding and stuffing away feelings, that things seemed "normal." Except that now these women helped me articulate what was going on inside of me. The classes I took in college examined women in contemporary society, and topics like rape in marriage and family dynamics. We looked at issues around class and gender and race. I had never met people so open and willing to tell their truths. For the first time in my life I was encouraged to focus on myself, and for the first time I asked what I really wanted.

"Don't think, don't feel, don't talk" was something I learned happened in dysfunctional families like mine. "Get married and live happily ever after" was the script I expected to live for the rest of my life. I didn't know anyone else who loved more than one person. I began to talk long distance to my siblings about this. I visited childhood friends and told them what I was going through. No one offered any suggestions, only "You'll get over it."

My college friends went off in different directions, and I took a teaching job near home feeling somehow abandoned. I still attended women's groups, but because of working full-time and doing most of the shopping, cooking, and laundry, there wasn't much time. My husband and I interacted less and less, and soon he developed a relationship with another woman, and left. I felt very alone, as my three children were ready to graduate from high school and be more on their own.

I didn't like women much at this point. How could a woman abuse a child? How could a mother ignore her daughter? I wanted to meet my husband's girlfriend, but he was threatened by this idea. My own mother and sisters were busy with more new babies in the family. My aunts were getting older and wrote less. I was never able to confide in them anyway.

I didn't like men much either. My husband and my father both continued to drink and make life difficult for those around them. My own teenage sons were beginning to use alcohol and tobacco. My brother and his wife lived close by, but were engrossed in their own babies. Questioning everything I ever learned about love and sex and family, I wanted out of relationship with everyone. I needed time to myself, to evaluate what it was I wanted. During this period of celibacy, I joined several groups of women who discussed the boundaries where sex and spirit meet, and started on the road to recovery....

We are women who practice the old religion of "Wiccan," sometimes translated as paganism. We come together to study the cross-cultural medicine wheel. We sit in a circle and listen to each other. This involves creating a sacred space which intensifies and directs the energy. The circle is endless, and ever flowing as is life. By celebrating the solstices and equinoxes, we are reminded of the rhythm of the seasons, the wheel of life, death, and rebirth. Our earth and the female aspect of all creation are symbolized by the circle. Within the circle we sit or stand, and dance and drum as our healing and life-affirming rituals unfold.

Ten years later I continue to feel as if I have a new family. This circle of friends includes both men and women, sometimes the same, sometimes different, who feed and nurture each other with words and openness. At first we are not all so willing to share our lives, our hurts and hopes, and dreams, some realized, some squashed. Eventually we open up as sacred space is created. There is no overt sexuality, just a juiciness in our conversation and hugs that feed my soul. I always leave feeling fuller and more abundant than when I arrived and look forward to going back.

"Coming out" as a bisexual has helped me feel powerful. In circles we share control, rotating leadership: actually we don't even use that word, we call it facilitation or being the "focalizer." It is easy. A rhythm and flow is repeated, but always varied. We create things. I have learned not to give myself away while still sharing and setting safe boundaries. I have learned the language of feelings. I know now that sex and spirit are not separate, not concepts to be thought about, but rather experiences to be enjoyed. As I learn to come from my heart rather than my head, I do not have to protect myself from relationships. Instead, I enter the experience with both feet, not just a toe in the water, or "straddling the fence." As I become continually willing to surrender, I want to share my power with both men and women without feeling out of control.

During the last few years I have made friends involved in "responsible non-monogamy" and "polyfidelity," or more recently the accepted term is "polyamory." From them I learned the word "triad." As a child, I contemplated the Trinity, trying to understand how three could be one. Now I want to develop a loving situation with both a male and female partner. As a bisexual female, I thought it would be easy to meet other bisexual women in this movement, but to my surprise most women were not interested in the same-sex connection. I found many couples interested in polygamy where the man wants to add a woman for his "enjoyment" or the woman is looking for another man. In these cases it is impossible to form a triad. Both partners are looking in opposite directions. This puts a strain on the primary relationship because the issue becomes who is going to spend time with whom, and one is left out unless both find someone new. This is too often the end of the relationship.

Some couples say they are more interested in *who* the person is rather than what gender, but they are often more into the theory of community than the practice of building relationships. My desire is for three people to love each other sharing power and energy equally without any one being in control. I want to live together with all of my lovers. Sleeping alone is not part of my ideal situation. I want to sleep in the middle, although I am willing to share that spot.

While living at Harbin Hot Springs, I met Paul who wanted to explore this possibility with me. But women we met were more attracted to him, and/or more interested in me as a friend, and unable to appreciate the gifts in both of us. As my relationship with Paul became closer, the perplexity increased. We are very different from one another and hoping to find someone attracted to us both seemed impossible. My original fantasy was that people would meet at the same time and develop a threesome simultaneously. Sometimes I considered breaking-up with Paul so this could happen. I knew from dating couples before I met Paul, that coming in as the third party, especially as "The Other Woman" was difficult. I also felt it could be different with us because I was the one who was most desirous of developing a relationship with a woman. It wasn't Paul who was looking. The ideal for us might be a lesbian exploring her bisexuality, rather than a heterosexual woman exploring possibilities with another woman.

We are interested in a relationship based more on common values and friendship than merely sexual attraction. We want to balance talking and touching with having a purpose in the larger society. We want the passion to flow between and among us as well as out into the world. It is balanced interaction, more than one-on-one sex: a holy union between people involving service not only to each other but to the community of others. Spirituality for me is not something I do alone on a mountaintop contemplating my navel. It is an active involvement with others; sex is only a small aspect of the fullness of relationship. We need to give our next generation alternatives. I am determined to live out my choices and move from theory to reality.

In the fall of 1993, Paul and I made a proposal to spend more intimate time with a friend he had known for three years. We both cherished and felt attracted to Tania, and gave her a copy of the *Polyfidelity Primer*, by Ryam Nearing. She had already purchased Dr. Deborah Anapol's *Love Without Limits*. Tania and I had some communication issues to work out, so we spent several nights talking till dawn while Paul slept. Then, an opportunity for us to sublet a beach house with Tania opened up a whole new series of questions. We struggled with what an equal relationship might look like. Paul and I had been living together for a year and a half, and we love to sleep with each other every night. Tania and I wanted all three of us to sleep together, and Paul agreed as long as he didn't have to be "squashed" in the middle. We liked the idea of taking turns, knowing Paul would be, what we jokingly referred to but knew was true, the pivot point. So we rotated during the night, reluctantly giving up the coveted spot between the warm bodies.

In the morning he held us on each side, and we had some wonderfully warm and special sexual dances together. Paul is a magnificent lover, who enjoys sensual touch and lots of kissing. At other times, Paul found our communication style confrontational, and often tuned out while Tania and I engaged in lengthy discussions about the process and evolution of the three-way relationship. All of us felt fragile in our newness and vulnerable with unspoken boundaries, I wanted to spend more time articulating what we each liked and wanted from each other. But I was accused of trying to direct and script our time together, so I silently struggled to tune into feelings, to get out of my head and more into my heart … this is hard for me. I found I was jealous, both of him wanting her and her wanting him. I knew I was getting touched less, because I was so used to having Paul's full attention focused on me. And although Tania was "doing a stretch" to touch me also, it was more me who wanted her. This caused Paul to feel ignored by me since he was accustomed to my fully focused attention on him.

On the spiritual level it is me who desires more ritual and a Tantric sexual experience. I always want to continue the touching, kissing, and stroking. Each time I want to remember the innocence of youth, come into each experience with a "new mind," and practice the gazing and titillation that preserves the newness. I want to be in touch with the divinity of my partners, and for them to know they are making love with a goddess.

The "wait and see" approach is not as appealing as focusing. Aware of my own power and ability to direct energy, I was scared to be too forceful or intentional because Tania expressed how unsafe and unheard she has felt in the past. I missed talking with Paul, and begged him to join our conversations. When he told us he didn't feel the three-way lovemaking was working, because he preferred one-on-one, I argued with him and tried to talk him out of his feelings. This made Tania furious with me, because as she rightly pointed out, his feelings are his feelings. But I was still longing for both of them to want me and each other equally and simultaneously.

Neither Tania nor Paul "understood" the language I would use about achieving "bliss consciousness" and seeing them both as manifestations of the divine ... as the Gods and Goddesses that we all are. Paul was more attracted to the sexual aspect, Tania to the political, and me to the spiritual.

We continued to sleep together every night, trying to find three-way ecstasy, but someone was always feeling left out. I would joke we just needed more practice, but Paul insisted he still wanted "alone" time with me, and that he was content to sleep without either of us. He felt sexually attracted to her, but not "in love" with her the way he was with me. I wanted to sleep alone with Tania, but her preference was for Paul. Obviously this triangle did not work for any of us, and after six weeks it was time to let it go.

This experience made Paul and I revalue our relationship and the place for fantasy within the context of what we expect from each other. We need to move to a higher spiritual plane for desire to flow three ways. He was raised Southern Baptist and over the past fifty-six years has become closed down to his feelings. He experiences a special union and bond with me, and is tolerant and encouraging about what I call my sexual deviation, but he is not exhilarated by sex the way that I am. He thought that having two women at once would be special, but found it was not as sweet as developing the intimacy we have between us.

There are not many people interested in the amount of engagement it takes for TWO to come to ongoing agreements about every detail of daily life, let alone be willing to work on THREE-way communication. It is precisely the communication issues that I am interested in pursuing with more than one person. It is that unity of trinity I am searching for. It is breaking down the old paradigms that say we are only capable of loving one at a time, and that heterosexual, monogamous relationships are the norm. As gays and lesbians fight for the right to be seen and heard, a bisexual, non-monogamous contingency who want to love and be loved by more than one is also emerging. Many young people, conceived during the open and free lovemaking of the sixties, ask "Why not?"

An issue for me has always been my dislike of "being in the closet." Although some friends are anxious to hear about our "ongoing soap opera," I am not willing to reveal my "perversions" to everyone. I intentionally use the words "deviation" and "perversion" because this is how most people view my preference, including Tania and Paul. Although they both said they loved me and expressed willingness to honor my preference—both admit it was not theirs.

Some people fall unconsciously into non-monogamy as a choice; for others it is a conscious preference. Being convinced there is a "gene" for monogamy I do not have, does **not** mean that I am interested in promiscuity. My wish is to build an ongoing relationship with equal power and love flowing in all directions with both a man and a woman. I am encouraged by the love and acceptance I receive from my own children and siblings as I talk about my desire. We are not as open with my parents and other relatives, nor with many co-workers, but we have created a supportive network of friends in whom we confide. It is in their support I find the union of sex and spirit. It is in being able to discuss the things that matter most to me which provides motivation for continuing this search for alternative relationships.

Two years later, Paul and I met Claire. We were attracted to her when we first met, and noticed she was flirting with both of us. As we talked, we learned throughout her life she had relationships with both men and women, although they were kept secret and separate. When we expressed our interests to her, and introduced her to other people involved in this changing paradigm, she was excited about the possibilities. Once again we made a proposal for the three of us to spend more time together.

I adore having a sister as a lover, surrendering to the longing, passion, and desire we feel. As women we have an easier time expressing our feelings, and Paul often feels left out of the intensity between us. The attraction Claire and I feel for each other has strained my relationship with him, but not diminished my feelings for him. He is still not as willing to engage as much as I have wanted. He is attracted to Claire, but remains aloof, which makes it difficult for us to know where he stands. Our housing situation is also not conducive for the three of us to live together. The ups and downs of this new triad are often frustrating, but, for me, worth the effort.

Now that the primary focus of my life is no longer being a "good Catholic wife and mother," there is more time to devote to relationships. I often wonder how I will explain things to my grandchildren. What their world will be like? Right now, none of my three children are interested in having babies. This is so different from the way I was raised. Their father and I encouraged them to be independent, and provided them with choices. These young adults know we will approve of any lifestyle that is not self-destructive. They know the union of sex and spirit is important. Although their father is monogamous and generally disapproving of homosexuality, we maintain a level of friendship, in spite of our different loving styles. Perhaps time will change his mind and open the minds of others who have limited the way they relate.

In the meantime, I am happy to have the support of other Catholic sisters like Mary Daly, Rosemary Radford Ruether, and Mary Hunt, all prolific authors who are teaching and living their belief that the world can be different in regard to sex and spirit. I am happy to be involved in ongoing discussions regarding addiction and codependence.

Many available books on the importance of enjoying a fully satisfying sex life address issues of power and control, suggesting these issues be discussed among and between lovers whatever gender they are. There are also many other books dealing with spiritual topics, especially those which instruct how to meditate, that talk about surrendering to transcend one's finite world and open oneself up to others, the cosmos, and the Infinite. Unfortunately, I have not found many books which bridge my dual interest in sex and the spirit, or talk about how to connect sexuality and spirituality. Hopefully, these stories of sexual diversity will encourage others to come out from the closet of their desires, and provide some fresh insights into the many more possibilities which exist when relationships begin with honesty and openness.

14. My Personal Story of Connecting Spirituality and Sexuality

Peter B. Anderson

First, I need to comment on my reasons for choosing to attach my real name to this story. For my entire adult life I've been different from all of my friends and family. It hasn't been a burden, just a reality. I've also been very happy and proud to be who I am and to meet the challenges that I've invited from life. Part of that pride and joy comes from being "up front" about who and what I am, and what I want out of life, even when who I am and what I'm looking for in life is different. Writing anonymously would diminish that honesty for me. As a result of this personal choice, I've made another choice, and that is to refrain from using any specific names in my monologue. As much as I value my freedom to speak personally, I value the right of others who have touched my life to remain unnamed. I would not violate their privacy. Therefore, my approach will be somewhat different in focus and content from other stories told in these pages.

How I incorporated my childhood and my study to be a Jesuit priest into a lifestyle of sexually open relationships doesn't seem to me to be a particularly remarkable story. I am writing it with the hope that as you follow your path you may gain some strength from your connection to my experiences.

The connection between my self as a sexual person and my self as a spiritual person was not a conscious choice, nor did it grow out of a recognized need in my life. The connection simply is and I simply am. I believe that our culture, through its codes of silence, suppression, and forced ignorance, supports a separateness between the sexual and the rest of life. I have never been able to accept this separateness. Perhaps a part of my rebellion was to make the sexual spiritual when everyone and everything else seemed to want them to be separate. Among the more important spiritual challenges I strive to meet is the struggle to be my "best" self in all facets of life. To be my best self means to recognize and acknowledge the "God" in every other person and treat them with the love and respect that they deserve. Certainly I have not always accomplished this in my life or in my sexual relationships, but I continue striving so that I can have the inner peace that I value. And that only comes, for me, when I am living my life as I believe I should.

All of my adult life I have had what for me has been the best of sexual lifestyles. I've typically been involved with one primary partner, usually someone that I am living with, and one or more other partners who were friends and lovers. One of the blessings of my lifestyle is the ability to create each relationship on its own merits without external controls and constraints. Another blessing is the continuation of relationships throughout my life that change focus from lover to confidant and the opportunity to create new relationships without ending enduring ones.

One of the most difficult aspects of being involved with me as a primary partner/lover is my demand for sexual openness and non-monogamy. I have always chosen to be completely open about my relationship desires from the beginning. I believe that it is much more difficult to change the course of a traditional relationship after some period of time than to begin the relationship with an initial understanding of my desire for a marriage-free, child-free, non-monogamous life. Obviously, a lot of people run away as fast as possible, but the ones who stay are a blessing forever. Living an open lifestyle offers me many gifts. Among them is the ability to create any kind of relationship that is mutually desired with another person. Many of my life-long and closest friends are former partners. I will love and cherish them in my life for who they are and what they have been. They know me at my best and worst, and love me regardless. The relationships that evolve, grow, and continue to provide spiritual nurturance throughout our lives are miracles as are the relationships that provide any one moment of wonder, joy, and fulfillment. I believe that it is my ability to see the greatness, awe, and wonder of any relationship that allows me to measure relationship success by the strength of its positive impact, not the length of its existence. All positive relationships are miracles in their existence. Any time one human being can risk the pain of rejection, failure, and hurt to open themselves in love to another is a miraculous event. When that openness includes their physical expression of love the connection established is complete — body, mind, and spirit!

My connectedness with myself is reflected in the reverence I have for each of my seven dimensions of health. Expressing this reverence involves positive behaviors in my life that promote my self-connection and self-worth. These behaviors include a healthy diet, daily exercise, spiritual expression, masturbation and daily orgasm, relaxation, socialization, volunteer work, and reading. Since I am an embodied spirit, my love of my physical self reflects and enhances my love of my spiritual self.

I believe that our spirituality and our sexuality are the two most closely linked dimensions of our health. In fact, I would argue that in my cosmology the highest reality of each is identical. I see spirituality as our "connectedness" with the "ultimate" life force. I define sexuality as our "connectedness" with other embodied spirits. This connectedness is transformational. By connecting to the "ultimate" or to another embodied spirit, we transcend the ordinary routine of our daily lives and live beyond ourselves wrapped in the transformational love of another. Transformational love is a love that is so accepting, trusting, and embracing of us that it promotes our growth, change, and inner drive to live out our genuine inner desires. This is the love we hope all parents will have and express toward their children and that special people can express toward us throughout our lives in sexual and non-sexual relationships.

Transcending and transforming my regular life allows me to recreate myself in the loving image of others and become my most meaningful and best self at all times. The transformational and transcendent powers of spirituality and sexuality are also the greatest healing powers that I have available to me.

Transformational and transcendent powers support us when we are hurt. They reach us in the voice, touch, or smile of a close and trusted friend. They also serve to inspire us when we are strong, like the encouragement of an outstanding teacher, parent, or coach. When the slings and arrows of everyday life are burdensome the loving expressions of others allow my sexual-spiritual self to rise above the pain and replenish my soul.

My cosmology is based in part on my understandings of incarnational theology, the belief that "God" is embodied, manifested, or revealed in each and every person regardless of their status within a culture, family, or the world community. I also find it in quantum physics and certain ideas borrowed from Eastern philosophies. These sources lead me to recognize "God" in everyone, to know that I am one with everyone and everything in the cosmos, to understand that all things exist in each infinite moment, and to trust that the path that I chose to follow is what is ultimately best. I know that to follow any self other than my self, or to deny the connection between me and all other embodied spirits would be a violation of my spirituality. Given my spiritual philosophy, the only acceptable moral or ethical code possible is openness to universal love, which in essence is love of self. Any other code would be self-hatred. In my world of universal love and connectedness, if I express myself sexually with another person in a way that enhances us I am expressing both my spiritual and sexual self to the highest possible degree. It is only through our sexual selves that we are able to express our connectedness to the "God" in all of us in such a direct and powerful way.

My journey began as the second oldest son in a large Catholic family growing up in a small farming town in Minnesota. My four brothers, two sisters, and I were very close and all attended a small Catholic school. While in the second grade I decided that I was going to be a priest. I didn't become holy or anything. I'd guess that I was a pretty rough and tumble kid—lots of fights and plenty of mischief. It was during this time that I learned a couple of the early moral/spiritual lessons that have stayed with me all of my life. The one my mother taught me, in response to all of my fights and in preparation for me getting my driver's license at fifteen years old, was that all human beings are valuable. She didn't care if they were ugly, dumb, or mean; they were valuable because they were the children of God. She was always worried that I would hurt someone, "Wouldn't it be awful if you weren't looking for just one second and a little kid darted out into the street and you hit them," was one of her regular admonishments. This particular lesson served me well when I came home from the seminary years later and became a conscientious objector during the Vietnam war. "Mom, wouldn't it be awful if I let myself go over there and kill someone?" was my response to her and my father's arguments for my going to fight.

My grandmother "Bobe" taught me one of the other great spiritual lessons of my life while I was still a child. Her love for me was unconditional and her trust in me was among the most empowering experiences I have ever known. A part of what makes her relationship with me remarkable is that even as a child, I was always the rebel. My issues with authority and conformity were apparent early, but Bobe trusted me regardless. At the time I thought that one had to become old to have that level of love and trust for others. Later I realized that it was who she was in my life, not how old she happened to be. Her lesson was, like my mother's, a simple one. "Peter, as long as you know in your heart that what you believe and do is the right thing, it doesn't matter what anyone else, and I mean anyone else, thinks of you. Follow your heart!" was her loving counsel. I couldn't have learned a more powerful lesson from a more loving person.

The other great lesson of my childhood, and the lesson that has allowed me to comfortably integrate my physical and sexual self with my ethereal and spiritual self, came from my father. This was not a lesson of word, but of deed. The four oldest children in our family are all boys. Somehow, during the 1950s and 1960s, in middle-class, middle-America, my father was able to show a great deal of genuine love and physical affection for all of us. While my classmates were living lives devoid of touch from virtually everyone in their lives, my life was full of touch and affection. I don't know how my father was able to break the barriers to physical affection with his male children, but I am forever grateful that he was the instrument that allowed me to learn the value of physical connection with those you love.

Following my commitment to become a priest in the second grade, I decided to reject the athletic scholarships offered to me and enter a Jesuit seminary my freshman year of college. It was because the Jesuits have a reputation for being the best and most demanding of the Catholic order of priests that I chose them. Studying to be a Jesuit priest altered my relationship with the world in a variety of ways. The first two years of the Jesuit experience are intended to parallel Christ's experience in the dessert. Self-denial, isolation, and singular reliance on yourself within your relationship to God are the pillars of the Jesuit novitiate. I'm not certain what great spiritual answers I was supposed to glean from this experience. I'm not even sure what questions I was supposed to ask, but I learned much. One of the great lessons that I learned was detachment from all things not spiritual. Experiences can be spiritual, relationships can be spiritual, cars, houses, televisions are not spiritual. Things not spiritual are burdens. They tie me to places and experiences that are limiting, repetitious, and that diminish my freedom to explore, grow, and exult in life. The knowledge that I can walk away from anything at any time is comforting and strengthening. The self-reliance that I learned from Bobe was greatly reinforced by my seminary experience. Her lesson combined with the isolation and self-reliance of the seminary also taught me that I could move through the world alone if I had to. I've certainly never wanted to, but the knowledge that the only relationship that I can't do without in my life is with myself is a powerful understanding. This perception has allowed me to live a lifestyle that has perhaps not been available to others.

Leaving the seminary was perhaps the single most difficult decision of my life. The prevailing message in the seminary is that God brought you here for a reason; obviously, to be a priest. Leaving meant turning your back on God, your Church, and your "calling." While I was in the seminary, I came to realize that I entered for altruistic, not religious reasons. I left because I needed to live out my altruism as a regular person immersed in life and its struggles, not as someone separated and segregated from the ordinary discourse of life.

The combination of detachment, spiritual strength, and inner peace that I developed has dramatically influenced my relationships with family, friends, and partners. I have been able to be very in love and deeply devoted to people in my life, and at the same time been able to realize that if I had to, I could walk away from anything. It is my inner spiritual strength that allows me to survive life's chaos, to take risks, to endure the pain of relationships ending, and still recognize and revel in all of life's experiences.

I've also been able to live an open sexual lifestyle with all of my partners and never feel jealous of or threatened by what they had in other relationships. My love for a partner directs me to desire the best for them. If they find another relationship that is better for them, I want them to have it. My hope is to continue to be included in their life, but my love for them requires me to respect their choices and play a continuing role in their life that is as mutually beneficial as possible.

My own involvement with relationships and struggles with relationship styles began after I left the seminary. Leaving the seminary led to leaving the Church and questioning all of society's rules and regulations, including traditional marriage and family. Even in high school I had been uncomfortable "going-steady" or promising myself exclusively to any relationship. This made no more sense to me than having only one friend, playing tennis with only one partner, or learning from only one teacher. Why would anyone in their right mind do this?

I was able to break with cultural norms because of the independence I'd gained throughout my life, coupled with an awareness of the cultural upheaval going on around me. At the time, I believed that marriage and monogamy represented the ownership of women and children by men, that marriage was a failed institution that made it more difficult for men and women to continue to communicate successfully with one another, and that relationships were measured by their longevity, not their interpersonal or spiritual value. The values of my religion were expressed so narrowly as to welcome only those who lived the most conservative lifestyles. The official position of the Catholic Church continues to be exclusionary and embraces all of the worst characteristics of a highly patriarchal establishment that continues to control its members through imposed traditions like the "sacrament" of marriage.

Also, I saw parents abandoning or neglecting their children, and our culture supporting an unethical war. I became very outspoken about all of these issues. I led demonstrations against the war, became a sex educator, and spoke openly about my "alternative" lifestyle of open sexual relationships. Even though I spoke openly about my sexual life, I never attempted to convince anyone that they should live life as I do. I always believed that my choices were best for me, but not for anyone else. The difficulties that I encountered throughout my life have convinced me that only someone who had come to this lifestyle as a result of internal need would have the strength to carry it out successfully.

My goal was to provide an example of someone successfully living an alternative lifestyle. I was the first conscientious objector to do an alternative service working for Planned Parenthood/World Population as a contraceptive and overpopulation educator. My life and work influenced me to consider the ethical issues involving the sacredness of the earth, social justice, and the well being of the human community. These considerations helped me realize an ethical commitment to limiting human numbers and facilitated my decision to have a vasectomy at age twenty-five. The other ethical component involved in this decision is taking responsibility for my own reproduction and not placing the women in my life in the disadvantageous situation of having to risk contraceptive and pregnancy complications in our relationship.

Living a sexually positive life in a society that is very sex negative is a difficult task. My growth and enlightenment has been facilitated by many people in my life, including some important colleagues and guides. Kirk— Lester Kirkendall, my first mentor in the field of human sexuality — taught me some of the more important lessons about sexual morality, the value of friendships, and how to live a life full of love for all of humanity. Bill Stayton's appreciation that everything in our universe has an erotic — nurturing and spiritual — potential helped me place my life in the context of the history of sexual expression and repression in human experience. Bob Francoeur taught me about the process of becoming a sexual person while James Nelson's powerful and beautiful writings about the spiritual aspects of sexuality opened other important vistas for me. Ron Moglia was and continues to be my teacher and friend as I progress through my career as a sexologist.

As people challenge my sexual choices it is most often from the perspective of evidencing a lack of morality. I am usually quick to respond with the sexual values I challenge myself to follow: promoting positive self-worth for each person who is directly involved; advocating for everyone to follow their own path by encouraging communication, honesty, and openness; refusing to violate relationship contracts or contribute to others' violations of contracts; relationship equality, non-possessiveness, love for self and others; and connecting the spiritual and sexual through genuine affection and physical expressions of love and care for self and others. Perhaps a fitting end to this current installment in my life process is to recognize the challenge for each of us to live up to a value system that involves introspection and communication between partners, that promotes the welfare of the human community regardless of the specifics of the lifestyle behaviors, and to combine our spirituality and sexuality in positive ways.

15. Slippery Rocks and Sparkling Waters

Kathryn Burnett

I have been thinking about writing this story for months and feeling quite hesitant, even reluctant. First, how does one put into words the feelings of the soul so that they are understood? And how does one write about something that runs so counter to the prevailing culture, or at least to its myths, and something at the same time so personal? Do I really want to hold up my lifestyle as a model? Maybe I am not quite convinced myself that it is "right." Despite these reservations, as I began to write, sharing my story simply and honestly, I found the telling both clarifying and healing.

Twenty years ago I walked into a university to register for a course and heard the richest, deepest, most soul-stirring voice I had ever heard. "I hope that man is in my class," I said to myself. Then I heard someone address him as Dr. Farrare. I knew then he would indeed be in my class, for he was the professor. It was instant attraction for both of us.

Since my keenest sense is auditory, I frequently remember people not by their faces, but by the sound of their voices. This voice, along with the wonderful physical vitality and joyous energy that went with it, caught my full attention. His skills as a group facilitator and teacher further captivated my intellectual interest. And his commitment to spiritual values rounded out all the areas I need for a deep relationship. You see, I am an ENFP in the Myers-Briggs Personality Indicator—extroverted intuitive with feeling and perceiving—and so is he. ENFPs, according to Keirsey and Bates in *Please Understand Me*, are complex individuals who strive for authenticity, and require connection on all four levels of the physical, intellectual, emotional, and spiritual, in their intimate relationships. This is an idealistic requirement that ENFPs are seldom fortunate enough to attain, or at least maintain in the every day realities of a marriage.

So how could this thirty-seven-year-old married woman with children deal with the intensity of this friendship? Let me say first and foremost, it was difficult and challenging. It put many values to the test for both of us—values of traditional marriage, roles, and expectation, values of honesty, integrity, and loyalty.

Twenty years have passed since that encounter. I have had many other encounters and meaningful relationships, but none has survived the rigors of balancing marriage and a significant other as this one.

We have maintained a relationship that many would deem impossible. Although both of us had experimented briefly with some openness in our marriages during the "open marriage" era of the 1970s, for various reasons we decided not to be involved in sexual intercourse. We were both in committed marriages. We were both professional people with public reputations to protect. And we wanted to be open with our friendship both with our families and in our communities.

I also had a commitment of loyalty to his spouse. As women, as "sisters," I was committed to protecting her relationship with her husband, to never participate in violating their relationship in any way.

We also agreed that our primary families would always come first. If we ever had plans to get together and something came up in our families that required our attention, our plans would be postponed. Thus trust and understanding were established.

However, sexual energy is not confined to intercourse. Sexual energy is the creative energy innate in all of us. It is the fire, the passion that supports all of life. It fuels the flame of spirit. It opens our hearts to love each other as well as all of life.

The yearning for oneness is akin to our yearning to be one with the Great Spirit. Wherever that energy is shared it is "heaven on earth." It is our reminder that if "God-Goddess is Love," then "Love is God." When we share this deep, loving energy with anyone we bring to this existence an influence for healing and peace. "Making love" in the spirit of love is literally raising the love consciousness of humanity.

Since we were committed to certain boundaries we were required to be more creative in finding other channels of sharing deep and satisfying intimacy. Yes, there has been much physical intimacy. There has been emotional caring and support as we shared deeply our joys and sorrows, our failures and successes, our dreams and fantasies. There has been intellectual intimacy as we helped each other in our professional pursuits and other learning experiences. And there has been spiritual intimacy as our souls soared together in places of union and deep contentment. We have also challenged each other in areas of integrity, honesty, and spiritual exploration. As all these areas mingled and flowed together, our connection has been deep and satisfying, although there was always a longing for more — more time and more physical expression.

It has been a balancing drama which needed to be reviewed again and again. When one forgot, the other remembered what our intentions were, and what we were about. When the passion in both of us threatened to override our commitments, some unforeseen circumstance seemed to present itself. We laughed at the universe's ways of holding us to our word.

Since we were not locked up in some bedroom, we had to find other places for our times together. Streams, lakes, oceans, woods, meadows, and gardens became our sanctuary, as well as concert and lecture halls, classrooms and quiet corners in lovely restaurants. We frequently sat on slippery rocks in the midst of sparkling waters, symbols of our path together, with feelings of deep gratitude for what we enjoyed.

This friendship entered my life when I was searching for a vocational direction for my life. It appeared like an angel. Although I had a wonderful husband and children, the kind of creative energy I needed at that time would have been impossible for them to provide. This friend was a model of professional achievement that stimulated and supported my need for growth and evolvement professionally, which I had not had, either as a child or as an adult, in the community in which I was involved. I had to make difficult choices to leave behind old acquaintances and a church group because they did not support my professional development as a woman. Mark was the friend who always believed I could do it. He continually affirmed my journey. I know I have equally enriched his life with support, pleasure, and challenges. This equality was very important to me. It was a necessary factor in the success of our long-term relationship.

There were many times of struggling with questions. Was this special friendship in any way sabotaging or undermining my marriage? Was it presenting an unhealthy model for my children? After all, were not all these needs supposed to be met by one's spouse? Would it be possible to be married to someone with whom I connected so easily? Or would the intensity of daily living ruin everything? Would we burn each other out?

My husband and I married young and had a wonderful family. We created a healthy family life style where our differences complimented each other in parenting. However, these very unique personality differences made it difficult to understand and be understood.

We both belonged to large extended families where the tapestry of family life runs deep and wide. This additional significant relationship allowed me to honor the commitment to the family system, without keeping me bound by its traditional limitations. I need a broad and varied existence with its many challenging and learning experiences. Had I been married to someone with more similar interests and passions, would I have pursued this extra relationship? I don't know.

My life story still contains its mysteries. Could I have developed as a whole person had I not had a primary relationship with all its challenges? Could I have come to understand the many differing needs and dynamics of intimate relationships, if I had not had these two very different kinds of long-term relationships? These questions have motivated me into deep studies of the human experience and our different needs for connectedness. This has greatly enhanced my professional career.

Would I encourage others to take this path? No, the rocks are too slippery for the young and those less grounded. Would I support someone who already finds themself on this path? Yes, of course. I know I have been richly blessed. I have had many loves in my life. No other has so profoundly impacted the person I have become as this friendship with Mark. Without it I fear I would have lost my way. I am indeed grateful.

I am also very grateful to both of our spouses for the time and freedom they have given us to be together. Without their acceptance, our relationship would not have lasted and flourished. There were issues of jealousy and insecurities on all our parts which needed to be faced. I said it was not easy, and it has been glorious!

16. Playing Pygmalion

Robert H. Rimmer

An Introduction by Robert T. Francoeur

You'll find a warm magnetism about Bob Rimmer's candid story of "Playing Pygmalion." He's not the typical graduate of Bates College and Harvard Business School one expects. True, he and Erma have been happily married for sixty years — an unusual longevity in our divorce-riddled society. That fits the aura of conservatism one expects of a quiet 80-year-old business man who has lived quiet years in a book-packed home in Quincy, Massachusetts, just south of Boston.

What is out of character for a Harvard Business School graduate is Bob's celebration of the wholeness of sexuality and the spiritual in his own life. So is Bob's steady missionary zeal that led him to weave threads of his personal quest into a dozen popular utopian novels about women and men struggling to find new ways of relating that transcend the conventional romantic boundaries of "forsaking all others" in the oneness of "two in one flesh." Bob's many characters are as driven as he by a positive view of their sexuality and thrilled by its potential for growth and wholeness.

Bob's first best selling novel, *The Harrad Experiment* (1967), describes an experimental college where the students are assigned a different roommate of the other sex each semester. *Harrad* quickly became an underground "must read" among college students wrestling with sexual values and relationships in the new freedom of coed dormitories, and eventually a movie starring James Whitmore and a young Don Johnson. *The Rebellion of Yale Marratt* (1967) tells of a man and his two lovers' effort to get the state of California to legalize triad relationships. *Proposition 31* (1969) deals with legalizing group marriages based on a corporation model. College student activists quickly pushed their professors to create new courses exploring the sexual revolution, cohabitation, and new lifestyles described in Rimmer's novels.

From the late 1960s through the 1980s, Bob's novels inspired thousands of Americans to break with the conventional and explore new ways of loving

137

and bonding in a world few of us are willing to admit has changed as radically as it has. The novels and new courses sparked more dialogue as students and older Americans wrote to Bob, sharing stories of their own explorations in the sexual underground of that era. One volume of letters, *The Harrad Letters to Robert H. Rimmer* (1969), led to second, *You and I ... Searching for Tomorrow* (1971), and a third, *Adventures in Loving* (1973). It was obvious. Many Americans were exploring new ways of meeting their need for intimacy in sexual fulfillment and long-term relationships that were adapted to their rapidly changing social environment. That Americans are still exploring the unconventional in 1999 is evident in the tolerance the majority of Americans expressed at the likelihood that the President and First Lady had some kind of unconventional agreement. Perhaps the First Couple also read Rimmer's novels. Less speculative is the fact that many of the men and women who share their stories with us in this book trace their adventures back to seeds they discovered in Bob's novels and collections of letters.

Having known Bob for over 30 years, I naturally wanted to invite him to share with us the story of his own attempt to redefine marriage and intimacy in a world most Americans find confusing, disturbing, and even frightening. So here is Bob and Erma Rimmer's own story of their sixty-year marriage and their partnership with another couple.

PLAYING PYGMALION

As I write this in 1998, I've been married for fifty-seven years to Erma ... one wife for a lifetime. But in 1955, if she hadn't discovered that I was having an affair with Virginia, and if she hadn't sobbed her anger to David, the last of a breed of caring general M.D. practitioners, who told her that all men, including him, were led around by their cocks, I never would have met David's wife, Nancy — or finally discovered a woman with whom I didn't have to play Pygmalion. She was Galatea! And if I hadn't met David and Nancy — whose names I have fictionalized and who are similar to one of the couples in *Proposition 31* — I never would have discovered just how anti-Semitic my father and mother were, nor way past mid-life would I have found the focus for my first novel, *The Rebellion of Yale Marratt*.

Girls ... later, women! Since I was five — for sixty-five years — I've loved them all, the long and the short and the tall. But like Henry Higgins in Bernard Shaw's *Pygmalion*, I would eventually begin wondering not, "Why can't women be like men?" but "Why can't women be like me?" Before I entered the first grade, most of my friends were girls. In the summer, in pup tents in the backyard and in the hot attics, it was a happy, giggly game to touch and kiss each other's forbidden parts. In my childhood, I was perfectly familiar with the hairless female pudenda. After I was seven, I never saw a girl/woman naked until I was seventeen, Like my peers, I spent many hours searching through *National Geographics* to see what women—black natives, of course—looked like. I probed the library for art books with a few reproductions of classical paintings where bulgy ladies out of mythology reigned supreme without clothes.

At sixteen, just before my final year in high school, I was a rebel without a cause. An exceptional student in English, fair in languages like Latin and French, mediocre in science, and dismal in math—compare with Yale Marratt in my novel—I fell in love with Rosslyn, a young girl who stayed with her aunt in Quincy during the summer so she could enjoy swimming at the private beach in Merrymount. Very pretty and very sophisticated at fifteen, Rosslyn's home was in Brookline, some ten miles away. Somehow, blushing, I dared to ask her to go to the movies with me. Before the summer was over, I finally had once again seen and touched a naked girl/woman and held her pretty breasts in my hands, kissed her nipples, and touched the lovely triangle of hair between her legs. I was delirious, totally in love. That summer, I practically lived in her aunt's house. Blanche and FH, my mother and father—later in life when I worked for my father I found it easier to refer to my father as FH for Frank Henry than as dad—both knew where I was. Of course, neither Rossyln's aunt nor uncle knew what we were doing.

I was so much in love that I didn't care if I went to college or not. When you made love to a girl every possible moment that you were with her, I was sure it was time to get married. It was now or never, especially since when summer was over Ross would go home to Brookline. I had a license to drive but with only one car in the family, I couldn't compete with the army of really affluent Brookline guys who could take Rosslyn anywhere in their own cars and, God forbid, make love to her.

During the first six months at Bates, I slowly became aware that I was much more sexually sophisticated than most of the guys I met. Very unusual for its time, Bates was a coed college. It was only twenty miles away from Bowdoin, a kind of male monastery with six hundred guys who depended on special weekends when they could bring in female companionship. Thirty years later, when I wrote *The Harrad Experiment*, I contrasted a fraternity weekend with the saner sexual environment of Harrad. But Bates College was no Harrad. Young women went to class with you, but dating rituals soon set in. By the end of your freshman year, you were "going steady" or you were one of the social outcasts who stood on the sidelines at the Saturday-night dances and prayed for some person of the opposite sex to smile at you.

I soon discovered a female rebel who managed to get through her 7:15 A.M. classes without breakfast, but needed chapel time to recover with a cup of coffee, English muffins, and a cigarette. An only child, her name was Margery McCray. Her friends called her Bunny. With wide-apart blue eyes and deep brown hair, Bunny was as tall as I was. Later, she called me "Napoleon," because she was an inch taller when she wore high heels. She was a fast learner, received straight A's in French and fairly good marks on other subjects. She could play popular music on the piano with great charisma and sing along with herself. I was soon very much in love with her, but couldn't resist trying to remake her in my own image.

I was soon reading everything I could find—and it wasn't much—on the vagaries of human sexuality. Scarcely a month went by during these three years that Bunny and I didn't think our college days would come to a sudden end. She often had irregular monthly periods, and once, when she was a week overdue, we were sure that she was pregnant. We both hated condoms, and although I knew about diaphragms, in the mid-1930s it was difficult enough to find a doctor who would fit a married woman to one, let alone a single girl.

On graduation day from Bates, although I had commuted on weekends to Hartford for two summers, FH and Blanche met Bunny's mother and stepfather for the first time. They were all aware that Bunny and I were in love and wanted to be married quickly. Bunny had been accepted for a buyer's training position at eighteen dollars a week at Jordan Marsh in Boston. I proposed my plan to FH for the first time. In those days there were no married graduate students living on campus at Harvard Business School, and very few off campus. I told him he could pay my tuition, but give me the cost of room and board at Harvard (equal to more than eighteen dollars a week), and together, Bunny and I could support an apartment in Harvard Square and get married. It wouldn't cost FH any more than he was already prepared to pay. In 1939, however, such ideas were outlandish, to say the least. FH refused. He had nothing against Bunny and thought she should be happy to wait two years until I finished my education. The problem was that Bunny couldn't support herself in Boston on eighteen dollars a week. With a combined income of thirty-six to forty dollars a week, there would have been no problem. The only solution was that she would have to go home to Hartford, get a job, and live with her parents until I graduated. How could I explain to FH that I now needed a regular bed companion? As well as a friend to save me from the Philistines at Harvard Business School. Before classes began in September at Harvard, Bunny wrote me a good-bye note. Her mother agreed with her. Two years was much too long to wait.

The shock of losing Bunny was compounded by the first lecture from the nationally known dean Wallace Brett Donham, who had, with the help of a multimillionaire, George Baker, practically created Harvard Business School. Dunham told us that we could now forget our easygoing college days. At HBS, unless you devoted seventy hours a week to classes and study, you were sure to flunk out. He assured us that 10 percent of the 1941 class would be gone after the first midyear exams. Paul had graduated from the Wharton School at the University of Pennsylvania. Unlike me, he had four years of undergraduate business training. Within a few weeks, I was sure that I should have been studying on the Cambridge side of the Charles River, getting a master's in psychology or sociology from Harvard, which I knew several of my Bates friends were doing. I was sure that I had probably been accepted because Harvard Business was experimenting with a new philosophy and accepting a few people like me who might add a new kind of creativity to the business world and not be so one-dimensional as typical HBS graduates were. My new roommate and I did have something in common. Paul, too, had lost the love of his life, Virginia Carnes, daughter of a wealthy physician in Massillon, Ohio. He had met Ginny and slept with her occasionally at the University of Pennsylvania, but now she had gone to Western Reserve and met another guy.

In the fall of 1940, I met Erma. My mother had mentioned that the family dentist in Boston had a new dental hygienist, Miss Richards, who was a very nice girl. Since I was constantly looking for dates, why not ask her? Why not? I needed my teeth cleaned, and soon a very pretty blue-eyed brunette with a wholesome, clean-cut face and firm breasts was leaning close to my face as she scaled my teeth, creating an aura of sexual intimacy. When she finished, I asked her point-blank, with a clean mouth, "How about a kiss?" There was no kiss, and no date. Dating clients was against the doctor's rules. But she warned me I must be sure to come back. I needed some new fillings and missed appointments were charged. When I purposely missed the next appointment, I told the doctor it was because Miss Richards wouldn't have a date with me. He changed his mind. The Rimmers were good customers, and he was only too happy to relax his rules and play Cupid.

Erma was a most affectionate and loving woman. She had been recently deserted by a former high school boyfriend who had decided to marry the daughter of a more prestigious Melrose family. Not only didn't Erma reject me when we were finally naked on her parent's sofa, but she encouraged me. Even though I was sure that her father would soon stomp downstairs and put an end to me, we were frequently making love in her parent's living room.

At twenty, a year younger than me, Erma needed to be loved as much as I did. To my amazement, she seemed very willing to be molded into my ephemeral ivory Galatea. I soon convinced her that while we were most certainly sexually in tune, if a long-lasting relationship were to develop, we must be able to communicate mentally. The business world didn't matter, but I told Erma that she must read and acquire what a quarter of a century later Edward Hirsch would define as "cultural literacy."

I was falling in love, and I was sure that I could recreate Erma, who was already smarter than I was in the practical world, and make her more literary than all the women I had known with bachelor's degrees, including Bunny. I told her all she had to do was read ... read and take a few courses, particularly in psychology. I had it made—a woman who loved me and was eager to learn all the things she had never been exposed to. Was I playing Svengali? Not quite. Time would prove that Erma had a mind of her own.

Before I graduated, after playing Russian roulette in the baby-making area for nearly a year, Erma and I set the wedding date: August 2, 1941. FH couldn't believe what was happening. A year and a half ago, I had been in love with Bunny. Since she couldn't wait two years, he agreed it was just as well I hadn't married her, but Erma Richards? A girl who worked for Dr. Tracy and cleaned teeth? What did I have in common with her? Unknown to me, he called Erma, interrupting her at work, and asked her point-blank why she wanted to marry me. "Does Bob really love you? Did you know that he was madly in love with another girl just a year ago?" Obviously, FH was still trying to direct my life. In tears, Erma assured him that we were in love. If you read *Yale Marratt*, you'll find a similar story, but fused to FH's anti-Semitism, which I didn't discover until fifteen years later.

So Erma and I were married. She soon discovered that, along with our other wedding furniture, we had to make room for my close to one thousand books in our four-room apartment. I wasn't making vast progress in sculpting my Galetea, but we were newlyweds who had many things to do, and we enjoyed sexmaking.

Erma continued to work as a dental hygienist for a couple of months, but then we bought a dog and were affluent enough for her to stay home. Not to read, but to cook and sew and decorate, at which she was very competent. In addition, for a few happy months, she was able to flit around Melrose in the handsome Ford convertible that FH had given me.

We had many Saturday-night parties with just-married friends and dating singles. Sexual flirting with others in their twenties, aided and abetted by plenty of booze, was a way of life. The idea of playing strip poker was often bandied about, and not being adverse to seeing how female friends of Erma's looked in their birthday suits, I devised a variation on blackjack, or twenty-one, which made it possible to play for several hours with a slow and tantalizing divestment of clothing—you'll find it described in detail in Yale Marratt. Within the first twelve months of marriage, although Erma and I were quite monogamous, I managed to hug at least half a dozen of her female friends after they had shed their last stitch of clothing and didn't know whether to run off or be embarrassed. But then, on December 7, 1941—Pearl Harbor Day—the top blew off and our happy daydream was nearly over.

A year later in 1943, Erma kissed me good-bye as I boarded a train in South Station for Miami. I'll never forget the sight of her standing on the deserted track, sobbing as the train pulled out. In my pocket were a dozen pictures I had taken of her naked and three-months pregnant. Would we ever see each other again? Both of us doubted it. The United States was not only bogged down in Europe fighting Hitler, but we were trying to defeat the Japanese island by island across the Pacific. World War II would never end.

In India, I discovered Indian yoga, and particularly tantra—the wine, women, and song approach to nirvana for those who couldn't pursue the ascetic Brahmin yoga disciplines. I soon had my own fully illustrated copy of the *Kama Sutra*, which in the 1940s and 1950s, along with James Joyce, Henry Miller, and D. H. Lawrence, would have put a United States bookseller in jail permanently if he dared to offer such a picturesque view of human sexuality. I also discovered tantric sex in 1945 and the potential of extended sexual intercourse without ejaculation to achieve a blending of the yang and yin as a path to nirvana. I also learned about tantric rituals where sexual merger with a loved one wasn't necessarily monogamous. Joy of sex, tantric style, is discussed in the middle section of Yale Marratt, and it's one of the goals of a Harrad style of education that I wrote about many years later. Subconsciously, although I didn't realize it until later, my Galatea daydreams and tantric sexual merger were opposite sides of the same coin.

In August 1944, after finally receiving a telegram that my son Robert, Jr., was born on July 3, I was running a finance office in Chengking, China, on a base with three thousand men and an equal number of Chinese "coolie" labor. A few weeks later, the United States dropped the atomic bomb on Hiroshima and suddenly it seemed that I might get home after all.

A civilian at last. Neither in the business world nor in my social life was I meeting anyone who was as obsessed or fascinated with music, the arts, and literature as I was. Nor, spending my days as a salesman, was it easy to make contacts with anyone with equivalent interests. As a result, during the next ten years, I became a totally split personality—a kind of Dr. Jekyll and Mr. Hyde who no longer bothered to play the Pygmalion game with Erma. She was proving to be a fun companion and a wife in many other ways. As Dr. Jekyll, I was a sober citizen and a hard-driving businessman who soon proved that I could sell major accounts.

As a benign Mr. Hyde, I was an enigma to my family and friends. As an antidote to the business world, I was reading many current novels and collecting anything and everything that had been written about human sexuality as well as more abstruse books in the areas of psychiatry, psychology, religion, and economics. I was omnivorously searching for answers to questions about life and death that I couldn't even formulate. I was also buying and listening to a wealth of music that was suddenly available on LP records, discovering chamber music, ballet, concertos, and symphonies along with the world of art, all of which I had been exposed to at Bates, but had put aside during my HBS and war years.

With business friends or people that Erma met through women's clubs that she joined, I rarely revealed my Mr. Hyde inclinations. With a few drinks of bourbon, I was one of the boys, a hale fellow well met and a kindred spirit for men and women with whom I had very little in common. I told Erma that we were like two people on different trolley cars—they still existed in those days—going in different directions, but waving at each other as we passed. But in many areas, we were well mated. Erma soon proved her abilities on our thirty-year-old bungalow, personally painting, wallpapering, laying cement walks, expanding the house, and, in between time, cooking gourmet dinners and taking care of the boys. We had many goals in common, but little mental companionship.

Early summer in 1946, a few months after I was discharged from the army, Paul Williams—his friends called him "Willie"—whom I'd roomed with both years at HBS, came to Boston and phoned to see if I'd survived the war. He had—also as a naval lieutenant—and during the war finally married Virginia ("Ginny"), whom Erma and I had met one night in Boston a few weeks before Paul and I graduated from HBS. They had two children. Paul thought we should get together and celebrate with a picnic at Crane's Beach in Ipswich, which had always been a springtime rendezvous area for HBS students. In May, a few months later, they arrived with their kids. A brown-eyed brunette with almond-shaped eyes, coolly sexy, Ginny thought nothing of sitting on a sofa with her arms around her knees, well aware that she wore no panties and her nether parts were beckoning. She was a sharp contrast to Erma. Before she settled down with Paul, she had known quite a few boys and men intimately.

Arriving in Quincy, she couldn't believe her eyes. Here was a house filled with more books than her father-in-law owned, plus hundreds of records. Paul read a bit, listened to some classical music a bit, but was an entirely different cup of tea than Bob Rimmer. I was charmed. Erma wasn't, but she liked Paul. During the weekend, I discovered that not only was Ginny an omnivorous reader, but she wrote poetry which her father-in-law, William Carlos Williams, thought was great. Ginny told me later that she loved Bill, as she called Paul's father, more than her husband, who was now a rising executive at the Abraham and Strauss department store in Brooklyn. Paul was more interested in his career in retailing (a subject he had majored in at HBS) than his wife's poetry. During the weekend, I managed to take Ginny alone on a fast auto tour of Quincy. We soon stopped for a torrential embrace during which she told me that their marriage was falling apart and she was having an affair with a buyer she had met at Lord and Taylor who was divorcing his wife.

The weekend ended with a few more discreet hugs from Ginny and an invitation from Paul to spend a weekend (without kids) in a cottage owned by his father on the Connecticut River near West Haven. Within a few hours after Erma and I arrived, we were all drinking gin, and Ginny whispered that she really had to talk to me alone. How we were going to escape our spouses in such confined quarters was a mystery to me, but by nine o'clock, eating very little except hors d'oeuvres, Paul and Erma had drank so much that all they wanted to do was go to bed. And very definitely not with each other! Ginny's hope that they might end up in bed together never materialized. She and I went for a walk along the river. We were soon feverishly undressing each other. Despite the discomfort of bugs and sand, we nervously make love on a lonely inlet.

During these years, Ginny and I mailed books we were reading back and forth to each other. She wrote me five-to-ten-page letters daily, care of Relief, my business address. I had never been privileged to enter any person's mind so completely. Ginny was like a dammed-up, pent-up river bursting through the dikes of an unhappy marriage. She flooded me with a million works, seeking answers for herself and for me. At one point, I had four file drawers jam-packed with every letter she ever wrote me, and I often thought if they were ever published, they would be among the most intimate revelations — Ginny was a colorful writer — ever put down on paper by a female.

Then, the bubble burst. Carelessly, or on purpose, Ginny left a long letter she had been writing to me on her desk, and Paul read it. Within a week, I received at home a certified letter. Erma opened it and it was from Paul's lawyers. "Cease and desist seeing Virginia Williams," they wrote, or be sued for alienation of affections.

I thought it was silly, but needless to say, Erma was hysterical. Did I want a divorce? No. I loved her and Steve and Bobby. I didn't believe in divorce. We might not be riding on the same streetcar, but we had a lot of good things going for us. I simply needed a female friend. I was mentally lonesome and I knew I would never meet a man like me in the business world. Surprisingly, after a rocky month or two, Erma stopped asking details about my extracurricular love life. She was sorry that I couldn't have my cake and eat it, but Paul obviously wasn't as lenient as she was. Six months later, I discovered why Erma had suddenly become so complacent. She had told David, the doctor she took Bobby and Steve to with various childhood ailments, about me. David had even been in our house and seen my overwhelming collection of books and told her: "My wife, Nancy, would go crazy if she saw these. She'd never leave. She reads all the time." But poor Nancy who read so much was a recluse. In her childhood, she had had a severe attack of rheumatic fever which damaged her heart. Although she had survived and even given birth to two very much wanted children, at thirty-nine — because of her heart specialist's orders — she spent much of her time resting in bed and wondering if the next time she was out of breath, or her heart started fibrillating uncontrollably, it would be the last time.

With David, Nancy was a loving but limited sex partner. David couldn't understand how I could neglect such a pretty, healthy, and competent woman as Erma, but he told her she should accept male reality. Man had invented monogamy, not for himself, but to keep his women under control. If men, married or not, ever lost interest in the joy of loving and being loved by a loving woman, the world would come to an end. Erma was dubious, but ready to let him prove it.

Now, without me (or Nancy) being aware of it, Erma and David became like young lovers champing at the bit. It wasn't easy for a wandering husband and wife, with four kids between them, to find a place to be alone. Erma didn't know Nancy, but she assured David that Bob would enjoy a woman with whom he could share all of his "damn books." The die was cast. David convinced Nancy, who rarely went to social events, that she should attend a local hospital ball and he'd introduce her to a man who had enough books to keep her reading for two lifetimes. Nancy was very pretty. Nearsighted with big, luminous brown eyes that you could drown in, she sighed when I asked her to dance. "I really shouldn't. My heart isn't very good." I told her that I wasn't a great dancer. "My heart is pounding too," I laughed. "We don't have to move fast. We could dance on a dime and just hug each other." And we did, most of the evening, to the exclusion of everyone else—including David and Erma.

Although we realized that our spouses had been making love for years, Nancy was under no pressure from me to have sex together. She knew about Ginny, and much later, I told her the finale.

Arriving at the front door of the Relief building one morning at eight o'clock, I was shocked to see a woman smiling at me a few yards from the entrance. It was Ginny. She had left Paul and her children, but not wholly because of me. "You knew our marriage was on the rocks from the beginning," she sighed. I reminded her, as I had many times before, that I didn't think divorce was the answer. I had lived with Paul at HBS for two years and I really liked him. I was sure that he loved Ginny, but she shook her head. "Paul was too possessive. He doesn't give a damn about my mind, but he wants my body exclusively," she said. Adamantly, she added, "If you don't want me, don't worry, I can take care of myself." I saw her occasionally and kept trying to tell her to go home, but then she met a man who was evidently free to take off with her. She sent me a postcard from Florida. Years later, I received a letter from her. She'd gone back home to Massillon, Ohio, divorced Paul, and converted to Catholicism. She was living with some Sisters of Charity and was occasionally housekeeper for a priest.

During the next twenty-five years, Erma, Bob, David, and Nancy became "the inseparables." This was no *Bob and Carol and Ted and Alice* Hollywood scenario. We saw the film much later and shrugged at the silly ending. We weren't swingers. We never made love as a foursome. Our travels together eventually took us to Florida, the Caribbean, Europe, Africa, Greece, and Israel. We were often casually naked together and slept with each other's spouses, but we never made sexual comparisons to each other. During the first year, we passed through occasional moments of jealousy, but it became increasingly clear that our love for each other was "in addition to and not instead of." Sexual and mental sharing became a natural way of life between the four of us, but we were careful never to reveal our sexual exchange to anyone. We never merged households, but perhaps we would have, as I proposed in *Proposition 31*, had we all lived into our eighties. We maintained separate families in our attractive middle-class homes. We loved our biological children as well as each other's kids, who ranged from five to thirteen years of age. Many years later, as a foursome, we enjoyed the fun of being both biological as well as surrogate grandparents.

Each of us grew emotionally and mentally in the unique marriage that later I would fictionalize (to Nancy's horror) and expand into alternate lifestyles in *Proposition 31, Thursday, My Love, Come Live My Life,* and *The Love Explosion* (the last title was not my choice). Seeing Erma through David's eyes, I learned to appreciate her abilities to tackle almost any project that required mechanical and physical adeptness and to do it all by herself, if necessary. Seeing Nancy through my eyes, David began to realize that her wide reading from childhood, her love of music—she introduced us all to the joys of opera—and the fact that she had me as a lover was making his wife a much more exciting woman. Seeing David through Erma's and my eyes, Nancy slowly became aware that David might not have had a Park Avenue-style medical practice, but he was one of the most caring medical practitioners around: a man who loved all of his patients, although many never paid him and tried to barter for his services. David blended his love for his family and ours with caring medicine and a never-ending sense of laughter and joy of life. Whenever you find laughter in my novels, in scenes like the meshugah ape in *The Harrad Experiment* or partying on Trotter Island in *That Girl from Boston*, David was the inspiration.

Continuing to live a split life, which now encompassed David, Nancy, and Erma, we were soon under fire from Blanche and FH. They belonged to a popular local club which excluded Jews. FH's argument was that Jews did the same. There were no Gentiles in their gold or yacht clubs. Spending a week on Cape Cod with Nancy and David, I was shocked to discover that there was no room at the inn when they saw David. But I was totally horrified when FH and Blanche refused to come into our house when David and Nancy (or any other Jews) were there. (Keep in mind that we lived next door!)

FH ardently believed that he wasn't prejudiced because he did business with many Jews. "They have their ways and we have ours. They don't want you either." He was wrong, even Orthodox Jews were delighted with my curiosity and need to learn about their customs and rituals. After my first novels were published, I was invited to speak at every synagogue (Orthodox, Conservative, and Reformed) in Quincy. Not a year went by when we weren't guests at Passover dinners.

I was now writing. My anger at religious prejudice slowly combined into a larger than life hero, Yale Marratt. When the novel was finished, I knew it was much too long. Two years later, seventeen publishers had rejected the book. I finally decided I needed an agent and picked Scott Meredith (today a millionaire literary agent). For fifty dollars, he agreed to read the novel. He liked parts of it, but told me that I had committed the ultimate no-no. Women read all the novels, and I would never sell one extolling bigamy. As Nancy had told me, chuckling, when I finished the book, one of the women had to die, and since Cynthia was Jewish, she was the most likely one. My ego was rudely punctured. The original manuscript, which I had trimmed on a power cutter several times so that it didn't show such wear and tear, was unsalable. I was a prophet without an audience. But I wasn't about to rewrite *Yale Marratt*.

If I hadn't known David and enjoyed him almost as much as I did his wife, I probably never would have written *That Girl from Boston* as my next novel. Most of it takes place on an island in Boston Harbor called Peddocks. David's hobby was fishing for Boston flounder — the harbor wasn't as polluted then — and he was also the preferred doctor for all residents on the island, who, over many years, had built unheated, untoiled, and unelectrified houses on Peddocks. To support himself, David had wrestled his way through medical school, and I included a wrestling scene in the novel. *That Girl from Boston* pits upper-class Bostonians against the lower-class Irish.

It seemed as if a heart operation, performed at Mass General, would alleviate Nancy's problems and prolong her life — people with rheumatic heart disease rarely live beyond their early sixties. We were all afraid that she might die suddenly if her heart began to fibrillate out of control. The operation was successful with a valve implant, but in the process, Nancy got an E. coli infection. After a terrible month, hooked to every possible lifesaving equipment, unable to talk to us for weeks, none of us believing that she wouldn't recover, she died. Our two-couple marriage was over. We were reduced to a potential ménage á trois, which didn't work. David thought that sharing one wife was an inequitable situation. Then, two years, later, though we remained good friends — a lonely man, missing the years the four of us had shared together — David died of a heart attack.

After twenty-five years of expanding our lives, as David and Nancy did theirs, in an interwoven mental and sexual involvement, still unable to tell our children who had long since married and were pursuing their own lives, Erma and I were alone. We tried once again with a couple ten years younger who had four children in college or their late teens, but the lifetime monogamous conditioning of the other husband made it an uneasy relationship. I fictionalized some of it in an unpublished novel called *The Trade Off*, which takes place in Guadeloupe.

What have I learned? That even before Nancy and David, I was on the wrong trip. I really wouldn't have been happy with a Galatea. Unlike Shaw's *Pygmalion* metamorphosed into Professor Higgins, I've learned the joy of really knowing many "Fair Ladies" with minds of their own. And rather than wondering why women can't be like me, I've learned how to function like a chameleon, and not only change color but to see and enjoy the world through other eyes and minds of women and the men to whom they may be attached. Is that rejoining sex and the spirit? Absolutely ... but it won't happen on any large scale until our leaders — teachers, politicians, and religious — and you who are reading this book, dare to become activists and pursue "freedom and dignity." If you want better, more loving people who can embrace multiple relationships, you must create environments and teach them now.

Families, Small and Big

Jerry Jud

The only form of family life approved and endorsed by our culture is the nuclear family, a man and a woman and children; one man and one woman married to each other for life. Many people think that this has been the only form of family life since the beginning with Adam and Eve somewhere around five thousand years ago. Nothing could be further from the truth.

In almost all cultures down through the ages, polygamy has been practiced. It is an embarrassment to many that the patriarchs had many wives and, that even in the New Testament, it was only prescribed that bishops be limited to one wife. Maybe this was because they had so many other things that needed their attention. When the mother and father of Jesus made their espousal to each other, there was no rabbi or priest to witness their covenant. And though they were only engaged, it was allowed, even expected they would enjoy the sexual union. Churches did not perform marriages until around the fourth century and not until the Council of Trent (1545-63) did the Western Church first assert that the use of the Christian ceremony was essential to a valid marriage. And although monogamy has only been prescribed since the fourteenth century, people still lived in extended families. In our country, it was not until after World War II, when there was a rapid movement from the small towns and countryside to the great cities, when corporations began moving people from job to job, that the nuclear family emerged as the only matrix in which children could be raised.

❖   ❖   ❖

Jerry Jud is a retired United Church of Christ minister, former U.C.C. administrator, and founder of Shalom Mountain Retreat and current founder-codirector of Timshel Retreat in the Pocono Mountains of eastern Pennsylvania.

The nuclear family is inadequate to be the sole bearer of the responsibility of rearing children. Remember that only half of the marriages entered into do not end in divorce—forget for the moment the level of happiness or unhappiness among those who do not divorce. Remember the huge number of children being raised by a single parent who also goes to work each day. Remember also the tragedy of the millions who do not have a partner, and are thus deprived of nurturing intimacy. Remember the totally unbalanced ratio of older women to older men. Remember these realities, and it is easy to see the importance of finding other socially approved forms of family besides the nuclear family. Surely the nuclear family will hold sway for an extended period of time. We can only hope, as we look at the stunted growth in personality development, at the lost capacity to live, at the deep wounding that goes on in the nuclear family, that there will be more openness to dialogue in this arena.

The stories in this book do not present an easy answer to the problem of the nurturing of children. In these stories the children suffer, too. The children are suffering and we do not know the way out, and we must find it. Children need to be raised where they feel loved and nurtured, where they can work through their conflicts, where they can unfold in an atmosphere of love and caring. In a world where 80 percent of all mothers go to work in the morning to jobs out there, where serial monogamy is the rule of the day, where disease and death also take parents away, we must find a form of family life that is different from the nuclear family. In the stories told here, there is some hope, but as long as children raised in these forms of family have to live under the opprobrium that their parents are not only wrong but wicked, the suffering is unabated.

A Watershed Paradigm Shift

In conservative religious circles it is decreed that sexual intercourse is for procreation only. In less conservative circles it is held that sexual intercourse is only to be engaged in within a blessed marriage. Things have changed and are changing fast in this arena. But it is also apparent that the old paradigm relative to these matters must lose its hold. In creating a new paradigm, is it too radical to urge a return to the biblical paradigm that allowed couples to celebrate their covenant to each other in the sexual union (Matthew 1:18-20); that held fornication or unchastity did not apply to sex within a covenant of caring, mutual justice, and loving kindness (Matthew 5:27-32; I Corinthians 7:15-19), and that saw nurturance and not procreation as the primary purpose of any sexual intimacy within a covenanted relationship (I Corinthians 7:2-5)?

Must the covenant of "two in one flesh" eliminate the possibility of a woman or man having more than one covenanted relationship?

Human sexuality is a great and wondrous gift. When it is expressed in love, it is surely the Gateway into the Divine Presence. The storytellers of this book know that and envision a time when we will again see sexuality and spirituality as one, as a means of celebrating the wondrous truth that the universe is one, that we are one. The critical issue of population explosion may now further this dialogue and open the way for a new perspective on sexuality in human life.

Great civilizations have risen and fallen. We are now in one of those critical periods when important dialogue is going on, and indeed when life-death decisions which will affect the future of human life on the Earth are being made. We must look to our renewal, which alone can come from re-visioning, from honesty in dialogue, from the adventurous love of the self and of one's neighbor, from the love of the Earth, and from the recognition of the Divine within us all and in all things. I believe in the dialogue method provided by this book. I believe in dialogue itself as a way of renewal. The Earth is old; it has its own story. Our story is lived within the story of the Earth. The human population of our little blue planet is in serious trouble. The resources of the Earth are limited and the cancerous growth of the human population has the potential of destroying its host and, in the process, destroying also itself. We must be a people of hope and act always on the side of renewal.

Part Three

The Healing Power
of Sacred Sex

An Anguished Prayer for Sexual-Spiritual Wholeness

God, damn it!

Stop the torrent of shame and shaming flooding the moral landscape of the people.

Empower us to withstand with life-saving dignity the rapids of righteousness surging from the shamers.

It is enough that we bear our own guilt for withholding loving sensuality and erotic pleasure from those around us hungry for caring touch.

Intimidated and lacking moral courage, we hide with fear of the shamers, and weep inside our souls with rage and sadness.

Let the light of your creation shine to dry the rivers of shame and tears.

Let us see the good news of our becoming whole in the freedom of sexuality for loving, friendship, comfort, intimacy and pleasure;

a freedom from the old bondage of unwanted procreation and the oppressive sex ethics of an older time.

Above all, may we cease to blaspheme your creation by going to the grave before we have ever lived.

Reverend Ron Mazur,
author of *The New Intimacy*

Painting Outside the Lines

Jerry Jud

There is scarcely any area of human life where the forces of outrage and punishment rear their heads more than when someone is discovered deviating from the accepted sexual mores. Not too long ago at the fiftieth anniversary celebration of Kirkridge Retreat Center in eastern Pennsylvania, I said that now that the lesbians and homosexuals have taken the risk of coming out of the closet, it is time for the heterosexuals, bisexuals, and other folk living non-traditional forms of family life to come out of the closet, too. The stories in this book are a small but important step in that direction.

The women and men who tell their quite different and varied stories here have been compelled by their sincerity to disclose both the "slippery rocks and sparkling waters" of their attempts to connect their sexual lives and spiritual needs. Their stories of relationships lived outside the conventional norms of our religious conventions are evidence that our society is in the midst of a paradigm shift. There is no way we can escape the radically new social environment we and our parents have created in recent decades. Because it is a tidal wave, we are being forced to explore new solutions, a new flexibility in the ways we meet, bond, and build our families, in the ways we meet both our spiritual and our sensual-erotic needs.

So it is very important that all of us, especially leaders in the religious and counseling communities, begin at least opening the door and taking a step or two out into the light of day, revealing the diversity that lies just under the surface of our public lives. We also have to listen to these courageous voices.

❖   ❖   ❖

Jerry Jud is a retired United Church of Christ minister, former U.C.C. administrator and founder of Shalom Mountain Retreat, and current founder-codirector of Timshel Retreat in the Endless Mountains of Pennsylvania.

157

Although millions of Americans paint outside the lines of conventional mores as far as sexuality is concerned, most of us are forced by the strictures of our society to stay underground and not share some of the most important and treasured parts of their loves with any but the most trusted friends. To acknowledge openly their unconventional lifestyles would be to risk being punished by their employers and ostracized by family and friends. Fortunately, the times are somewhat changing, and some of the folk witnessing here are in situations where they can use their own names; most have not. Those who have used our own names are either in a less vulnerable position in our society, or feel for various reasons that we want to take the risk of identifying our names with their story.

Whether or not the writers put their real names on their stories, there is nothing in these stories which says: "You should go my way. It's the solution, the best way." Rather hear: "This is what we have experienced. Here is what we learned and here is why we tried to do what we did. Maybe it will shed light on your journey and increase the dialogue among us."

Most of our storytellers started out in one place and ended in another. I myself have gone from squeaky clean and role-bound church pastor to church executive dealing with church and culture, to a founder of a psychological-spiritual retreat center, to a founder of a center for mystics; from strict monogamy to open marriage, to a triangle, then again to husband with one wife, and now with a deeply loving relationship with two other people in our marriage.

In the realm of sexuality and spirituality, many would say these women and men have marched off the map. They are sojourners. To live one's life under the paradigm of journey is to choose to find one's own way instead of taking one's direction from the dominant culture. It is to travel with a vision of the unfolding self and of trusting vision over doctrine or dogma. I like the saying, "My karma ran over my dogma." That is the way the folk presenting their stories here also feel. These stories are of people who have been courageous and grounded enough in their inner being to believe that sex and spirit can be joined, and that some times, for some folk, painting outside the lines of social convention and traditional religious boundaries is the way to go. Hopefully, these adventures outside the lines will illuminate the way for others, open our minds to new realities, break through the comforting walls we have built around our world, and open the way to more creative, more spiritual, more loving ways of coping with our rapidly changing world.

"New occasions teach new duties.
Time makes ancient good uncouth."

17. Growing Beyond an Open Marriage

Ryam Nearing

I'm one of those people who really likes being married. I consider myself a pack animal and find intensely intimate partnerships the juice that glides me through the tough times in day-to-day life and also sweetens each good moment.

My story is that I married my high school sweetheart, Barry. We were both only nineteen years old, so lots of folks doubted we would last. Now that we've made it twenty-five years so far, I feel satisfied in seeing us as a successful marriage. Obviously, time isn't the only thing we have going for us, but these days it's clearly noteworthy. We're still best friends, working and playing together. I look at us as fellow travelers on this life path, having made it through plenty of adventures.

But there's more to our marriage than just the two of us. For the past fifteen years we've lived with another partner as a triad. Lots of people didn't think we three would last either. But we have.

I just never thought about limits to loving. Krishna-murti, Alan Watts, and Plato introduced me to images of loving way beyond the couple framework while I was still in Hamilton High, an inner city school in Los Angeles. But I didn't automatically connect love with marriage, since my parents' marriage, the one I first had contact with, looked to be completely without it. I really didn't believe I'd ever make the mistake of getting married myself. Love sounded fine, especially if you approached it from a very high, spiritual perspective and expected nothing in return, but being a bride sounded deadly.

So at sixteen I was a free love advocate and practiced what I preached. My summer job at a mental hospital in southern California put me in daily contact with several young male co-workers who found my philosophy intriguing. But charmingly enough, they seemed to feel wounded when I didn't act like the fact we'd had sex meant that we were forever bonded or that I'd feel jealous if I saw them with someone else. They acted like children, I thought, even though they were over twenty-one and I was still in high school. How could they think that the simple kind of sexual exchange we engaged in meant a commitment? When they'd tell me they loved me, I'd laugh and say, "How could you? We hardly even know each other." I guess they thought they had to feed me a line, but it was the last thing I wanted to hear.

But, those who were Vietnam vets broke my heart with their emotional war wounds. Give them two beers and they'd start crying, reliving their stories until they were desperate just to be held. I saw the war's damage and sometimes felt like I had to fill up those horrible holds with my life force, like holding my finger in a giant dyke, trying to keep it from collapsing.

A stretch of this kind of relating convinced me that I was on the wrong track. Friendly sex like warm ice cream or cold coffee, lacked pizzazz and could do only in a real crunch. I wanted more. The brief heart connections I'd managed felt so rich, they led me to believe that what I craved was sex with real love: to experience it with a soul mate, a best friend, a partner as a bond and expression of our connection with each other.

In the Catholic school years of my childhood, I'd been told that marriage was a sacrament: the union of two souls in a loving relationship building a life together. I'd become cynical about the specific superstitious and dogmatic aspects of organized religion, and had it out with my parish priest when I told him I no longer believed in his God. But still the nuns had me until age seven, and as they say, that's all it takes. So I carried the idealistic images of perfection, pure love, total honesty, and a divinely inspired union of souls. And after my bout of casual caring and straight sex, I wanted more.

Back at my high school, I figured I'd found my match. He didn't know it, but I did. Barry had no big religious background, just a jack Jew, and he and I could talk philosophy and life purpose, and planned our escape from the city (Los Angeles). Our relationship developed in stages, gradually becoming more and more intimate. By the time we started UCLA, we were best friends, lovers, and even shared a checking account for mutual purchases.

Alas, in those days the Vietnam war still kept eating young men. Barry was unlucky at the lottery (number ten), his conscientious objector application was denied, and Canada sounded like a last resort, so he went to Navy boot camp. The absurdity of this was a great teaching: Nothing like being a slave to learn the preciousness of freedom.

When he broke out of his training, Barry wanted to get married. Of course my mother loved the idea. I knew I wanted to spend my life with him and somehow in the glow of our love I dropped my horror of the institution, imagining that I could make a marriage that stayed fresh and healthy and fun.

From my studies of cultural anthropology I'd learned to look at human custom as a dance of infinite variety and quite arbitrary in its specifics. Every place on earth seemed to have some way for men and women to publicly demonstrate their particular bond to each other. I chose to see my wedding as just one out of countless ritual forms. Bemused by the idea of a white dress and wedding cake, Barry and I made our vows out under the sky, pledging to be lovers and friends to each other with a small group of friends and family witnessing.

While some people say that getting married changes everything, for me it changed nothing. If anything it just made logistics easier: living together and sharing money and decisions. In a couple years we acted on our high school plan and managed to get out of LA to Idaho where we settled onto some land.

This is when we first opened up our marriage. I got involved with a coworker. Just a few months before, I'd graduated summa cum laude from UCLA with a B.A. in psychology/sociology, but the job I got was as the first woman laborer on a small city's Street Department. Funny these days to hear the subtle nuances that are considered sexual harassment! I learned to wear steel-toed boots, swear as good as any man on the crew, and outdo any dirty joke they told me. I also fell in love with a wild young guy who was intrigued by my vegetarian diet and other "strange" ideas.

He'd never heard of open marriage, but I'd read the O'Neills' book and Rimmer's *Harrad Experiment* so had a context to imagine healthy multiple relationships. Still, remember this was Idaho. The other men on the crew kept warning my friend Bill that my husband was "gonna come after him with a shotgun." Actually, my husband was a bit unsettled by the situation. While I told him immediately about my involvement with Bill, we were still faced with a major shift in our lives as they'd been together so far. When someone close goes through a change, it changes the whole relationship. So we had to find a new equilibrium in our partnership. I needed to explore and expand, and Barry needed to rely on his own confidence and curiosity to understand what the changes really meant.

We both knew it didn't mean that we had stopped loving each other. Or that either of us wanted a divorce. In the face of this newness, all three of us stretched with the situation and even managed to find some outings to enjoy together as a group. We took it day by day and Barry got to experience some of the benefits of my having another lover. For instance, he hated the idea of attending my work Christmas party. So I went with Bill. This managed to mess with the minds of many of our coworkers: that my husband would let me party with another man! While it shocked them silly, Barry slipped out of an undesired social event and Bill and I enjoyed the party. We three saw it as win-win even if the rest of our world just didn't get it.

But eventually my lover Bill and I found our dating relationship had nowhere to go. He wanted a full-time girlfriend, and I couldn't fill that need, so our relationship wound down into a warm friendship, sans sex. Although I'd enjoyed this experience, it was a little bit of a relief to go back to life as usual. Having a husband is so easy to explain and so socially approved. Having another person involved seemed to set people's teeth on edge. They didn't know how to relate to us: we were socially awkward to deal with. Who should they invite to their parties or over for dinner? Were they being disloyal to Barry if they enjoyed spending time with Bill? Was I still an okay person, or a shameless slut for having two lovers? So when things cooled down with Bill, I definitely relaxed back into being a known and accepted social quantity: a wife to Barry.

A couple years passed, and in central Washington State, I grew to love another man, Joe. I again imagined that he'd be an outside relationship to my marriage with Barry. A simple positive addition to my life. As you can tell, even with some experience under my belt, I was still a bit naive and idealistic. It didn't take long for Joe and I to get very involved in each others' lives. We worked together on projects that both of us found totally engrossing. He was publishing a book, and I was his assistant, learning many new skills and providing him with support he needed. Barry could see the progression, and struggled with jealousy and insecurity, although I again had no thought of leaving him.

For me, the realization that I could feel so close to Joe made me reconsider my idea of open marriage. I liked really loving two people. Both men were completely different types, although they also had much in common. When the three of us got together, we had hilarious and expansive conversations, and work parties that produced major results in little time. Joe, as opposed to my first outside lover Bill, shared so much with us in the way of lifestyle and values that it made spending time together simple and rewarding all around.

In this phase, our relationship style was still as a primary couple, but we were also part of an intimate network. In our small rural university town, a whole circle of us worked together and knew each other's lovers and friends.

And, of course, any friend might any day become a lover. Barry explored relationships with a few women. One had been part of a four-person group marriage that blew up. She'd left her original husband for a sabbatical, and met Barry in his glass blowing class. She cooked him gourmet meals and introduced him to Southern Comfort. Joe took me dog sledding and taught me Amslan. While Barry and I enjoyed the expansive energy of this phase, it still left something lacking. There didn't feel like there was anywhere for the relationships to go. Were these people just "dates"? Was seeing them once or twice a week "enough"?

When Barry's lover, Anna Marie, left town to return to her husband with only a brief phone call to let Barry know, we had to reflect on the quality of the intimacy we had chosen. Here was another deflection. She'd obviously seen our situation as just a brief "affair," as had my first lover Bill. I just hadn't fully realized how programmed most people are to believe "true" love is a one-to-a-customer deal (or at least one to a customer at a time). And while everybody loves a lover in this culture, hardly a soul can believe that loving more than one other adult as a spouse is just as much a "real" relationship as any couple. Even people involved in these relationships seemed to look at them as transitory and "less than."

But there I was, really loving two men and not wanting to choose one over the other, not wanting to leave either of them. And I was struck by the insight that during a lifetime relationship, like the one I had with my husband, both of us would most likely run into at least a few other people we would truly love in addition to each other. Being a practical sort when push comes to shove, I decided to figure out a good way to have a long-term committed relationship with more people than the church and government issued twosome.

I already knew open marriage hadn't done the trick for us. Lovers either wanted us to leave our marriage for them, or else they were looking for something more casual than we wanted in our intimate relationships. When we had linked up with Joe, he was a best friend to both of us. His communication skills and dedication to honesty between us helped in processing the changing and difficult emotions that came up in our unconventional situation. But then even he backed off when we brought up the possibility of "group marriage."

Directly discovering for ourselves that we found having more partners, but within a committed relationship, most desirable, we realized we were in the funny position of being too straight for the world of "open relationships" and too "weird" for the folks looking for marriage-quality partnering. Still, Barry and I knew we'd found our fit and figured if we ever found someone we loved who also thought group marriage was a great choice, we'd go for it. (We were specifically attracted to polyfidelity where all partners in the group are equally valued as spouses.)

Amazingly enough, not long after this decision, we actually did it: we met and grew to love another man who desired a larger marriage, Allan. We courted for months, living next door to each other and talking a great deal about our life dreams. We also matched up our day-to-day lifestyle choices (like where we wanted to live, how we wanted to live, diet, politics, spiritual choices, etc.) to see if we could be together for the long run.

Our values matched up well, but this is not to say we're alike. You can't imagine three people with more varied temperaments and personal operating styles! But that's the spice of being three. With support from some friends who themselves were in a group marriage, we decided to make a commitment to each other as a family. We chose our name, Syntony, which means attuned to the same vibration, and began our life as a multiple-adult marriage.

Today it all seems very normal and natural for us. As to our home life, we live in the same house, operate out of the same checkbook, and run our own solar business together. Both men feel like husbands/partners to me and the two of them see each other as brothers/partners. It's so hard to describe intensely spiritual loving bonds in words, but basically, we're best friends who find we get more from life experiencing it together. And we feel quite fervently about this. In the different aspects of our day, we're a team, a crew, a gang, a family, a tribe, a marriage.

We haven't hidden our marriage in the woodwork either. Since we've been together, we've held discussion groups, written a book on the subject and a newsletter, appeared on TV shows, and hosted an annual conference for people involved in or interested in group marriage or responsible non-monogamy. Aside from a few folks who believe strongly that God said people should only share their life with one other adult, most either find us interesting or just leave us to our own personal life choice.

Our good friends just see us as people who live as three instead of two, but our biological families vary in their acceptance. My father and siblings have no problem with our particular choice and love both guys as part of our clan. Allan's relatives are friendly, but not too close, and Barry's mother disapproves, but is polite when we see her.

My philosophical and spiritual beliefs prioritize love and individual freedom above all other values, and my marriage style is truly an expression of both these. Group marriage is one actualization, on this earthly physical plane, of love and freedom for me. First, my relationships are based on deep and abiding love, which constantly teaches me new lessons in life. I've learned so much more through the fast pace and intense stimulation of multi-adult family life with two completely different, completely intimate, and completely committed relationships in my life.

There is so much to learn about being a loving human in the graciousness of long-term relationships, and having more beloveds magnifies the process. For example, it becomes perfectly clear to me what stuff I project, because there it is in both relationships. This makes it very difficult to blame it on the guys. There's not too much room to hide from myself in a threesome. Each of us has had to face ourselves, and learn our strengths and weaknesses together. We've all felt that great yogic stretch of growing into more of who we are with each other's support. And this is the essence of love to me: acceptance and evolution.

Then there's freedom. I thank the cosmos that I was lucky enough to break out of the patterns laid out by the standard culture and pursue a lifestyle that was more of a custom fit for me. I just would never have felt content limiting myself to one love this lifetime. My belief in the sanctity of individual freedom also helps me in staying in and keeping my relationships refreshing and rewarding over the years. Not that it's easy to stand back and let someone you're so involved with make choices you'd rather they didn't, but accepting my partners as free and separate adults provides space in our family for the natural change and growth of our years together. This is essential in keeping our marriage healthy and alive for the long run.

Actually, I feel that the ideals I was fed in Catholic school as a young child about marriage being a major life sacrament and about Jesus' words on loving one another have withstood my major disillusionment with Church dogma. I know for certain that in my life, love sustains me. And my marriage is built on love that stands alone without much in the way of societal support. I wish that many people in couples would realize that if they are so blessed as to find more love, they could expand their relationship instead of ending it. And my best hope for my personal future is that we three would meet and grow in love with another woman or dyad, expanding the family joy I already know.

18. Dancing to the Goddess' Drum

Carol Jud

We are a culture that has lost its ground. We live in a world where there are few maps or guideposts to understand the most basic of human relationships—our relationship to our bodies and our relationship to the divine. We can acknowledge that as humans we are sexual beings, and many of us will acknowledge that as humans we are also spiritual beings, but do we really know what we mean when we use these words? What does it mean to be sexual or to be spiritual and how do the two meet?

Traditionally, sexuality has been considered the epitome of embodiment, while spirituality has been considered to be a breaking loose from the body. We live, however, in a culture where sexuality has been disembodied. It has become a spectator sport and a matter of commerce rather than a deep body experience. Spirituality, too, has lost its connection to the life force. It seems to be imprisoned in old rhetoric and empty ritual.

I arrived on this planet with a body and to the best of their abilities, my parents helped me to love and honor that body. The culture, however, counteracted those teachings with double messages about the body. There were not-so-subtle teachings about the body being dirty, shameful and of a lower order than the mind. There were teachings that implied that it was dangerous to live in a body, that sexual feelings are bad, and that pleasure, especially sexual pleasure, is bad. There were messages telling me that being female was of a lesser order than being male, and there was increasing evidence that the feminine was being violated and disparaged.

My mother died when I was just moving into young womanhood at age thirteen. This cut me off from my most immediate teacher about the mysteries of womanhood and sexuality. I was left feeling that I had been separated from and abandoned by the community of women. I was given all of the facts about sexuality and I do not believe that I was flooded with undue negativity about sexuality, but it seemed that when the basic teaching of the child was completed, there were no new teachers available to teach the woman. A parallel situation occurred in my spiritual life. I was raised in the church where I spent my early days listening to God's word, singing the hymns, and carrying out the rituals. The church was a part of my family life and my community life and yet as I grew to be a woman, the teachings no longer seemed to speak to my life in a relevant way. I felt an undeniable spiritual longing that seemed to have no container. There seemed to be no one to look to for guidance, and I am not even sure that I would have known what to ask. So I left that part of myself behind and went out into the world to marry and find a career. Perhaps the questions stopped temporarily but the indefinable longing remained.

It was not until I entered training as a core energetics therapist that I started awakening to my sexual and spiritual energies. Although I was well into my thirties, I am not sure that I had yet developed any deep understanding of either sexuality or spirituality. When I started to do deep bodywork, I was amazed to discover that my sexual energy was my most immediate connection to the spiritual. In this work, I started to actually experience my body as the gateway to both sexual and spiritual realms. Ironically, these most significant sexual and spiritual experiences did not include anything that might be considered sexual activity or spiritual practice. They simply involved being fully present in my body—breathing, moving, listening, feeling. I learned that my body is my place of truth. Knowing in my body comes from experience, not from teaching. My experiences came in direct opposition to the culture's teaching that sexuality is not sacred and that to be truly spiritual, one must remove oneself from the desires of the body. I felt the sacredness of the sexual and the sexuality of the sacred and the meeting place was my own body. In my body, the sexual and the spiritual are not merely connected, they are one.

I became aware of this union during one of my training sessions when I unexpectedly experienced a profound sexual and spiritual initiation. It began as I danced to intensely rhythmic drumming with an almost hypnotic beat. I danced alone with my eyes closed, feeling connected to the ground, and to my body. Moving with a slow and swaying motion in my pelvis and arms, I kept my feet firmly planted on the ground. I worked with rhythmic pelvic thrusts to the beat of the drum. Moving slowly and then in double time, I felt pleasurably grounded and very powerful. Gradually I quieted myself and felt the vibrations that were pulsating through my body. I reached out. I was aware of a difference between extending my arms with the palms at right angles to the ground and reaching out with the hands open. In the open position, I felt both softer and more receptive, while continuing to feel powerful—a strange combination for me. As I stood in this flowing position, the music shifted to Gregorian Chant. This music brought me to a totally new place of consciousness. My arms felt full, as if by reaching, I had finally satisfied my longing. I raised my arms to the top of my head and allowed the energy and vibrations to move through the Crown Chakra.

The following is an attempt to bring words to what I experienced.

> "I am still vibrating—needing to be alone, not wanting to get involved with any social activity. The experience had been too powerful. It almost seems that concretizing it into words might take away from that power. What to say? I felt (no, I knew) that I was in the presence of the Divine. I saw God, Goddess, the Ground of Being—the name didn't matter. First there was the longing. My arms were outstretched and the music began—seeming to emanate from within, not from without. The pain of the longing was intense—longing for what I did not know. At first it felt like the longing I feel for my Beloved, but then it went far beyond. I saw that my longing and my love for a Lover give me a model, a container, a starting place, a channel to know God. I realize it would be a mistake to make a human lover into my God but I also know that the human lover opens the pathway to my God."

So what did I experience? It was an opening of myself in vibration with something above, around, and within—awesome, terrifying, and yet full of peace and love. There was no form. Perhaps there was only color, like a brilliant sunset—moving, vibrant, spacious. I opened myself fully to the light even though I felt vulnerable and almost overwhelmed by the awesomeness. The vibration within was so powerful that I began to see it as a mirroring of the powerful vibration on the outside. My smallness and my insignificance melted into the knowledge that I was a part of this power—part of the universal web. It was here that I was able to begin to touch the divine within. Because God is all and I am a part of that whole, I become God when I become a part of the whole. This is the source of my power. This power, however, is not something that I own or which I can claim that I earned. Rather it is something that flows through me as it flows through all things and sets me on fire—connecting me, opening me, moving me. The Fire and the Rose: the Fire burning through—destroying the old and warming the new with life; the rose—soft, vulnerable, and sensuous. I vibrate and become a leaf drifting through the skies. I vibrate and the vibrations are channeled and focused, cutting through like a sword, grounding my consciousness.

I have wrestled with God for many years. I was mad at the guy who sat on the throne and judged me, never being quite satisfied with anything that I did. I was mad at the guy who took my mother from me when I was thirteen years old, leaving me with the feeling that I had been cheated and that somehow I was to blame. He was supposed to be the God of Love, but the words seemed empty. There were too many rules and too many judgments. Yes, I left that guy a long time ago.

His departure, however, left an empty space within my soul. I surrounded this vast emptiness with a thick wall that kept it from my sight and out of my consciousness. I was so successful at this deception that I almost forgot that my soul had once known some other way of being. But now Miracle of Miracles, my body has brought me back to this divine place. My body has brought me home.

How ironic that the Christian Church has blocked off the most obvious channel that we humans have to experience our divine selves — THE BODY. It is almost as if the fathers of the Church were threatened by the idea that by allowing us to know and love our bodies that we might suspect that the divine is within and not enthroned on a cloud somewhere. It is amazing how much fear and energy have been poured into making sure that we will never arrive at this simple and basic truth that **we are divine**. What a mystery! We don't have to do anything to be divine. We just have to allow ourselves to be.

Listening to my body in this special way gave me a glimpse of what it is like to just be. For a brief moment I felt myself to be nothing but pure energy — no name, nobody special, maybe not even a body since the energy was flowing so freely in and out of me. Such surrender brings its own terror because in giving up all that gives me my own unique identity, I come close to the experience of my own death. Yet by giving up that part of myself, something new is born that is much larger, something eternal. I have a sense of being not an isolated individual, nor even an individual part of the web; the feeling is that **I am the web**. All that is outside me is also within me and all that is within is also outside. There is nothing that is foreign. There is nothing that is separate. What I hate is part of me and what I love is part of me.

This was such a breathtaking idea that I feel that I could hardly contain it. But that misses the point. Energy is not energy when it is contained. **Energy moves**. That is what it is about. So to contain this idea or to own it, is not to **be it**. Perhaps even formalizing it into a theory is an attempt to own it and to contain it. But without understanding, I was afraid that I would lose the powerful impact of the experience. Then I realized that this was the illusion that I believed all of my life—that if you cannot prove something logically, it isn't so.

But there is another kind of knowing, a deep knowing that is the consequence of experience. This is a knowing beyond logic. So now what little I do know about my spiritual self and the spiritual aspects of the universe, I know through direct experience, not through scientific proof. This is stored and grounded in my body, not in my head. I still need to bring my consciousness to these body experiences. Without the consciousness, the moment is lost and cannot be integrated into the flow of my life. With this experience, I am changed. The vibrations in my body no longer feel only like a personal expression. These vibrations are my connection to all things and so they are my connection to the divine that moves through all things.

It is sad that I spent so much time during my training years looking for a book that explained how the body is connected to the spiritual aspects of a person's life. I see now that even if I had found the book that I would have missed the message. Spiritual truths cannot be passed on by word of mouth. That is why such truths have traditionally been referred to as Mysteries. They can only be the outcome of direct experience. Passing along the Word can easily become religion or law. What starts as truth becomes rigid and dead. But true spirituality must be experienced, and the most powerful and perhaps the only source of direct experience for me is my own body. My body is my teacher. I vibrate and I celebrate the universe through my body. I vibrate and I celebrate the Goddess through my body.

It was many years later before I was able to experience the intensity of this sexual/spiritual channel with a partner. The process required an opening of the heart that went beyond all boundaries I had known before. In this place of expansion and trust, I felt catapulted into space and came face to face with the Goddess. She told me that her name was Aija and I stood at her feet in awe and wonder. At that moment, I felt that she possessed me totally and called me into her service. She told me that she is the Goddess who says "Yes." She says "yes" to life. She says "yes" to the body and she says "yes" to sexuality. She says "yes" but that "yes" requires that I be awake and aware and know the consequences of my actions. This "yes" requires me to listen to the place where she lives in me and not to the external law. She promises unknown worlds and demands total commitment to truth and essence.

It was surprising to me, once these new spaces were opened within me, that they did not close down when the lovemaking was ended. This awareness seems to have become a permanent part of my internal landscape, even when I am not actively making love. It is as if I experienced the Goddess flowing through me with such extraordinary power that I know the reality of her presence in the same way that I know the presence of the sun's warm rays on me or the cool water of a lake or the delicious taste of a wonderful meal. She is no longer a spiritual idea but a concrete presence. It feels to me that the distinction between the sexual and spiritual no longer makes any sense to me. In my body they are truly one.

I did not understand what was happening or why, but something in me knew that this process was bringing me back to my essence. My body went through months of opening to prepare for the Goddess' work. I watched my body become transformed in my lovemaking. When I felt the sexual energy move through my body, I became acutely aware of the places where it got stuck and I was moved to find ways of breaking through the barriers to free up the energy. I felt a need to crack open my chest, my heart chakra, my throat, release my jaws, and stretch my body. I heard myself utter new sounds as I heard my body find its voice. There was pain and there was pleasure. Every part of my body called for life and motion. Sometimes the violence of the opening frightened me and made me want to retreat into safer territory, but something kept pressing against the boundaries that held me in. I felt that the Goddess was throwing me into the fire, tempering me and shaping me.

Through all the experiences of ecstasy and wonder, through all the explorations of new worlds, I found myself shaking my finger upward in what seemed to be contempt or derision even while I was calling out the Goddess's name. My partner asked me why I seemed to be addressing the Goddess in such a derogatory fashion. It took me some time before I realized that I was not addressing the Goddess but the old bearded God on the throne. Finally I heard the words that accompanied my defiant gesture. I heard myself saying, "Never again! Never again will I submit to living out a 'No' to life. Never again will I betray my body. Never again will I feel that my body is anything less than a sacred altar at which I can celebrate the Goddess and her creation. I no longer belong to you. I have come home." The Goddess calls and I must answer her call.

My path has helped me realize that my definitions for spirituality and sexuality were much too small. The old definitions created tiny separate categories that limited the worlds that they could encompass. I believe that deep spirituality is being wide awake and utterly aware. It means being fully present in the body, in the senses, in the heart, and from that vantage point, celebrating whatever is being experienced. From this point of view, watching a sunset could be spiritual, or listening to great music, or petting a kitty cat, or making love, or even eating a ham sandwich. The crucial point is the showing up in one's fullness. Similarly, one could also say that if you really show up in your body and your energy is flowing and your senses and chakras are open, then everything is a sexual experience. Communing with a starry night or feeling the deep vibrations of a Beethoven String Quartet could be just as sexual as making love with a lover. **The real union between the sexual and spiritual does not come out of sexual activity or spiritual practice, but out of being fully present in the body.** The separation of sex and spirit is an unnatural disjointing resulting from the separation of the body from the mind and soul. When the body is whole, sexuality and spirituality flow together and are one. The Goddess Aija calls me to celebrate her in my body and in my life. She calls me to guide those who have lost their bodies back home. She calls me to teach that living deeply in our hearts and bodies provides a healing connection to the earth.

And so I sing …

BE STILL MY SOUL.

BE STILL MY SOUL AND KNOW.

BE STILL MY SOUL AND KNOW THAT I AM.

BE STILL MY SOUL AND KNOW

THAT I AM GODDESS.

19. Enriching Deep Friendships with Sexual Intimacies

Jeremy Masefield

All human relationships have roots. No one can have a deep, meaningful, significant relationship which does not have deep roots. Towards the end of his life, Bishop John A. T. Robinson, the famous (notorious?) Bishop of Woolwich of *Honest to God* fame, wrote a book called *Rooted and Radical*. A tautology, perhaps, but so few appreciate that to be and act our radical behavior, humans must have been anchored with deep roots.

For thirty-five years, my wife and I have lived in the professional world of American academia. We are both, quite separately in our different fields, regarded as very successful. Hence, we are also very visible in the Midwestern college community in which we live—I as a professor of business, and she as a well-known practicing psychotherapist. Almost all of our activities, speeches given, public stances taken, TV interviews, political connections are well known.

Not quite all. For a third of a century, we have lived in a network of what some refer to as "non-traditional intimate relationships." We have maintained a veil, not a hard barrier, between our very public lives, and the details of our personal lives. We have very deliberately and thoughtfully chosen this "partly closeted" option. Our judgment, fully reinforced by the history of what has happened to others who chose to go public, was and remains that there is virtually no gain either to ourselves or "the movement." Yet the cost in complexity, in personal hurt, or professional injury by what one of our closest friends called "promiscuous sharing" of intimate details can be very high. Hence everything in this vignette is "coded," but everything is as accurate as one can make in such personal recollections.

The story starts in Chicago to which I had emigrated from Britain. By birth (I carry a well-known family name, hardly recognized in the U.S.) and by education (Harrow and Oxford), I came honestly (!) by my slightly elitist attitudes. Tempering that elitism, however, was a much more significant value

175

from my upbringing—a robust, well-informed, rounded Christian faith. Nurtured in a home where bishops and archbishops and radical leaders like Paul Tillich, and the Niebuhrs, and John Bennett were often around, my liberal Protestant (albeit Church of England) fitted into the America of our campus neighborhood during undergraduate student years.

When I moved to an assistant professorship at the State Land Grant University and there met my very American, reared on a farm, wife Susan Davis, the complementarity seemed too good to be true. There also we met as fellow faculty Barbara and Luther Schmidt. They shared our Christian faith, although they came from more pietistic Midwestern churches. As ecumenism, civil rights, nuclear war, and all the social issues emerged on the Church's consciousness-screen, we shared with Barbara and Lew, among a dozen others, both ideas and action. And by the sixties, "sex" had reared its lovely head in our thinking. Barbara had gone to a national conference, and our local study group was deeply into the issues. Homosexuality and premarital sex dominated: abortion and sterilization were minor issues. Extramarital sex was an emerging, but endlessly discussible topic, but a little unreal.

Two books, however, raised questions, which we knew at the gut level were basic: both *The Quaker View of Sex* and Rustum and Della Roy's *Honest Sex*. (Years later we met Della and Rusty.) They suggested that co-marital, "honest," relationships including sexual intimacy could sometimes be a Christian choice. The Schmidts by then had moved away to a Chicago suburb. The Masefield's first involvement in co-marital sex started with Susan and a widowered close friend. That relationship was to last a lifetime. Since then, for over three decades, my wife and I have each had several sexually enriched friendships. Most of these friendships have lasted for years to decades. Among them, there have been two "foursomes." This is the story of one of them.

Go back in time and mood—if you can. 1968: Martin Luther King's assassination. I was visiting at the Schmidt's that evening on one of my frequent business trips. Robert Kennedy's assassination, the Democratic Convention, Nixon's election: downers all for liberals. The public arena was bleak as a venue for self-expression. Not so the private. Sex was very in. Esalen beckoned, encounter groups proliferated. Bodies and souls were being bared all around us. The Schmidts and Masefields were at the center of all these swirling vortices of ideas and participation. It was Lew who "popped" the question to Susan on a football weekend when I was out of town: Why shouldn't or couldn't these four who'd known each other so well and so long increase their intimacy, strengthen their friendship by adding a new partner? That question did it. The lid was off. It did not lead to any increase in intimate contact but to, literally, hundreds and thousands of hours of discussion, reading, worrying, being stimulated by the idea, and so on. That this went on for two or three years was evidence of how seriously and deliberately we entered into that new relationship. Our values were paramount.

Sexual Dynamics in a Foursome

Although both marriages were very secure, entering into a parallel sexual relationship has to bring an element of threat and competition. It is not as crude as penis or breast sizes, but there was a "shake down" period of half a dozen to a dozen overnights or weekends together before the four of us were fully comfortable with the idea that once or twice a month we would simply pair up in a hotel or at home with the other spouse. Recall that Susan and I had a decade or more of experience in this "lifestyle." That in fact we both had other sexual partners in parallel and you can see that in some ways we were the initial tutors—psychologically and, as it happened, sexually. Both couples claimed to have rich, full sex lives. They were. But one was a meat-and-pota-toes kind, the other a multi-course meal. Susan was not only very multi-orgasmic, but she had many "erogenous zones" that led to orgasm. I smile with pleasure at the recollection of Barbara's "unmaiden" voyage.

Intercourse for the Schmidts was in the missionary position, and with careful attention to detail, which in most cases brought Barbara to a vaginal orgasm followed by Lew's very energetic and noisy orgasm! So on our first time out, Barbara with all the enormous excitement, came very quickly and was surprised and puzzled that I didn't "come," and wondered what she had failed to do. I said, "Nothing," and continued very gently inside her. She couldn't believe that she was "getting excited" again. And when she came the second time with a profound shaking and shuddering and sobbing, she couldn't get over it. Twice in a night!! She became suddenly "guilty"—I would recall this later. "This never happened with Lew ... perhaps it isn't right ... It's too good!! ... " Should she have "richer" sexual experiences out-side the official pair? This issue haunted her for years. Barbara also was some-what anxious about how well Lew was doing with Susan. He seemed almost too happy, too relaxed, too self-confident. After about six months, we agreed that rather than "keep score" and try to balance things out when the visits were not symmetrical, that it simply made sense to maximize the co-marital sexual contacts, since they were infrequent anyway.

Within a couple of years, Barbara and I had an extraordinary sex life. She turned out to be omni-erogenous. Not only vagina, clitoris, nipples, ears, but she would orgasm in response to kissing or biting on any part of the body. Quite literally she would have a couple of hundred orgasms an hour. Oral sex, if not brand new, was experienced liberally by Barbara for the first time. She was sure vaginal entry from the rear was "impossible for her body," until she became addicted to it. Lew Schmidt, while very watchful and wondering what his wife could be doing for so long when he went to the bathroom, had himself gained a new self-confidence. He was enormously proud of the fact that another man's wife, with her husband's permission, would take his cock in her mouth, and even bring him to orgasm that way.

The four of us always showered together. Barbara reveled, with Lew's approval, in filling two hands with two erect penises while the two men massaged her breasts and other parts. The two couples shared very active church lives, vacations, and visits to the extent that the cross-marital sexual activity (averaging well over once a week) was much more than the average for married couples of their age. Moreover, it was of much higher quality. Indeed, the fact was that each couple spent more time and sexual energy in the crossed pair than in the straight. This didn't bother Susan and me—we had even other partners, but it may have worried both Lew and Barbara for different reasons.

Barbara by this time was a public advocate for experimentation within marriage with new sexual partners. She "flirted" to sub-intercourse levels with several men, but she seemed reluctant to "go all the way." The reason for this, it eventually transpired, was that she could not grant Lew the same freedom. Each of them had (at least) one other "consummated" relationship—again with good friends—but the sexual component lasted only some months.

The foursome became inseparable for about another fifteen years. Then warning signs appeared but went unrecognized. First, health. Both Barbara and Lew had major surgery, on more than one occasion. Lew retired followed by Barbara. The Masefields were still working. Life patterns were changing. Grandchildren played a bigger role in the Schmidt's lives. They took long vacations to Europe, Latin America, China—and they took along other couples on these jaunts. In our conversations, again Barbara could not articulate why, but she felt that the sexual component should be cut back. Of course this was done—with the backing and filling that the ambivalence demanded.

Barbara and Lew were socially and religiously moving to the center—away from radical church views and radical social postures.

Forty-five years of friendship, twenty incredibly enriched by adding sexual intimacy, are now on hold. No one quite knows why. In the context of this volume, it is not inappropriate to speculate on the why. Susan has it all sorted out, when the professional therapist in her appears. Lifestyle and values, she says, make such co-marital relationships last.

The Schmidts' home has returned to a more traditional church where they can never champion, leave alone provide reinforcement for such alternative lifestyles. Age and diminishing sex drive play into it, and the lifestyle of upper-middle class retirees. Deep down, however, as I recall Barbara's early reluctance, her cries of "Why should such good things happen to me.... It's too good ... Not again ... It can't be true...." I agree with Susan's analysis. Her values have changed back to Midwestern, mainstream church. If once, why not again. All we need to work out now is to restore the friendship to a non-sexual, warm supportive one.

Looking back over this history, I find it resonates perfectly with the title and theme of this book. Susan and I could never have become involved with Luther and Barbara had we not shared with them a specifically Christian commitment. Our radical faith stance made possible our radical social stance. The later stages of our forty-five year friendship shows even more clearly how closely the spiritual and sexual are intertwined, and how closely the spiritual controls the carnal. As Barbara and Luther's faith stance became increasingly traditional, in spite of three decades of affirmation and experience with another style of incarnated (in the flesh) self-expression, we could no longer continue on that level when the spiritual backbone that gave form to that self-expression was no longer there. One solid fact stands out above all others: Susan's and my sexuality are inseparably intertwined. This is just as true for our dearest friends.

In the late eighties, we traveled to a retreat led by James B. Nelson on "Embodiment" at a place called Kirkridge. Something Jack Nelson, a founder of Kirkridge, said during that conference has stuck firmly in my mind because it was something I am finding increasingly difficult to avoid admitting. Jack was recalling a conversation he and William Swartley, a long-time student of Carl Jung's in Zurich and founder of The Center for the Whole Person, had years ago with the Kirkridge retreat leaders who dealt with sex and marriage. Swartley was talking about the deep pain even avant-garde clergy and laity experience in affirming non-traditional sexual patterns.

"Jack, we are trying to get traditionally-raised Christians to really live and affirm sex. To be honest, I think that is impossible." Our experience has certainly proved that. Only those who remain **rooted and radical in their faith** can explore and grow in sexual patterns that run counter to the traditional church values.

One God, One Spouse?

Robert T. Francoeur

Basic in both the Jewish and Christian faiths is belief in a "jealous God," who does not tolerate any rivals, any idolatry. At the same time, although the kings and patriarchs of Israel had many wives and concubines, the creation story of Adam and Eve clearly spells out monogamy, one spouse for life, as the basis of our sexual morality and ideal of marriage. No idolatry, no adultery! But does belief in one God necessarily require that sexual love be limited to a husband and wife?

For 3,000 years, religious thinkers have linked monotheism and monogamy. Phonetically they go together nicely. Consequently, we believe that when it comes to one's girlfriend or boyfriend, one's husband or wife, a little jealousy is a sure sign of healthy, true love.

Besides, any deviation from sexually exclusive pairbonding takes a lot of effort. Everyone knows how difficult it is to keep a marriage healthy, dynamic, and faithful when we marry in our twenties and expect to, but often do not, remain together until we die 50, 60, or more years later. It has to be more challenging and difficult to include one or more satellite or co-marital friendships within the living fabric of a primary relationship than to maintain a sexually exclusive marriage. How does one nourish the love and responsibilities of a marriage or other primary relationship, and keep that love up front, when a co-marital or satellite friendship starts up with all the fascination of new passion and intense communications? How does one balance the old and the new, the primary and the satellite? Maybe it makes sense to link

❖   ❖   ❖

Robert T. Francoeur, one of the editors of this volume, is a Fellow of the Society for the Scientific Study of Sexuality, a married Catholic priest, and author of *Hot and Cool Sex: Cultures in Conflict* and many other books.

belief in one God and one spouse, "forsaking all others, until death do us part."

But does monogamy, the commitment to a single spouse, necessarily require sexual exclusivity? These stories, and the long and varied history of marriage in the Jewish and Christian traditions, clearly challenge the assumption that monogamy equals sexual exclusivity. Many people may equate the two, but some, like our storytellers, are struggling to explore their sexuality and spirituality with new definitions of fidelity and commitment and new patterns of loving friendships.

In his many creative writings on sexuality and spirituality, theologian James B. Nelson reminds us that Jesus taught and lived a radical monotheism that relativizes everything else. Neither monogamy nor sexual exclusivity qualifies as absolutes. But Jesus also taught a radical incarnationalism that bids us take very seriously, though not absolutely, our fleshly commitments and limitations. We live in tension, without absolutes — save one God — but also with serious commitments like love, fidelity, and responsibility for the ongoing creation of ourselves and others.

We live "between the times." We are not yet in the New Age, because we still live with our distortions, limitations. Some still see these distortions and limitations coming from our "fallen" nature. I prefer seeing them as part of our still rising and converging consciousness and nature, part of our ongoing creation. The radical consciousness of the New Age, the New Kingdom announced by Jesus, has dawned and is invading us. The ambiguities of our pilgrim lives "between the times" require that we not make absolute claims of what is right or wrong for all people. Convinced that love is central, these storytellers ask us to listen to their experiences, share our own stories with others, and pray that our paths have integrity and are life-giving.

20. A Single Woman's Journey

Cynthia

I used to think that being married was the be-all and end-all of happiness; that is, until I was married. Having remained in partnership for fourteen years and divorced for sixteen years, I have enjoyed and abhorred quite a number of relationships along the way, making for a fairly nontraditional lifestyle.

Quietly dancing on the edge has been a lifetime experience for me so far — sometimes pleasurable, other times agonizing and depressing. I have managed to fit into the "real" world and yet carry an enigmatic eccentric quality — a professional with an artistic flair and a never-ending smile on her face. Still unmated, a melange of experiences, adventures, and escapades has been synthesized into my present-day life.

I began a caravan of short-term relationships while still struggling in my marriage. My partner was a fine human being, a caring husband and father and yet, I was miserable and restless. After a few affairs and the incessant oppression of guilt after having been discovered during the final affair, rage and personal upheaval led to counseling and finally, a divorce.

As a newly released woman in her mid-thirties, vibrant and filled with a healthy zest for life, I began a relationship with a twenty-five-year-old wild sort: biker, drug-user, night-owl. Lovemaking was exciting and dangerous; we were almost always "high." Pot, LSD, hashish, amphetamines, and cocaine accompanied us everywhere. After a year and a half, my vibrancy and zest for life had been expended. This runaway train ride was over.

After a few months recovery, I set out every weekend to investigate gay bars. Throbbing music, flashing lights, and sweating bodies drew me in. I danced unabashedly, flesh sliding over flesh, arms and legs writhing in an unbridled rhythm, exchanging hot breath and intermingling sweat — lewd movements butt to butt and pelvis to pelvis: sex with clothes on.

Sometimes I would take home a man, sometimes a gay couple, and the tempestuousness continued through the night. The next day was perpetually followed by remorse. I sat musing, nursing an aching head and spirit in an empty house. I began to recognize the misery and restlessness I perceived during my marriage. It was time for some serious self-examination.

I then embarked upon a rather unorthodox psychological growth process, focusing upon reshaping my own relationship with myself and healing my woundedness. During this time, a period of twelve years, I engaged in various heterogeneous partnerships lasting on the average of two years each. My lovers included a business manager, a chemist, a school student, a carpenter, an accountant, a private school fundraiser, and a college professor. As my relationship with myself had healed and deepened, so had my relationships with others become more intimate.

A few summers ago, I encountered a most mystical relational experience when I met T.J. We were visiting mutual friends in a secluded spot in the mountains. A few days passed as I took time to surrender to the gentle, delicious, restorative gifts of nature. Breathing in the clear, warm air, soaking up the sun's healing rays, and dancing with the trees and grasses brought me into a state of joyous relaxation.

In this ecstatic state, T.J. and I made love in many ways as we connected our breath, bodies, and energies. Sometimes we sat perfectly still, watching the bees pollinate the flowers. Sometimes we lay spine-to-spine, sensing the energy flow up and down, in and throughout. When we made love physically, we breathed alive our passion, purposefully intensifying a vibrating electric energy which encircled our own bodies and spun like a whirlwind through each other.

While embracing, we mutually visualized what was happening in the meeting place of our hearts as we held each other close. We both saw an endless green meadow strewn with bright, dancing flowers and gamboling sheep. A boy and a girl were soaring on a swing which hung from an apple tree branch, their feet reaching for the sky, their faces lit with sunshine pleasure. They were young and free and happy as could be! We snuggled together in that warm, loving energy, luxuriating in the mystical embrace. These times were for us, a very high experience of lovemaking and intimacy. After many years of searching, I had finally been gifted with a taste of the marrow of the kind of relationship for which I longed so intensely.

Fifteen years ago, I began my sexual/spiritual quest without really having a clear picture of what I was searching for. Seeking body/spirit oneness is quite a mysterious process. I had heretofore gathered and tended to all the essentials of life my mom told me would make me feel fulfilled, satisfied, and happy: a good education, a secure job, a comfortable home, a responsible husband, and beautiful children. This combination just didn't do it for me. There were the makings of a huge fire out there somewhere, still left unkindled. Were they there for me to seek out and find outside myself, or were they really, perhaps, somewhere inside my soul?

I struggled with staying in my highly successful, conventional life. For many this would have been the realization of an ideal. I knew, however, that I had to break free and so chose to follow a persistent call — the call to light the fire and to connect with the divine. Through the practice of yoga and going into deep psychological-spiritual work, I began to tear down walls and to open myself to the discovery and knowing of my own soul. This was a bone with a lot of meat on which to chew and much marrow to suck out, and I continue, even now to relish these delicious morsels.

Through picking and savoring, and even sometimes spitting pieces out, I have assimilated some of the wisdom contained in the bone. A part of this wisdom tells me that the physical body is an essential vehicle for knowing God. Through yoga, exercising what Margo Anand calls "the inner flute," and practicing rebirthing techniques, I have been able to strengthen my body and open her to know, accept, and receive the spirit of the divine. This spirit, I believe, brings itself into us as the very air we breathe. Air, to me, is the manifestation of the divine spirit. It is nothing and everything and is absolutely essential for our fully realized alikeness. In our deciding to unfold, we extricate ourselves from the armor of our former lives and then expose the tender, vulnerable self within and create the possibility of nurturing and intimately sharing this new self.

There are many ways we can shed our armor, unlock our souls, and strengthen our physical beings. The practice of erotic sex is an avenue of empowering and maintaining the body/spirit connection. In practical terms, the combination of sensual body movement and deep conscious breathing can ignite passion in every cell of our beings and bring us thoroughly to life. This awakening, culminating in total-body orgasm, shows us the way to the treasure of knowing the oneness of the flesh and of God. In this state I become consciously submerged into the deepest parts of my physical self, while simultaneously, I am released from the constrictions of this corporeal entity so I soar with wild abandon in the realm of the divine.

Through dancing, doing yoga or T'ai Chi, lifting weights, engaging in sexual experiences, and following other similar disciplines, we can keep the body strong and flexible. Exercising, practicing specific breathing techniques such as rebirthing, and spending time in the wondrous realm of Mother Nature, enlivens our souls and bodies. For the fire of light and passion to roar, the fuel of the flesh and the air of the divine spirit, two essential components, must unite. We have the choice of taking in this fire energy, passion — the eternal flame that surrounds and penetrates us at every moment — and use it to expand our sexual/spiritual union. We can learn to surrender to the fire and to the music of our own being in everything we do. For example, sometimes I dance the passion-fire of my inner music with a partner, sometimes with a friend, sometimes with a tree or a dragonfly, and often with myself. The mystical union is not relegated to the sexual act alone. As our experiences in the integration of sex and spirit grow, we become more and more conscious of our burning alikeness and the many opportunities we have to live and express this alikeness. I am truly thankful for my time with T.J. and the many mystical revelations of our union.

I encourage anyone of any age to practice breathing techniques, to keep the body in excellent shape, and to surround oneself with nature. For me, these are the ingredients of the fire of life, the highest connection of Heaven (the Spirit) and Earth (the Body). It is a gift we may all choose to receive and to cherish. Say "YES" to the fire of the union of Sex and Spirit!

21. The Runaway's Story

Judy Harrow

Sometimes the blessings come hard. It was that way for me. Sometimes the only way to get Home is by running away from somewhere else.

I was born in 1945, in New York City, Jewish. That means I was raised among firsthand memories of the Holocaust, and in the first, triumphant years of Israeli independence. There was not much actual religious education in my family, even less for the girls. Instead we were taught an intense tribal loyalty that bordered on xenophobia. We were constantly reminded how many generations of our ancestors had endured intense persecution to preserve our heritage. We, who were safe and free, were beholden to the memories of those martyrs. We must always cherish their legacy.

Yes, I felt that pride, and I still do. And yet, my heritage did not nurture me psychologically or spiritually. As a female, I was to be hidden in a balcony, behind a curtain. Public participation in the religion, let alone any leadership role, was completely denied me. At that time, there was no celebration of a young girl's religious coming of age, as there was for the boys. We were told that our place was at home, preparing meals and raising children—that religious study and prayer was something for men to do.

It seems to me that people have different talents and temperaments, which we express, as we grow up, as different interests. In a healthy community, every talent is nurtured so people can contribute their own unique gifts to the vibrant, complex life of the whole. Nobody is held back from their own potential by irrelevancies such as gender. But back then, years before the ordination of the first woman rabbi, there was no place in the Jewish community for girls with the temperament for spiritual exploration and the talent for ritual.

It's just a little bit ironic that my spiritual path began at a summer camp sponsored by the Jewish community. Some summer camps specialize in sports, community service, theater—these days, even in computers—but the one I went to back in the fifties specialized in camping, in "woodcraft." We did hikes, cookouts, nature study, and sometimes we would sleep out on the ground, under the moon.

There I first heard the forest speak. Only in a whisper, way back then. Most of the message eluded me, perhaps because I lacked the words and concepts with which to explain Immanence to myself. All I could ever retain was a sense of Presence, of the living, and loving, spirit of the woods. But I was tantalized.

In due course, I acquired a college degree, my own apartment, and my first lover. Seems a little quaint now to have done them in that order, but it was still the early sixties. Two years later, that first sexual relationship came to an end. And then I spent two lonely years, involuntarily chaste, in that little apartment. In retrospect, I went through a major depression. I slept most of the day and listened to radio talk shows all night. The first year of that behavior flunked me out of law school. The second year, I was just plain unemployed. Well, sometimes the blessings do come hard.

Had I not been a lot lonely and a little desperate, I probably would never have listened to Brian. He wanted an open relationship. I was afraid and embarrassed. No one had ever said such a thing to me. I took the risk only because I felt I had nothing to lose. I was so lonely and without purpose, anything had to be an improvement. Freedom, I have since learned, is very much more than just another word for "nothing left to lose." Still, sometimes emptiness creates the space for fullness to come.

Brian and I first made love on the fourth of July in 1972. We still count that day as our anniversary. Our relationship was open from the beginning. It still is. Back at the beginning, though, both of us were new at open relationships. We had no role models to go by, no support systems, nowhere to seek advice. Does this sound familiar? We thought we were the only ones in the world. And we didn't know what to do about jealousy.

Somewhere I heard about Family Synergy, a support group that existed at that time (and today) for people in open and group marriages. We contacted them, and joined. Soon, I read in the newsletter that they were asking people to serve as Area Representatives, to begin to create groups and activities outside Los Angeles. Brian and I volunteered, and got a New York chapter going.

We had a monthly meeting. Each month we invited a speaker. Anybody even halfway local who had written a book or article on alternative family forms got invited. The authors responded generously. Brian and I claimed the organizers' privilege of taking the speaker out to dinner before each meeting. Our elders, our guides answered some of our own beginners' questions, even though they constantly reminded us they had "no answers, only some better questions." Those evenings included delightful, informative discussions with Jim Ramey on *Intimate Friendships,* Bob Francoeur on *Hot and Cool Sex,* John and Mimi Lobell on their open marriage, and others.

Through being active in Family Synergy, and having contact with people in alternative families all over the country, I became concerned about the lack of family counseling services for people like us. More than once I heard the story about some complex family that had some very normal conflict about money, or housework, or childrearing (or even jealousy). When they sought counseling help, they were told that the first thing they needed to do was to become monogamous.

In September of 1975, I enrolled in a graduate program in counseling. I completed my master's in 1979. The woman who flunked out of law school nine years earlier earned a perfect 4.0 average in the counseling program.

The study of counseling is, in part, the study of the communication between people. Marriage counseling for alternative families was my primary interest in entering graduate school. But the study of interpersonal communication soon leads to the issues of personal psychological growth, because, if I am not clear who I am and what I need, how can I tell you? And if I am stuck in my own blockages, how shall I hear you?

After all these years, I still can't say where psychology stops and spirituality starts. My experience was that one leads to the other, very fast.

And my interest in Goddess worship, in Earth religion, was dawning. The forest had spoken to me, since childhood. She was beginning to speak more clearly. But, again, I thought I was the only one. And again, I was not.

Actually, Goddess worship had been revived in England during the 1930s and 1940s, brought to this country by English immigrants in the early 1960s. By the time I found it, in the mid-seventies, it was beginning to take root and grow here. In 1979, that growth was to be multiplied by the publication of two remarkable books. But that was later. In 1975, followers of the Earth religions were many fewer, far harder to find than we are now.

I vividly remember sitting in the classroom on my first evening in graduate school, waiting for the professor to arrive, reading the first issue of my first subscription to a neo-Pagan magazine. Still, I did not look for people to worship with, nor tell anybody but Brian of my interest. It was just too weird.

And besides, how could I betray all those Jewish martyrs by changing my religion?

Sometimes the blessing comes hard. Sometimes freedom really does begin after we have nothing left to lose. Brian and I were talking marriage. Both of us feel strongly about keeping vows once taken. We could not in honor marry "according to the laws of Moses and of Israel," vowing ourselves to an exclusivity we had no intention to live.

At some level, I believe that all religions are human creations. The Sacred is what It is, beyond our capacity to understand or describe. All our descriptions are necessarily limited, neither more nor less than our best approximations. The symbols, stories, and rituals we create are a way of telling ourselves and each other what really matters to us, expressions of those values on which we base our lives. For me, one of those core values is that love is infinite, and should be free. Another, if the things of the Earth are sacred, is the holiness of passionate, physical loving. I needed a religious path that could wholeheartedly affirm these values, but I was not yet aware of that. I was still trying to fit myself into a familiar, but Procrustean, bed.

There was a conference on alternative family styles held in Washington, D.C., sometime during those years. If you were there, you might remember me. I was the one asking if anybody knew a Rabbi willing to help us create a wedding ceremony expressing our own values about marriage. Nobody at the conference could make a referral.

When I got home, I called a Jewish feminist magazine. They suggested a local Rabbi known for his radical views. We called him. He agreed to meet with us. And then he asked me out. I accepted the date.

I knew the Rabbi wanted to have sex with me, and I was willing. We lived in a tiny, one-bedroom apartment then, so Brian arranged to be out for the evening. Then the Rabbi asked if we could move our date to another night the same week. I told him that would mean no privacy, and he agreed.

We sat on a park bench, watching the sun set over the Hudson. The Rabbi got crude. He began to grope and to pressure me for "more" like a sweaty-palmed high school boy back in the fifties. He had neither sensitivity nor respect for my feelings about privacy. It didn't go all the way to date rape, but it got too damn close. By the time I got home, I felt shocked, soiled, and thoroughly disillusioned.

I had run into the old double standard, the assumption that a woman who says yes to more than one man has forfeited her right to say no in any circumstances, even on a public park bench. He was not a progressive, just a hypocrite.

This is not to imply that all Rabbis are that way. The vast majority of Rabbis would have been far more shocked than I was by that guy's behavior. They are, by the teachings of their religion, committed to a monogamous lifestyle. But, because they do honor their traditions, neither would the vast majority of Rabbis have considered helping Brian and me create an honest wedding ceremony for ourselves. So, it seemed, there was no place for me in Judaism.

Of course, there are plenty of secular Jews living in open relationships. Many of them have participated in conventional marriage ceremonies without thinking seriously about the public pledges they were making. But I love ritual, and take it seriously. And I wanted a religion in which I could participate fully, even lead.

In retrospect, perhaps I could have found an appropriate Jewish context for myself, somewhere, if I had only looked hard enough. In retrospect, I suppose I really didn't want to. The forest had spoken to me. My Mother the Earth was waiting for my love and service. But those generations of martyrs held me in bonds of guilt. How could I abandon them? It took a strong psychic shock to break me loose. It hurt, at the time, a lot. The loss set me free. The blessing came hard. No other way it could have come, I think, and I am only thankful that it came at all.

I found a group and a teacher. I was initiated as a priestess of the Goddess in September of 1977. At Midsummer of 1980, I started a Circle of my own, which is still flourishing. In 1984, I served as national president of our church, Covenant of the Goddess. In 1985, after a five-year legal battle, I became the first of our clergy legally empowered to perform marriages in New York City.

Those are historical events, numbers on a calendar. What is far more important, but much harder to describe, is what has happened with my inner life. I have found a symbology and ritual that expresses my own deepest values, and a young, vibrant, growing community and culture that supports my development.

We call ourselves neo-Pagans. We are polytheists. Polytheism gives mythic and theological validation to all forms of diversity, including diversity in relationships. And we are immanentists, worshipers of Mother Earth, who place ultimate meaning and value in this life on this Earth, here and now.

We celebrate our bodies as part of the Nature we hold sacred. We are taught that all acts of love and pleasure are rituals of the Goddess. When we open to each other in love, we can see the Sacred Presence shining from each other's eyes. At those moments of high intimacy, giving pleasure is giving worship. We listen to the Sacred voices in the forest.

The forest speaks to all of us. With help, I have learned how to hear Her much better. My life is coherent now. My values, my religious practices, and my daily life all reinforce each other. In a very real sense, the process began when I took that Fool's leap off the precipice into an open relationship with Brian. The reality of our love eventually forced me to reconsider all my other habits of mind and spirit. The blessing came hard, yes, but it came in abundance.

So, in July of 1993, Brian and I celebrated our twenty-first anniversary. We threw a great big party at a friend's house out in the suburbs. "All these years of adultery," we joked, "and now the relationship is finally an adult." We thought that was as good as it would get. Well, Aphrodite still had some surprises left for me.

In September, I met Gwyneth. Since I was a lifelong heterosexual, I figured she'd be a close and fascinating friend. At Vernal Equinox, 1994, we became betrothed, and we married at Summer Solstice in that same suburban backyard. Gwyn and I purposely deferred physical expression of our love until after we'd exchanged our vows. We were saying to each other, our friends, and our Gods that we chose to commit to each other without first proving that I could make the transition to bisexuality. So I got to be the last thing I ever expected to be—a virgin bride. That hour of privacy we took after the ritual and before joining the reception surely was Aphrodite's own marriage gift!

A Handfasting ritual is what it sounds like. The guests were invited to bring something, some sort of ribbon or cord that would symbolize their wish for us, their personal blessing, as they joined our hands together. One was a beautifully hand-crocheted band in symbolic patterns and shades of Aphrodite's own pink. Another was a brown scapular of Our Lady of Mount Carmel. One friend used computer cable to connect us, since we live in different cities part of the time. One used saran wrap "to keep your love fresh." You get the picture: a huge bundle of bright bindings, a talisman of our marriage.

First and best of all was Brian, my best friend and lover of twenty-two years, blessing us from his heart, happy to see me happy, happy to share.

Brian and I never actually did marry, although we still live and love together. Religion and ritual are simply not his cup of tea. Gwyneth, like me, is a priestess, and now she is what Brian did not care to be, my working partner, co-leader of my Circle.

It's worked out just exactly as the O'Neills said so many years ago in their book *Open Marriage*. People are complex and multifaceted. No one person can fill all of another person's needs. No two people are interchangeable parts. With each lover, I can express a different aspect of myself. All of them collectively do what no one of them individually ever could: they love me into wholeness. Generous Aphrodite be thanked!

Sometimes I wonder about the father of my old tribe, Abraham the runaway, and what he might say to me now. Although I left the home he made, perhaps I still followed his example. Centuries ago, God told Abraham: "Go forth from the land of your kinsfolk and from your father's house to a land that I will show you" (Genesis 12:1). So I heard the voice of the forest, of the Goddess, my Mother, the Earth. By running away, I found my own people, my own Home.

22. Reclaiming Lost Sexuality– A Man's Journey

Lawrence Davies

Being an obedient Baptist child of the clergy meant that I did not dance, drink, smoke, or masturbate. I was a virgin when I married at twenty-five, an important accomplishment, I thought, until I realized that I did not know the first thing about my own sexuality, let alone the sexuality of a woman. It made it very difficult connecting with her. But, being raised to be good meant that if anything was wrong, it must be her fault. I was safe in my righteous tower. She of course did not agree with me. In fact she went to great lengths to point out my faults, of course to no avail. I was not home. I was too busy sprucing up the exterior of my life to pay much attention to the interior. With the best of intentions, my loving parents along with the churches they served, groomed me to be innocent. And the goodness for which I strove resulted in a subtly covered righteousness that learned to direct others in the journey but not to take my own journey. I had mastered the skill of ironic detachment. Underneath, I was always longing for someone to approve of me. My wife definitely didn't.

I finished a couple of master's degrees in theology, considerable clinical pastoral education, and a whole new set of techniques that *helped me think my feelings without really feeling them.* Then, with the advantage of being a male in the culture, I used all of these systems to protect my righteousness. Looking back, I see that she must have been going increasingly mad at having no confirmation of the reality she saw in front of her. Alas, I had been betrayed by my upbringing in righteous innocence. She was being betrayed daily by the denials of the man she wanted to love.

My first test came when my shaky thirteen-year marriage fell apart. We did everything we could, both to make it work and to destroy it. But it had been a death embrace from the start. Now everything was in ashes with no sign of a Phoenix anywhere. I still wanted her — but only because I think I lost the competition with an old lover she had embraced. I found it harder and harder to cope with simple things in my life. When picking up my children,

195

I found it excruciating to knock on the door of a house in which I had once lived and for which I still paid the mortgage. I remember moments when I could barely formulate words with my friends where before I had functioned with silky grace. I had been president of everything I joined. I had moved with courage in challenging the old order with new leadership in a radical experimental house church, but now slunk off out of the limelight into a small office where I could counsel with people who were as wounded as I.

Strangely, my life had finally begun!

I met a woman. Because I had failed in the first marriage so totally in spite of my best efforts, I eyed this new woman a long time before I let myself fall in love. That certainly was a newfound ability. It was incredible to me that anyone could love me, this empty shell. But she seemed open, loving, and intent on having me in her life. I could see that she was sought after by many others, so it was not by default. I was clearly her choice. She said that God told her that I was the one she was to go with.

Ironically, it was partly because of that love that I became aware of the inner work I had to do. The work was the exploration of other women, work I had neglected in the earlier years of repressed sexuality and Baptist piety. It was no longer acceptable to me to attempt to commit myself to this woman if I were secretly wishing that I might be with several others on the side. The legalistic commitment in my previous marriage had not worked. It was time for me to gather up all of myself. It was time to make a total commitment. It was time to offer all of myself to this woman who surely deserved my full presence.

I did it with the guidance of a story. One of the benefits of growing up in the church and taking part in the bathrobe-costumed dramas is that you see your life always as part of a larger story. Therefore, I had never been in any situation that did not have a Biblical story to speak to it. For this journey, however, I had to look beyond the Bible into Greek mythology where sex was more openly embraced. The story that jumped into my consciousness was the ordeal of Ulysses returning from the Trojan wars finding his way back to his wife, Penelope. He had heard about the enticing sirens who called to sailors from the bank of the river. He had also heard that these men became so entranced by the sounds of these beautiful women that they crashed their boats on the rocks below. So he crafted a way of listening without being destroyed. He blocked the ears of his oarsmen with wax and had himself bound to the mast with ropes. His blood ran hot, just like my own. I understood perfectly why he had to see and listen to the sights and sounds of the sirens beckoning from the bank. Like his, my blood longed for the mystery of woman, indeed the mystery of the Goddess. It was time to move into my manhood. It was time to lose my innocence. I knew the danger of crashing on the psychological rocks but I had to do it.

But in order to do it I had to have a context for exploring the excess that leads to wisdom. I needed a loving community where I could be forgiven not only for the Pharisee that I had been, but also for the licentious sinner I was consciously choosing to become. By the grace of God, I found such a community, where we were focused on process rather than outcome, where success was not the accomplishment of a dream but the willingness to dream the biggest dream you could imagine, where we were forgiven before we sinned, not after—a true world of grace. It made an otherwise impossible journey possible.

It turned out to be a glorious time. I realized the power of being a man. I did not have to talk a woman into anything. She seemed turned on simply by the power, by authentic presence. She was even more turned on, in fact, entranced, by gazing into the full extent of a man's dark and light energies. I started to know, from the inside, the power of Shiva who holds a focused energy, who knows the importance of simply "being there," who calls to his Shakti to enter into the full power of her vulnerability, to trust finally that she can let go of her wild energies, without reserve. I knew that a woman's deepest fear was not like a man's—that she would be powerless. Rather she feared that if she fully let go, she would go crazy, flying into a million pieces. She needed focused consciousness to compliment her diffused awareness. Castenada's words rang daily in my ears, "A man contains, and a woman leads." I began to understand that the "containing" of a woman was not to build a box around her, but rather to hold a focus on which she could gaze, a focus centered not only in his phallus, but also in his whole being. With her eyes on that living tree, she was safe to let go into her full nature.

There were several times when I simply got drunk with the power of it all. And several times when I was not able to sustain that focus and I collapsed in an ignominious heap. But by some amazing grace, I struggled to my feet and stood. I expected no approval for this behavior and got none. In fact, much of what I got was anger, judgment, preaching, disdain. There was also a patronizing, "Oh, he'll get over his womanizing soon." But for me, it was not a matter of getting over it but of going through it to the other side. After I completed the "ordeal," I felt as though I was bringing to my woman the greatest gift I had ever given to anyone. Not surprisingly, she was not overwhelmed with gratitude or delight. She had gone through her own ordeal, feeling very bruised along the way. Nevertheless her willingness to "hang in" with me over what turned out to be seven years, left me feeling as though she had held a light in her window, a light that guided me home not only to her but also to myself.

Curiously I was not punished by those around me as severely as the law might have demanded. I have wondered if it was because of the loving intent that I carried throughout the process. Or because people, especially women, intuitively knew the extent of the hollowness of men in our culture, and were willing to support the journey of a man who was at least trying to open the gates of his interior strength. In a strange and surprising way, even though I did not deserve it, I felt supported underneath.

The journey led me to believe that it might be possible for a woman in her full power to join a man in his. This led me to a great optimism between the sexes. I got visions that it might be possible for men and women to be radically different, an out-of-step thing to say when so much of our culture is screaming for equality and sameness. In the workplace, yes. But in the bedroom, a meeting of radically different but equally powerful energies. That a man needs to explore the full extent of his focused masculine power, to maintain and sustain his erect consciousness. And that a woman needs to open every cell in her body to the possibility of letting go, not in helpless submission, but in powerful surrender. When these two energies meet, they spin together into the presence of the Divine, giving men total access to the feminine mystery, and women total access to the masculine mystery. With this vision, I discovered that I was not just on a journey to come home to a woman. I was coming home to myself.

Sex Before and After the Resurrection

James B. Nelson

As a Christian, I affirm the words of the ancient creed, "I believe in the resurrection of the body." What the resurrection of the body means after death is a mystery to me. But whatever the symbol means, it does affirm bodies. The Christian resurrection vision attempts to say that in whatever mysterious form God's eternal love holds us, we are not now and will not be disembodied spirits. Matter matters to God. God loves bodies.

The trouble with those theologies that urge us to kill off the body by denying its goodness and spiritual significance, is that we do not kill the body so much as consign it to hell. And hell is the place of the dead who cannot accept their death—it is, indeed, the place of the "undead." In fact, the lifelessness of our flesh may be our world's most serious danger. For when bodies are deprived of eros they inevitably become champions of thanatos—and take distorted pleasure in death and destruction.

But there are many different ways that persons of faith have been attempting to name themselves with an ethics of bodily life—and resurrec-

❖   ❖   ❖

James B. Nelson, professor emeritus of Christian Ethics at United Theological Seminary of the Twin Cities in Minnesota, has been a pioneer in the quest to reunite sexuality and spirituality in a holistic Christian perspective. Among his many important books are *Embodiment: An Approach to Sexuality and Christian Theology* (1978), *Between Two Gardens: Reflections on Sexuality and Religious Experience* (1983), *The Intimate Connection: Male Sexuality and Masculine Spirituality* (1991), *Body Theology* (1992), and *Sexuality and the Sacred: Sources for Theological Reflection* (1994).

tion. Some are lesbian, gay, and bisexual persons of faith who have refused the intolerable choice that many in religion and culture try to force upon them—between choosing God and becoming desexualized or claiming the goodness of their sexuality and denying their spiritually. That is an unholy choice, and in the face of such oppressive attempts many gay, lesbian, and bisexual persons have refused to give up their passion for life-giving touch and connection. They have named and claimed an erotic body spirituality.

Another example: many feminist women are renaming their menstrual experience. No longer a taboo, ritual uncleanness, or the curse. Nor is it simply a regrettable inconvenience. It can be sacred power. Such women thus are experiencing and renaming this connection to the flow of life itself. They are naming their body's Sabbath time of renewal and rebirthing, the rhythm connecting them to the deep cyclical rhythms of creation's divine energy. I take it that such renamings of menstruation are far more than a romanticizing of an unpleasant reality. They are ways of embracing a new kind of sacred bodily power.

And the examples provided by the stories in this book. I do not minimize the mixture of motives with which persons can enter into nontraditional sexual relationships. Nor do I minimize the risks to the very values that such persons at their best seek to express. Not everyone will find blessing in what is pictured herein. But some will. And some obviously have. And these are blessings that I, for one, hope that our religious institutions can be more open to in the future. I hope that this book will help that breaking in of the fresh winds of the Spirit.

A Reflection

The 1990s: A Turning Point in Human Relations

Timothy Perper, Martha Cornog, and Robert T. Francoeur

We Americans have changed more in the last thirty years than our ancestors did in the previous three hundred years. In fact, historians commonly agree that no other generation in human history has been confronted with so many radical social changes in such a short time as we have faced since the 1960s.

Whether or not we like these changes, we are being forced to adapt the way we live our lives to fit this new environment. We can't escape to some island paradise of "the good old days." Willing or not, we are changing our fundamental ideas of what love, sex, love, marriage, and family mean to us.

In the twenty-two family snapshots shared by our storytellers, one can easily find a hundred or two men, women, and children more or less affected by the main characters. In a stage play, the main actors are up front, with supporting players. But the stage setting is also important to understanding what the actors are doing. The stage setting provides an essential perspective. Having orchestrated these twenty-two stories, we would like to include in our role as editors a brief stage setting and interpretation. We're comfortable with this because the three of us have been longtime active members of the Society for the Scientific Study of Sexuality. Sexology is one of the professional hats we wear. Combined, we've spent about a hundred years studying and writing about the evolution of human relations.

After we present our stage setting, we would also like to share with you some new insights into what neuroscientists and psychologists have discovered recently about the connections between mystical/spiritual ecstasy and sexual ecstasy and communion. We hope our stage setting and insights into the varieties of ecstasy will give our readers a clearer understanding of the messages in these stories.

Our Stage Setting: A Backdrop of Torrential Social Change

We start with two major brushstrokes:

- LIFE EXPECTANCY
  - Never before in our two-million-year history have humans been expected to marry in their twenties or later and stay happily married for fifty or sixty years.
  - An infant born in 1997 in the U.S. has a one-in-three chance of living for more than a century!

- CONTRACEPTIVES
  - Never before in our two-million-year history have we been able to enjoy sex without the risk of an unwanted pregnancy and with growing protection against sexually transmitted diseases including AIDS.

Doubling our life expectancy in one century and the discovery of hormonal contraceptives and antibiotics make us unique in human history. The reality of "until death do us part" and "forsaking all others" changes significantly when we are talking about fifty, sixty, or more years of marriage instead of ten or twenty years. Especially, when we add in the immediate consequences of our increasing life expectancy and pregnancy control.

Consider some other elements in our stage setting. Please add to our list if you can think of some other important details:

- In this century, women have gained the vote, flooded the workplace, pressed for gender equality, celebrated their sensual/sexual needs, redefined the nature and purpose of sex, challenged sexism, and rejected marital rape and sexual harassment, as they became increasingly independent both economically and psychologically. Since the late 1980s, the ratio of women over men has been increasing in American colleges, with women now outnumbering men on most campuses by two or three to one. The women are also outperforming the men academically.

- — Never before in more than three thousand years has male dominance and social control been so seriously and successfully challenged!

- With effective contraception, legal abortion, and the increasing economic burden of raising children, today's women spend far less of their lives rearing children than their great grandmothers did.

- In the past two decades, thanks to AIDS and the White House scandals, anal and oral sex, masturbation, condoms, affairs, gay and lesbian partnerships and marriages, and even open marriages have become a regular part of public and media discussion.

- Our shrinking families and kin are scattered across a continent, putting a greater than ever burden on the network of friends we include in our "intentional families."

- By the year 2000, three out of every ten American households will be single men and women living alone, yearning for closeness and intimacy, surrounded by neighbors but often acknowledged only by a passing "Hello."

- We travel farther, more often, and faster to enjoy more leisure and variety than any generation in human history, and this mobility, leisure, and variety inevitably affects the ways we relate and the expectations we bring to our intimate relationships.
  - — Think how the automobile, leisure, women in the corporate world, and affordable motels with their readily available anonymity have made extramarital affairs much more feasible than ever before, despite attempts to squash office romance.

- Television, the cinema, magazines, and especially the World Wide Web and Internet have created a wild mix of sexual information and misinformation, along with new, sometimes unrealistic expectations for romantic love, intimacy, togetherness, and sexual satisfaction, for adults, adolescents, and children alike.

With an ever-increasing insistence, these social currents buffet us, the actors on the stage, from every side. Sometimes we adapt instinctively, unaware of how we are changing. Think of how we went from very few divorces in 1900 to our current divorce rate of one in two marriages. At other times, when we become aware of some impending change, we are knocked off balance, puzzled how we can continue to meet our needs for love, intimacy, and family. Panic is a common response, especially on the religious and moral right. "Let's go back to the good old days!" But we know that won't work. Nor can we shove these changes out of sight, out of mind. Sooner or later reality will catch up with us.

Whether or not we admit the radical, unprecedented social forces that surround us on the stage of life, they will continue to affect our lives.

- They have inevitably increased our expectations of our spouses and marriage, often unrealistically beyond the capacity of mere mortals.

- They fuel our sky-rocketing rates of premarital sex—95 percent and rising—single and teenage mothers, extramarital sex, divorce, and remarriage.

- In 1996, a little over half of the hundred million American households were married couples with or without children. That was down from 70 percent in 1970, a drop of 17 percent in just twenty-five years.

- In 1996, some 885,000 Americans were living with a partner to whom they were not married.

- In 1996, one in six Americans over age forty-five was living in a non-traditional family, with non-relatives or non-nuclear-family relatives.

- As we approach the millennium, less than one in six American married couples are following the traditional pattern of bread-winner husband and stay-at-home wife. Fifty years ago, two-thirds of married couples followed this pattern.

These ever-accelerating social forces have also enabled women to move to the forefront of a global revolution in the ways we view sex, love, intimacy, marriage, and family lifestyles. Women, especially single, married, and divorced women in their thirties, forties, and fifties, are forcing men to recognize that their definition of a successful date or a rewarding relationship based on their performance in bed doesn't work any more. Women are redefining sexual satisfaction in their own terms, focusing on intimacy, nurturance, whole-body sensuality, passion, and yes, ecstasy. As we develop new attitudes about our sensual and sexual nature and a new understanding of our complex need for intimacy and love, new lifestyles and more discerning and complex moral values are also emerging.

We are clearly developing more positive attitudes toward sexual pleasure, shifting from the unrestrained "free love" coupling in the 1960s and 1970s to a celebration and exploration of sensuality involving the whole body and the spiritual dimensions of our sexuality.

The widespread threat of AIDS has led to a social acceptance and endorsement of non-penetrative sex (NPS) — outercourse — a recognition that sexual intimacy and love is much richer than the traditional male performance obsession with penile penetration and coital orgasm.

Premarital sex was overwhelmingly condemned in the 1950s. Today it is tolerated and widely expected by most — even in the churches and synagogues.

In the thirty years since the Stonewall riot gave birth to gay liberation, the churches and synagogues have been forced to recognize the reality of gay and lesbian lifestyles, and learned to cope somehow with this reality within their congregations. Meanwhile, Hawaiians, Alaskans, and Vermonters have explored granting some legal status to same-sex unions, a move that will have unprecedented repercussions throughout American society.

This fills in some important details in the stage setting for our stories. It was this stage setting that prompted our storytellers to share part of their lives with us.

So What About Integrating Sex and Spirit in Our New World?

There is a good reason why our storytellers, and countless others around this country, are unwilling to accept the widespread conflict between sex and spirit. That reason lies deep in the history of our human spiritual/sexual nature.

SPIRIT — Thousands of years before our earliest written religious texts, our Cro-Magnon and Neanderthal ancestors ritually buried their dead in hopes of a life hereafter, leaving us powerful relics of their human search for the spiritual meaning of life. The neural circuits of our brains have been prewired to seek and experience the ecstasy of spiritual transcendence and union with the One.

SEX — Even more ancient are the biological roots of our sexuality. Our skin, like the skin of all our ancestors back to the earliest warm-blooded mammals, craves and thrives on the nurturing, sensual pleasures of touch and cuddling. The ancient pleasure centers of our emotional (limbic) brain have been wired to respond to nurturing sensual touch and the ecstatic pleasures of erotic, orgasmic explosions. Our sensual, erotic, passionate needs cannot be denied unless we get rid of our bodies—and our brains.

SEX and SPIRIT have coexisted for as long as humans have been human.

But connecting the two has never been easy, at least not in the past two thousand years. That's why, once we had settled on twenty-two stories from the over forty our invitation brought in, the three of us decided we should offer some observations about how we interpret these stories of connecting sex and spirit. A behavioral biologist, Tim has spent twenty years studying our courtship patterns. Both he and his wife, Martha, are ferocious readers of sexuality literature. Martha is a librarian by training, and an expert in sexual materials for libraries. Bob, also a biologist and theologian by training, has spent decades analyzing the connection between sexuality and spirituality. He has always been intrigued by trying to anticipate the impact that social and technological changes can have on how we experience love, marriage, and family.

While we debated which of the four dozen original stories to include in this book, we spent hours bouncing ideas around before we finally were able to ask the key question that underlies all the stories: Does mystical (spiritual) ecstasy have anything in common with sexual ecstasy?

Looking at the biology of our brains, altered states of mind, and how we become conscious of both spiritual and sexual ecstasy, we wanted to know whether there is any evidence that these two seemingly different ecstatic experiences might share the same bases and processes in the chemistry of our brains.

Earlier, we noted that we commonly use the same adjectives to describe our experiences with both sexual and spiritual ecstasy, words like "communion," "altered state of mind," "out-of-body experience," "entranced," and "enchanted." Both kinds of ecstasy involve a communion. Both are affiliational ecstasies.

But most attempts to experience mystical communion (union, ecstasy) do not result in a truly ecstatic, altered state of mind, out-of-body experience of transcendence and communion with the One, but rather in the calming reassurance one finds in everyday prayer and meditation. Similarly, attempts to experience sexual ecstasy (communion, union) more often result in a release of pent-up genital tension, rather than in the transcendence and ecstatic erotic communion Tantric Yoga practitioners seek.

Our questions eventually led us to identify six characteristics we believe are part of both mystical/spiritual ecstasy and erotic/sexual ecstasy. These links, we believe, are vital elements in each of the stories told in this book.

Transcendence is the first characteristic we identified in both sexual and spiritual ecstasy. Transcendence is based on the certainty that there is unity, a greater other of God/Love in this world, and "she is here." Transcendence involves communion with the Cosmos, the Plenum, Unity. In the sexual sphere, "I am her and she is me, and we are one." We're talking about a truly erotic ecstasy, not some pornographic experience of sex. A pornographic experience isolates us from our surroundings and concentrates on genital release. An erotic ecstasy creates communion—"I see her and she is the world." "In her is Eden" versus "what a piece of ass." Both are valid, even very different experiences. Only the first, however, can be ecstatic in the sense of a spiritual experience based on communion. Both mystical and erotic ecstasies are alike in breaking our finite boundaries. They bring an "epiphany," a shining through, a revelation. "I never knew that before." "*Amor novus est*—Love is always new, every time."

Joy, rapture, delight, laughter, wonder, and playfulness are a second characteristic shared by both sexual and spiritual ecstasy. No one can capture this trait in a single term or phrase. It is undescribed and undescribable because ecstasy is emerging, not static. It's alive, in process, fluid. Joyfulness and playfulness have been highlighted as a basic value in at least two pioneering documents on sexual morality, the 1970 United Presbyterian work-study document and the 1978 Catholic Theological Society report. (We didn't include "passion" in this list of adjectives because it seems too strong a word, possibly too angry an emotion. And yet, it too is used for ecstatic experiences in both the spiritual and sexual domains.)

Fulfillment. Whether we are dealing with our spiritual quest or our deepest sexual needs, personal fulfillment is why we exist. Being fully human involves a feeling of essential rightness, being in tune with ourselves, other humans, the earth that birthed us, and the transcendent Other. We're not talking about fulfillment as doing what is morally right, the dull satisfaction of a job well done, nor smug self-satisfaction concerning a long-sought goal achieved by hard work. These can give us a sense of fulfillment and satisfaction, but they don't in any way approach the "existential" ecstatic fulfillment that echoes through the awareness that "I am here for her/him. She/he is why I am." Spiritual writers and mystics talk about "spiritual love" or agape, in which the ultimate fulfillment becomes altruistic self-sacrifice. In the erotic mode, ecstatic fulfillment becomes a desire to give pleasure and joy that blossoms in a mutual communion.

Transfiguration. Whether spiritual or sexual, ecstasy involves a transfiguration, a metamorphosis. Ecstasy changes the meaning of everything. Reality is transfigured. Time is lost in an eternal moment, amid a heightened awareness, sensibility, and sensitivity. All the senses peak in ecstasy, but the involvement of the primal senses of touch and smell is unique to sexual ecstasy. The entire skin is recruited in the ecstasy of transcendence, joy/wonder, fulfillment, reciprocity, and hope. While touch is obviously part of sexual ecstasy, and vital to it, touch seems to be incompatible with spiritual ecstasy.

Reciprocity. Both sexual and mystical ecstasy result in an "entranced communion." There is a mutual, reciprocal togetherness, an "entraining," expressed in the simple awareness that she/he loves me too! The mutual feeding rituals one sees when a couple is in the fresh bloom of love is but one expression of reciprocity. One of the most charming characteristics of the recently discovered playful, bonobos chimpanzees of Zaire, our nearest relatives, is the way they sometimes exchange food as part of their sex play. Whether the mutual feeding is a spontaneous part of the playfulness of entranced lovers or part of a Tantric love ritual, feeding one's lover has its mystical echo in the communion ritual of breaking bread and sharing wine in his memory.

And finally, Hope. In our search for the aspects that sexual and mystical (spiritual) ecstasy have in common, we include hope. In ecstatic love, whether sexual or spiritual, all things are possible, and nothing impossible in Love/God. This shared hope is not the simple expectation that I will achieve some hitherto unachieved goal. Ecstatic hope is the certainty that the cosmos is a "place of hope." Not Pandora's hope of something better, but her belief that all things are possible in the here and now because of this ecstatic communion.

Facing the Challenge of These Stories

As our traditional lifestyles, expectations, and values are challenged, some vehemently denounce the changes, and call for a return to "traditional American Christian family values." Others experience a renewed interest in spirituality despite their skepticism about the ability of religious institutions and authorities to deal realistically with new dimensions and issues in sexual morality.

For centuries, orthodox church teachings have presented human passion and sexuality as a hindrance, if not a major obstacle to the spiritual life. Official Christian doctrine has never been enthusiastic about recognizing or celebrating sexual pleasure and passion as an acceptable path to the divine. This has changed somewhat in recent decades as married couples have increasingly forced moralists and clergy to recognize and deal with their personal experiences of the vital connections between sexuality and spirituality. Increasingly, unmarried couples, whether gay, straight, or bisexual, are challenging their religious leaders and communities to recognize that they can find in their intimacy the same kind of connection between sex and spirit as married heterosexual couples are proclaiming.

What is unique about the women and men telling their stories here is that they have recognized these changes as signs that we are moving into a new era, a new culture, where the tried-and-true traditional patterns no longer work the way they did so well for centuries. One of the surest signs that a culture is moving onto a new stage is when we no longer find the meaning and psychological-emotional support our ancestors found in traditional myths and superstories. For centuries, the biblical myths of Adam and Eve have given meaning to male/female relationships, marriage, and family. Our ancestors produced these myths thousands of years ago when they were moving from a hunter-gatherer, nomadic, clan-based society into a new culture structured around farming, written languages, and male-dominated hierarchies. Their myths about the origins of the sexes, love, marriage, and family have supported and inspired the progress of Western civilizations down to the present.

In our post-industrial culture, we struggle with a whole new stage setting for our lives. The signs of our changing world have inspired our storytellers to reinterpret the perennial truths in our ancient myths. They are trying to reinvent for our age the perennial meanings of "until death do us part," "forsaking all others," and "cleaving together in one flesh." In trying to find new dimensions in intimacy and marriage, they have explored paths and relationships that society and the churches frown on or condemn. But they have been spiritually rooted enough to be that radical. While their solutions are definitely not for most Americans, they will appeal to some as a realistic alternative to ignoring the signs of our changing times and the unrealistic "guaranteed recipes" for putting fire and passion into marriage after years of daily life together that regularly appear in adult magazines of every kind.

These stories have their own poignant quality. Each, in its own way, tells of something wonderful happening—even when it didn't last. These are not stories of compulsive, addicted, or promiscuous love affairs, pinned to the completion of some incomplete or interrupted adolescent fantasy. Instead, the encounters frequently begin with an effortless and almost preternatural clarity of awareness and purpose, a quest equally intuited by both the man and woman—although the women are more likely to be aware first of the implications and potential of what is happening. There is a basic trust, integrity, and honesty between the couple, even when their relationship must be kept private because it violates the norms of what the church or society finds acceptable. The stories are deceptive in their ease, but we know that each of the storytellers had great difficulty in putting their adventure on paper. Sometimes it took a year or more of encouragement to bring a story to paper.

These stories contain no moral or theological polemics. The storytellers plunge beyond the shallowness one finds in most religious discourses that try to grapple with the spirituality of sex. In some cases, the stories become parables, no more, no less. They present the reader with a personal narrative, not an analysis, with the poetic and qualitative, not the objective or quantitative. They are fascinated and riveted by their experiences, even though they do not fully understand their own stories. Some stories are clumsily written in prose a professional copyeditor would blue pencil. But the clumsiness is incidental to the stories. It arises because the stories are not contrived, but emotionally authentic, and tell of love and intimacy in ways one would only share with a trusted friend. While they are autobiographical and reflective, often dramatic and bemused, none has the pained quality of a confession. There is no pondering over how I can make sense of my life, no *mea culpa* for disasters, no regrets even when a loving and precious relationship fades.

These are not the kind of revelations one reads about in the multiple relationships sparked by the aphrodisiac lure of the rich, powerful, or famous, like the multiple affairs of Presidents J. F. Kennedy, Franklin Delano Roosevelt's years with Lucy Mercer and Missy Lehand, and others during his four terms in the White House, or Eisenhower and Kate Summerly, and, of course, the extramarital affairs we learned both Clinton and some of his accusers in the House and Senate had engaged in. The writers are ordinary people, except in the depth of their concern about the spiritual dimensions of their lives and in their awareness of the sensuality of the world that nurtures them. They are also different in their openness to those around them with whom they need to bond in order to participate in each other's growth. Their openness includes a special sensitivity, at once susceptible and responsive to the subtlest erotic signals.

At first reading, some stories might suggest the writer was drawn by the lure of finding the link between sex and the sacred in a forbidden love affair with an official or unofficial representative of God. Our reading suggests a different interpretation in which the woman and man approach each other as equals, drawn by a heightened sensitivity they see in each other, a skill in honest, open communications, a deep knowledge of one's self, and, for the women, a rich appreciation of the intimate connection that males in church ministry appear to have more than other men in our culture because they are taught to be sensitive and listen.

The women, in particular, do not play coy games of hard to get. They knowingly engage in the dance of intimacy. They, along with the men, know full well and exactly what they are doing. They consciously intend every step on the path to an intimate, loving bonding. The women in particular tell stories of a mutually and reciprocally activated cascade of signals sent and received.

Some readers may wonder whether these men and women are just using self-serving interpretations of biblical texts and theology as a pretext to justify what might be viewed as undisciplined amoral libertine behavior. Our view, often based on knowing many of the writers for years, is that these are deeply spiritual people embracing and celebrating their sensual sexuality and the sexuality of another human. In this openness, they discover new spiritual dimensions. In their quest, some have broken with traditional religion and ventured forth to find new spiritual wells of nourishment and refreshment. Others have stayed within their faith of origin, deepening and enriching their spirituality with new epiphanies.

The Future?

In the view of many skilled social observers and religious thinkers, human consciousness is on the threshold of a radical convergence in which the undeniable progress made during the 3000-year reign of male-dominated scientific, analytical thought can now be blended with the gender equality and integration of sex and spirit of prehistoric hunter-gatherer cultures to create a new epiphany, a reincarnation of passionate love and the sacred. One part of this epiphany, as many see it, requires breaking with the traditional male definition of "sex" as a penis/intercourse performance that affirms a man's masculinity and his procreative potency. The new experience of sexual intimacy will need to involve the whole embodied person that includes, but also transcends, the genital. This experience will bring with it a new sexual morality, no longer focused on genital actions and marital status but centered rather on the quality of the intimacy and on the mutual responsibilities people encounter of nurturing and promoting personal growth.

Does this suggest we are entering a new sexual revolution? We think not.

But the question suggests a different kind of question. Just because sex and spirit have been linked together since the beginning of recorded history, one can ask whether the desire to link sex and spirit expressed in these stories is merely a continuation of some arbitrary cultural link that tells us we should try to link the two, or whether this desire exists because both sexuality and spirituality are intrinsic to and inseparable in our humanity?

We cannot answer this question for you. Each of us has to find our own way into that "forest." Since no one can enter or exit the forest by another's gate, we leave it to the reader to draw her or his own answer to this question.

While many readers will hopefully find in these stories support, insights, and inspiration for their own quest to reunite sex and spirit, these stories carry a different but equally important message for the priests, ministers, rabbis, and other official leaders who are custodians and teachers of the official "traditional" doctrine and morality. These stories clearly suggest that today's religious leaders and spokespersons are going to encounter new and perplexing questions about human intimacy, love, and the link between sexuality and spirituality that traditional answers will not satisfy.

Traditional moral formulas, particularly when they arise out of an absolutist worldview of literally interpreted sacred texts, are no longer adequate to deal with the subtle and complex range of intimacy, sexuality, and the sacred described in these stories. As the authors of a 1987 Episcopalian Church statement on "Changing Patterns of Sexuality and Family Life" point out, those who approach the Bible as a book of moral prescriptions directly applicable to all moral dilemmas, ancient and modern, misunderstand and misuse the Bible. The Bible is rather a record of the quite varied responses Israel and the Church made to the word of God *throughout centuries of changing social, historical, and cultural conditions.* "The Faithful responded within the realities of their particular situation, guided by the direction of previous revelation, but not captive to it" (Thayer, 1987).

The men and women who tell their stories here respect the rich insights of their religious traditions, but they also realize that creation is an on-going process in which we participate. They are pilgrims, not captives to a fixed worldview.

Therein lie the appeal and the challenge of these stories and the adventures they describe of the rejoining of sex and spirit.

Suggested Readings

Abraham, Ralph. 1994. *Chaos, Gaia, Eros*. San Francisco: HarperCollins.

Anapol, D. 1997. *Polyamory: The New Love Without Limits. Secrets of Sustainable Intimate Relationships*. San Rafael, CA: IntiNet Resource Center.

Anderson, Peter B., Diane de Mauro, and Raymond J. Noonan, Eds. 1996. *Does Anyone Still Remember When Sex Was Fun? Positive Sexuality in the Age of AIDS*, 3rd edition. Dubuque, IA: Kendall-Hunt Publishing Co.

Boswell, J. 1994. *Same Sex Unions in Premodern Europe*. New York: Villard Books.

Buber, M. (collected and introduced by). 1996. *Ecstatic Confessions: The Heart of Mysticism*. Syracuse University Press. (Paul Mendes-Flohr, ed.; Translation by Esther Cameron).

Cauldron Productions. 1993. *The Union of Sex and Spirit*. New York: House Publications Service/Cauldron Productions.

Countryman, L. William. 1988. *Dirt, Greed, and Sex*. Fortress Press.

Cousins, Ewert. 1987. "Male-female aspects of the Trinity in Christian mysticism." In: *Sexual Archetypes: East and West*. Bina Gupta, ed. New York: Paragon.

Ehrenreich, Barbara, Elizabeth Hess, and Gloria Jacobs. 1986. *Re-Making Love: The Feminization of Sex*. New York: Anchor Press Doubleday.

Foster, Barbara, Michael Foster, and Letha Hadady. 1997. *Three in Love: Ménages á Trois from Ancient to Modern Times*. HarperSanFrancisco.

Francoeur, R. T. 1972. *Eve's New Rib: Twenty Faces of Sex, Marriage, and Family*. New York: Harcourt Brace Jovanovich.

Francoeur, R. T. 1974. *Hot and Cool Sex: Cultures in Conflict*. New York: Harcourt Brace Jovanovich.

215

Francoeur, R. T. 1989. "New Dimensions in Human Sexuality." In: Robert H. Iles, ed. *The Gospel Imperative in the Midst of AIDS*. Wilton, CT: Morehouse Publishing, pages 79-98.

Francoeur, R. T. 1992. "The Religious Repression of Sex." In: D. Steinberg, ed. *The Erotic Impulse: Honoring the Sensual Self*. New York: Jeremy P. Tarcher/Perigee..

Francoeur, R. T. 1994 (Winter). "Covenants, Intimacy, and Marital Diversity—Into the 21st Century." *Journal of Humanistic Judaism*. 22(1):16-19.

Francoeur, R. T. 1996. "Sexual Codes." In: *Encyclopedia of the Future*, George Thomas Kurian and Graham T. T. Molitor, eds. Macmillan Library Reference USA, Simon & Shuster MacMillan, pages 830-834.

Groff, Linda. 1996. "Social and political evolution." In: *Encyclopedia of the Future*, George Thomas Kurian and Graham T.T. Molitor, eds. Macmillan Library Reference USA, Simon & Shuster MacMillan, pages 854-861.

Haddon, G. P. 1993. *Uniting Sex, Self, and Spirit*. Scotland, CT: PLUS Publications.

Heyn, Dalma. 1992. *The Erotic Silence of the American Wife*. New York: Random House Turtle Bay Books.

Heyward, Carter. 1989. *Touching Our Strength: The Erotic as Power and the Love of God*. San Francisco: Harper & Row.

Jaspers, Karl. 1953. *The Origin and Goal of History*. New Haven, CT: Yale University Press.

Karlen, Arno. 1988. *Threesomes: Studies in Sex, Power, and Intimacy*. New York: Beech Tree/ Morrow.

Keen, Sam. 1994. *Hymns to an Unknown God: Awakening the Spirit in Everyday Life*. New York: Bantam Books.

Kingma, Daphne Rose. 1998. *The Future of Love: The Power of the Soul in Intimate Relationships*. New York: Doubleday.

Klein, Marty, and Ricki Robbins. 1999. *Let Me Count the Ways: Discovering Great Sex Without Intercourse*. New York: Jeremy P. Tarcher/Putnam.

LaChapelle, Dolores. 1988. *Sacred Land, Sacred Sex, Rapture of the Deep: Concerning Deep Ecology and Celebrating Life*. Silverton, CO: Finn Hill Arts.

Lawrence, Raymond. 1989. *The Poisoning of Eros: Sexual Values in Conflict*. New York: Augustine Moore Press.

Loving More: Magazine New Models for Relationships. PEP Publishing, P.O. Box 4358, Boulder, Colorado 80306.

Mazur, Ron. 1973. *The New Intimacy: Open-Ended Marriage and Alternative Lifestyles*. Boston: Beacon Press.

Murphy, Sheila. 1992. *Delicate Dance: Sexuality, Celibacy, and Relationships Among Catholic Clergy and Religious*. New York: Crossroads.

Nearing, Ryam. *Loving More: The Polyfidelity Primer*. PEP Publishing, P.O. Box 4358, Boulder, Colorado 80306.

Nelson, James B. 1978. *Embodiment: An Approach to Sexuality and Christian Theology*. Minneapolis, MN: Augsburg.

Nelson, James B. 1983. *Between Two Gardens: Reflection on Sexuality and Religious Experience*. New York: Pilgrim Press.

Nelson, James B. 1992. *Body Theology*. Louisville, KY: Westminster/John Knox.

Nelson, James B., and Sandra P. Longfellow, eds. 1994. *Sexuality and the Sacred: Sources for Theological Reflection*. Louisville, KY: Westminster/John Knox Press.

Ogden, Gina. 1994. *Women Who Love Sex*. New York: Pocket Books.

Parker, Rebecca. 1994 (July/August. "Making Love as a Means of Grace." *The World* (Unitarian Universalist Church Association).

Patterson, James, and Peter Kim. 1991. *The Day America Told the Truth: What People Really Believe about Everything that Really Matters*. Englewood Cliffs, NJ: Prentice Hall.

Ramey, James. 1975. *Intimate Friendships*. Englewood Cliffs, NJ: Prentice-Hall.

Ramey, James. 1975. "Intimate Networks." *The Futurist*. 9(4):174-182.

Reiss, Ira. 1996. *Encyclopedia of the Future*, George Thomas Kurian and Graham T.T. Molitor, eds. Macmillan Library Reference USA, Simon & Shuster MacMillan, pages 828-30.

Reiss, Ira. 1997. *Solving America's Sexual Crises*. Buffalo NY: Prometheus Books.

Rimmer, Robert H. 1990. *The Harrad Experiment*. (25th anniversary edition) Buffalo NY: Prometheus Books. (www.toexcel.com)

Rimmer, Robert H. 1964. *The Rebellion of Yale Marratt*. New York: Avon Books. (www.toexcel.com)

Rimmer, Robert H. 1968. *Proposition 31*. New York: New American Library: Signet. (www.toexcel.com)

Rimmer, Robert H. 1969.*The Harrad Letters to Robert H. Rimmer*. New York: New American Library Signet. (www.toexcel.com)

Rimmer, Robert H. 1971. *You and I ... Searching for Tomorrow*. New York: New American Library Signet. (www.toexcel.com)

Rimmer, Robert H. 1972. *Thursday, My Love*. New York: New American Library. (www.toexcel.com)

Rimmer, Robert H. 1973. *Adventures in Loving*. New York: New American Library Signet. (www.toexcel.com)

Rimmer, Robert H. 1998. *Dreamer of Dreams: Wondering — A New Religion Challenges Christianity*. San Jose, CA: toExcel Press. (www.toexcel.com)

Steinberg, David, ed. 1992. *The Erotic Impulse: Honoring the Sensual Self*. New York: Jeremy P. Tarcher/Perigee.

Thayer, N. S. T., et al. 1987 (March). Report of the Task Force on Changing Patterns of Sexuality and Family Life. *The Voice*. Newark, NJ: Episcopal Church of Northern New Jersey.

Timmerman, Joan. 1992. *Sexuality and Spiritual Growth*. New York: Crossroad Publishing.

The Editors

Robert T. Francoeur, an internationally known, widely published writer on sexual issues in today's world, is author/editor of the multi-volume *International Encyclopedia of Sexuality* (covering all aspects of sexuality in 32 countries, 1997), *The Complete Dictionary of Sexuality* (1995), and several college text books, including two editions of *Becoming a Sexual Person* and six editions of *Taking Sides: Controversial Issues in Human Sexuality*. His abiding interest in the changing future of human sexual relations is evident in contributions to *The Encyclopedia of the Future*, in a three-year monthly column on "Future Sex" in *Forum Magazine*, and in his earlier popular books, *Hot and Cool Sex: Cultures in Conflict, Eve's New Rib: 20 Faces of Sex, Marriage, and Family,* and *Utopian Motherhood: New Trends in Human Reproduction*. Besides over 200 articles for a variety of popular magazines, he recently co-authored *The Scent of Eros: Mysteries of Odor in Human Sexuality*. **Readers are invited to contact Francoeur by email at rtfrancoeu@aol.com. We are interested in hearing additional stories that reflect the philosophy and spirituality of our storytellers.**

Martha Cornog edited *Libraries, Erotica, and Pornography* (1991), which won the American Library Association's Eli M. Oboler Award for intellectual freedom in 1992. She has written articles on sexuality materials in the library for *Library Journal, Collection Building, Journal of Information Ethics, SIECUS Report,* and the second edition of *Gay and Lesbian Library Service*, many in collaboration with her husband, Timothy Perper. She has also published on sexual language and communication and contributed to *The Complete Dictionary of Sexology* (1995) and *Human Sexuality: An Encyclopedia* (1994). Her most recent book, also with Timothy Perper, is *For Sex Education, See Librarian* (1996). Her current projects include editing an anthology on masturbation, and collaborating with Timothy Perper on a book about the evolution of erotic love. Active in the Society for the Scientific Study of Sexuality, she served on the editorial board of the Society's *Journal of Sex Research*. Manager of membership services for the American College of Physicians, she holds an MS in library science from Drexel University and an MA in linguistics from Brown University.

Timothy Perper is widely known for his field studies of how men and women flirt, court each other, and develop relationships. He has described the fascinating details of our dance of intimacy in *Sex Signals: The Biology of Love*, on television, and in both popular and scholarly articles. His analysis of the dance of intimacy came from hundreds of hours observing men and women of all ages flirt and court in family and singles bars, college cafeterias, and hotel happy hours for business folk. His current project is a book on the evolution of eros, sex, and spirituality over the past several million years, and the effects this has on our relationships today. He is particularly interested in the commonalities of spiritual, mystical ecstasy and erotic ecstasy. He is also the co-author, with his wife Martha Cornog, of the award-winning *For Sex Education: See Librarian*.

Three Catalysts of This Book

A comment from Robert Francoeur, coeditor of *Sex, Love, and Marriage:*

A couple of summers back, Rusty Roy called to invite me to an informal weekend gathering of a dozen church leaders. I've known Rusty for years, ever since I was inspired by the bestseller he and his wife Della wrote in 1968. *Honest Sex: A Sexual Ethic by and for Concerned Christians* influenced me and thousands of readers looking for insights into the real meaning of the sexual revolution of that era. *Honest Sex* is just as relevant today at it was in the 1970s, Actually more so. Rusty and Della were co-founders of two Christian community experiments, Koinonia for students at Pennsylvania State University and the Sycamore Community for adults. I've always enjoyed and learned more about life today attending the many conferences and retreats on lifestyles and relationships Rusty and Della organized at Kirkridge Conference Center, an ecumenical retreat in the Pocono Mountains of eastern Pennsylvania.

I jumped at his invitation, and ended up being invited to edit a collection of stories everyone at this summer gathering would help me gather. It took some time to get just the right combination of people with just the right combination and variety of stories to create this book. Rustum and Della, who are mentioned by many of our storytellers, kept after me urging me to bring *Sex, Love, and Marriage* to daylight. I wholeheartedly thank them.

I also want to thank Jerry Jud, a retired United Church of Christ minister and administrator, and our genial host at Timshel Retreat in the Endless Mountains of northeastern Pennsylvania. Jerry was so enthused about this book project, he offered his own story, and was gracious when we suggested we found his daughter Carol's story a bit more suited to the flow of our final 22 stories. Jerry shares his insights with two reflections on "Painting Outside the Lines" and "Families, Large and Small."

Contributors: The Storytellers

Robert H. Rimmer Beginning in the 1960s, Rimmer produced a dozen novels about "achievable utopias," including *The Harrad Experiment*, *Proposition 31*, *Thursday, My Love*, *The Rebellion of Yale Marratt*, *The Premar Experiments*, *Love Me Tomorrow*, *The Immoral Reverend*, *The Birdwhistle Option*, and *The Resurrection of Anne Hutchinson*. Among his eight other books are several collections of letters from readers of his novels, sharing their own personal experiences, and the enormously successful *X-Rated Video Tape Guide*. He continues his exploration of critical social issues, writing from his home in Quincy, Massachusetts. Bob can be reached through **http://www.harrad2000.com**.

Peter Anderson, Judy Harrow, Susan Robbins, Carol Jud, Ryam Nearing, and Art Rosenblum have also attached their real names to their stories.

The Reflectors

Woven into this rainbow of stories of rejoining sex and spirit are some brief meditations, "Reflections" we call them. Our thought was that these might lighten the intensity of the personal adventures and give the reader a chance to pause and reflect on a particular theme or a few stories at a time, before reading on. These "Reflectors" come from a rich variety of backgrounds and perspectives so we hope they will enhance the reader's appreciation of the stories and their messages.

Annette Covatta is a member and former provincial of the Sisters of the Holy Names, former council member of the New York State Council on the Arts, a spiritual drummer, and founder of Fulcrum, a company offering programs in psychospirituality. She recently produced a cassette of guided imagery meditations, *Reflections in the River*.

Marilyn A. Fithian has been co-founder, associate director, instructor, researcher and counselor/therapist at the Center for Marital and Sexual Studies in Long Beach, California, since its inception in 1968. She is co-author with the late William Hartman, her life partner, of *Treatment of Sexual*

Dysfunction: A Bio-Psycho-Social Approach and *Any Man Can: The Multiple Orgasmic Technique for Every Loving Man*. She has also held several offices in the Society for the Scientific Study of Sexuality.

Jerry Jud is a retired United Church of Christ minister, former United Church of Christ administrator, founder of Shalom Mountain Retreat, and current founder-codirector of Timshel Retreat in the Endless Mountains of northeastern Pennsylvania.

Ron Mazur, author of *The New Intimacy: Open-Ended Marriages and Alternative Lifestyles*, and *Commonsense Sex*, is pastor of the Unitarian-Universalist Fellowship in Daytona, Florida. Mazur also created the terse, chewy "erotic meditations" that open each section of this book.

James Nelson, professor emeritus of Christian Ethics at United Theological Seminary of the Twin Cities in Minnesota, has been a pioneer in the quest to reunite sexuality and spirituality in a holistic Christian perspective. Among his many important books are *Embodiment: An Approach to Sexuality and Christian Theology* (1978), *Between Two Gardens: Reflections on Sexuality and Religious Experience* (1983), *The Intimate Connection: Male Sexuality and Masculine Spirituality* (1991), *Body Theology* (1992), and *Sexuality and the Sacred: Sources for Theological Reflection* (1994).

David Schnarch, a well-known clinical psychologist, has spent twenty years exploring the relevance of spirituality and morality to sexuality. He has described his integration of sexual, marital, family, and relationship therapies in the highly acclaimed *Constructing the Sexual Crucible: An Integration of Sexual and Marital Therapy*, and in *Passionate Marriage: Sex, Love and Intimacy in Emotionally Committed Relationships*.

William Stayton wrote the Forward. Bill is an American Baptist minister, has been a marriage and gender counselor for many years, in addition to teaching in the human sexuality graduate program at the University of Pennsylvania. An assistant professor of psychiatry and human behavior at Jefferson Medical College, he has also held several offices in the Society for the Scientific Study of Sexuality and the American Association of Sex Educators, Counselors, and Therapists.